PORT Essington

The British in North Australia 1838–49

Derek Pugh OAM

Forewords by The Hon. Tom Pauling AO QC
and Professor Bart Currie

Derek Pugh OAM: Author
Port Essington: The British in North Australia, 1838–49
Text Derek Pugh 2020
Original Photographs Derek Pugh 2020, unless otherwise attributed.

ISBN: 978-0-6481421-7-1
All rights reserved. No part of this publication may be reproduced, stored in a retrieval system, or transmitted in any form by any means, electronic, mechanical, photocopying recording or otherwise, without the prior written permission of the author.

Design and layout by Michael Pugh: michael.pugh@bigpond.com

Notes: Includes bibliographical references and index.

Subjects:
Cobourg Peninsula: Port Essington—Royal Marines—British Navy
Northern Territory: History—British military attempts at settlement
Australian Aborigines: Iwaidja—Early contact—Jack Davis (Mildun)—Flash Poll (Memorimbo)
Ships: *Alligator—Pelorus—Britomart—Essington—Rattlesnake—Bramble—Fly*
Shipwrecks: *Pelorus—Orontes—Heroine*
Pioneers: Northern Territory—social conditions—health—scurvy—malaria
Macassans: trepang industry
Diarists: Captain James Watson—George Windsor Earl—John Sweatman—Ludwig Leichhardt—John MacGillivray—Archibald Sibbald—John Lort Stokes
Commandants: Sir J.J. Gordon Bremer—Captain John McArthur
Missionary: Don Angelo Confalonieri

Also, by Derek Pugh:
Darwin: Origin of a City.
Darwin 1869: The Second Northern Territory Expedition.
Escape Cliffs: The First Northern Territory Expedition, 1864–66.
Fort Dundas: The British in North Australia, 1824–29.
Fort Wellington: The British in North Australia, 1827–29.
Turn Left at the Devil Tree.
Tambora: Travels in Sumbawa and the Mountain that Changed the World.
Tammy Damulkurra (2nd edition).
Schoolies.
The Owner's Guide to the Teenage Brain (2nd edition).
Front Cover: Port Essington, Louis LeBreton, *Voyage au Pôle Sud et dans l'Océanie, 1839.*

Contact: derekpugh1@gmail.com
www.derekpugh.com.au

A catalogue record for this book is available from the National Library of Australia

To the men, women and children who settled and endured life, or lost it, in Victoria, Port Essington, and to their Iwaidja hosts.

And to Captain John McArthur, R.M., perhaps the most patient of all.

> *Have patience and perhaps*
> *in this book you will find,*
> *A few and rough scraps from*
> *the pencil and mind.*
>
> John McArthur
> Victoria
> North Australia
> World's End

(The McArthur Notebook, 1849)

Acknowledgements

Finding appropriately erudite informants and then asking them—busy people as they are—to read the text and write a foreword for my books is always at the risk of a polite refusal. So, I was thrilled when my requests were answered positively and immediately, by two gentlemen who have long had an interest in and knowledge of Port Essington. And, as a bonus, from them came two unique viewpoints. I am therefore indebted to The Honourable Tom Pauling, AO QC, the 18th Administrator of the Northern Territory, and Professor Bart Currie, from the Global and Tropical Health Division, Menzies School of Health Research, Charles Darwin University and Royal Darwin Hospital, for their words.

As always, the writing process has been supported by several people who have been integral to its success. I particularly thank, once again, Peter Whelan, Liz Pugh and Lon Wallis for editing, Peter Dermoudy for the use of his architectural sketch of Victoria Hospital, and Michael Pugh for his excellent book design. Any mistakes in this book are mine. This project was supported by the Northern Territory Government through the Northern Territory History Grants Program of the Department of Tourism, Sport and Culture. Thanks go, also, to staff at the Mitchell Library in Sydney, the State Library of South Australia, and, of course, the Northern Territory Archives and Library Service in Darwin.

Iwaidja and other indigenous people need to be aware that as this is a history, it inevitably contains images of people who have died. This is an Iwaidja history, as much as it is British. Thank you for your past and continuing welcome to your ancestral lands.

Derek Pugh

Contents

Acknowledgements	iv
Contents	v
Table of maps	vii
Foreword by The Hon. Tom Pauling AO QC	ix
Foreword by Professor Bart Currie	xiii
Victoria settlement timeline	xvx
Victoria, Port Essington	xxvi
Preface	1
1. Captain Sir John James Gordon Bremer, RN (1786–1850)	7
2. Captain John Mcarthur, RM (1791–1862)	53
3. Health and happenings	99
4. Relief and reinforcements	113
5. The *Lizard* and the *Gipsy*	125
6. Overlanders	131
7. Iwaidja	145
8. The *Heroine* and The Priest	159
9. Decline and departure	173
10. And then?	193
11. And now?	215
Appendix 1: Lists	
1.1: List 1: Members of the Victoria Garrison and their families	238
1.2: List 2: Prisoners of the Crown loaned to the settlement, Nov 1844–Feb 1845	244
1.3: List 3: Others who died at the settlement who were not part of the garrison	245

Appendix 2: Letter: Sir George Gipps to Lord Glenelg, 1838	247
Appendix 3: Log of the Essington: First of the fleet to arrive in Port Essington	250
Appendix 4: Journal of the French Explorer: Captain d'Urville	256
Appendix 5: Reports, an Advertisement, and the McArthurs' Diary	
5.1 Sir J. Everard Home's report on the Victoria Settlement: 1843	263
5.2 McArthur's Report on the Buildings: 18 October 1847	265
5.3 McArthur's Advertisement for Land: 1845	270
5.4 The McArthurs' Notebook: Diary entries	273
Appendix 6: *Northern Territory Times and Gazette*	
6.1 Miller's story after the wreck of the *Wood Duck*, 1874	280
6.2 A Tourist Trip to Port Essington, 1874	282
Appendix 7: The McArthurs' Notebook: Poetry	288
Table of illustrations	295
Bibliography	300
Index	312
Further reading	

Table of maps

Map 1: The composite map drawn by Joan Blaeu, a Dutch cartographer, in 1659 (http://www.map.net.au/). — xxviii

Map 2: Settlements in North Australia 1824-69 (Pugh 2016). — 4

Map 3: Port Essington 'This fine Port must ere long, become one of very great importance, to all Ships bound from Sydney and Van Diemen's Land and from India' (Watson, 1838). (Google Earth, 2020). — 31

Map 4: Labelled image of the Victoria Settlement site (Approximate positions) (Google Earth, 2020, 11°21'46.96"S, 132° 9'9.89"E). — 51

Map 5: Charles Tyers' chart of Port Essington 1839 (NTL, Rare Map 56). — 58

Map 6: The McArthur Map 1847 (HRA 1 XXV 1 373). — 59

Map 7: The final leg of Leichhardt's 3000-mile journey from Moreton Bay (Leichhardt, 1847). — 138

Map 8: Confalonieri's map of the tribes of Cobourg Peninsula (Spillett, 1972). — 167

Map 9: McArthur's map of 1847 as he labelled it (Spillett, 1972). — 266

The British in North Australia: Port Essington

Foreword
The Honourable Tom Pauling AO QC

I went to Port Essington in 2010 as part of a group led by Heritage Architect Peter Dermoudy. We were to clear the cemetery of overgrowth, accurately locate and map the graves using ground-penetrating radar, and survey and report on the condition of the remaining structures. Having cleared a great deal of scrub and overgrowth the radar was put to work. After many hours, the results indicated 58 graves. This was unexpected and alarming. Who were they? The answer came when Peter produced a photo copy of a water colour painting of the cemetery skilfully done by John McArthur, the commandant of the garrison. It showed a massive tree where four of the 'graves' were found. More extensive examination showed the radar images lacked the characteristics of graves dug by soldiers. To Peter's great relief we were back to 54.

Standing in the Victoria cemetery the feeling of isolation is palpable. It is a terribly lonely place. The 54 known graves are mostly unmarked, so your attention is drawn to a significant monument erected to the memory of Mrs Emma Lambrick, the wife of the second in command Lt George Lambrick. She died in October 1846 of the fever. Buried with her are son George Jr and baby Lambrick. Neither child thrived. Lt Lambrick stayed on after their deaths, and at times was the person who kept the Garrison together, when all about him, including the Commandant, were sick with fever. He finally departed with his surviving daughter, Emma, on HMS *Meander* in November 1849, when the settlement was abandoned. What a melancholy scene we can now see. What a heartbreak to leave loved ones in such desolation. No Church Sexton oversees this burial place.

The settlement was erected with substantial buildings along a small rise between swampy mangrove mudflats and a cliff. From the swamp rose a *miasma*. Shakespeare might have called it a 'foul and pestilent air'. It brought the deadly fever that was malaria. Today we blame the *Anopheles* mosquito and the entry to the settlement of someone infected with malaria. It killed very many and it killed Emma Lambrick. It is difficult not to consider the COVID 19 Pandemic when reading of the speed with which the fever killed so many at Port Essington.

We continued to survey the remains of the stone structures, including the charming Cornish Cottages and the charcoal kiln, which was in remarkably good order. The extent of work generally showed the earnest effort put in to make a success of the third attempt at establishing British claims to the whole continent, through occupation of the North Coast. The author's earlier books on the failed settlements at Fort Dundas on Melville Island (1824–29), and Fort Wellington at Raffles Bay near Croker Island (1827–29), underline the need the British had to prove occupation. These settlements used convicts. Victoria settlement did not. The vision was of an entrepot to rival Singapore.

Of all the structures at Port Essington the hospital was the finest. It still has a grandeur. Near here, Owen Stanley, Captain of HMS *Britomart*, directed the play *Cheap Living* by Frederick Reynolds. It was performed by members of the garrison with males performing the female parts in borrowed or put together costumes. The date was 24 August 1839. Nearly 171 years later, it fell to me to direct *Cheap Living* for a second time—it was for this task that I was really recruited and not the chainsaw and axe.

We dressed the ruins of the hospital with a large Union Jack and some bunting and put up some basic lighting. There was no time or opportunity to rehearse, so marked up scripts were distributed (without audition) and I read the stage directions setting the scene very loudly. I then cued the 'actors' to read (as loudly as they could) the lines of the text and to move as directed. Word had got about in the boating community that there was a show to be seen and a small but engaged audience attended. From a scratchy start, while the cast got used to my unorthodox method of directing, the show began to flow. A good night was had by all, and a few welcome libations were shared in the 'green room' after the show.

I stayed a while, feeling for Emma and her children and Fr Confalonieri, who you will meet in this splendid book. The loneliness I experienced at the cemetery was even more powerful here in the hospital. The reader will find it in these pages.

This is a splendid read full of heartbreak, hope, despair, ambition, and resilience. And ultimately failure. There are surprises aplenty and contradictions too many to count. John McArthur was a complex man, in many ways admirable but in the eyes of others, deeply flawed. The author allows you to come to judgment by presenting the record.

This is a special work about a settlement that preceded Escape Cliffs and ultimately Darwin. It is an excellent work, vital to answering the question of how we got to where we are.

The Honourable Tom Pauling, AO QC
18th Administrator of the Northern Territory

Foreword
Professor Bart Currie

Victoria settlement was located deep into Port Essington on the isolated Cobourg Peninsula of the Top End of the Northern Territory. Visiting this third failure of British attempts at establishing a foothold on the remote north Australian coast prompted diverse emotions. First was how overwhelmingly oppressive it must have been during the build-up and monsoon seasons for those living in the cottages, with their 'Cornish chimneys', wearing the stiff British military uniforms and women's wear of the times. In the 'wet' Darwin is barely tolerable wearing stubbie shorts and loose singlets. What a relief to learn that—as uniforms wore out—men in the settlement adopted cotton clothing traded from the visiting Macassans.

The second impression on my visit was of the totality of the endless bush and the monsoon vine-forest encroaching back over the settlement. It was only held at bay by the curatorial activity of the Garig Gunak Barlu National Park rangers.

Derek Pugh's meticulous documentation of the chronology and seasons at Port Essington, and of reports from individuals from Victoria and the visiting boats, provides some clarity as to why and how 54 men, women and children died at Victoria settlement over the 11 years—almost a quarter of the settlement's population. When assessing health circumstances in the settlement through the prism of my own work, I had to ask: 'did they really mostly die from malaria, as suggested in the history books?'

In the early nineteenth century the training of doctors, surgeons and their assistants was extremely variable and often rudimentary, with surgical skills the most sought after by the military. Deaths were overwhelmingly either from trauma or from what we now know as infectious diseases, and during that period the 'miasma theory' of disease spreading from 'bad air' or 'night air' still prevailed. Malaria was a miasma (*mal'aria;* the 'bad air' of Roman swamp fever) until October 1880, when a French army doctor discovered the microscopic crescent-shaped bodies of the malaria parasite in the blood of a soldier with 'fever'.

The *Anopheles* mosquitoes that can carry and transmit the malaria parasite have always been present in the tropical north of Australia, but the malaria parasite was not itself present when the European ships began arriving. Sporadic incursions of malaria with some transmission to Indigenous Australians possibly occurred with the seasonal visits of the Macassan trepangers from the 1700s, but it required the fixed settlements of the early British military outposts to drive the establishment and endemic transmission of malaria. In the fifth year of the Victoria settlement malaria began filling the hospital and causing deaths. Subsequently deaths occurred from fever each year.

Reports from the settlement described the clinical features of the two main species of malaria. *Plasmodium vivax* caused 'remittent fever'. Vivax malaria rarely kills the victim directly but can relapse over months and years. At Victoria it resulted in progressive debility of the residents and the consequent deterioration of the whole settlement and its infrastructure. This was described so poignantly in the final year before abandonment as a 'garrison of yellow skeletons'. Vivax malaria may have become more permanently established, cycling through the settlement members and the ubiquitous mosquitos[*].

> [*] Vivax malaria subsequently remained endemic in some remote Northern Territory communities for over a century, with the last case of endemic malaria in Australia occurring in 1962 at Roper River mission (Ngukurr community), over 500km southeast of Port Essington.

Plasmodium falciparum, was the 'virulent, deadly fever'. Falciparum often killed its settlement victim within days. It was probably re-imported every year by visiting Macassan praus or supply ships as they returned from northern neighbour countries each year.

Support for malaria being the dominant cause of fever at Victoria comes from the patients' positive response to quinine when it was sourced from visiting ships.

Residents of Darwin have become increasingly aware of an enigmatic tropical infection called melioidosis. Melioidosis was little known until *Burkholderia pseudomallei*, the bacterium responsible, was declared a potential biothreat weapon, like the anthrax bacterium and the Ebola virus. The bacterium lives in the soil and water of certain countries and humans and animals are infected through the skin and/or inhalation of bacteria aerosolised from the soil during severe weather events or the ingestion of ground water.

The discovery of melioidosis is itself a story of colonial medicine. Captain Alfred Whitmore, a pathologist from the Indian Medical Service stationed in Burma, published *An Account of the Discovery of a Hitherto Undescribed Infective Disease Occurring among the Population of Rangoon* (1912). Melioidosis was not described from Australia until an outbreak in sheep in Winton in the arid north Queensland hinterland in 1949—exactly one hundred years after the abandonment of Victoria. The first case in Darwin was diagnosed in 1962, yet Darwin now has the highest incidence of melioidosis per population anywhere in the world. Soil sampling studies from the Menzies School of Health Research have recovered the bacterium from soils in gardens and sports fields across the city.

In the 1990s the Menzies School also recovered the melioidosis bacterium from Victoria's ruins, and melioidosis cases occasionally occur on nearby Croker Island. So, were any of the fever cases and deaths at the settlement actually from melioidosis, rather than malaria?

On the ledger in favour of melioidosis are: the presence of the bacterium in the soil; the seasonally wet environment of the settlement; the extensive exposure of the men to the environment in their daily activities, with footwear worn out and many working barefoot; the ubiquity of 'grog' and an amazing diversity of liquor in the records of victuals, with apparent frequency and longevity of alcohol consumption, including binge drinking (alcohol is second to diabetes as a risk factor for melioidosis, with high alcohol levels dramatically diminishing the ability of the immune system to kill the bacteria after initial inoculation); recognition that melioidosis is 'a great imitator' with many clinical variations, with the chronic pulmonary form of melioidosis still frequently being mistaken for tuberculosis; and the documentation of deaths in imported sheep, which like camels and alpacas are magnets for melioidosis and do poorly in melioidosis-endemic locations. On the ledger against: following the severe tropical cyclone of November 1839 in which eight sailors drowned, it was noted that there was no subsequent sickness—melioidosis case clusters typically follow, but not invariably, severe weather events; ingestion of leaves from toxic plants is an alternative explanation for the sheep deaths; and the majority of the descriptions of the fever illnesses and deaths were consistent with introduced malaria.

The generally friendly relationships between the local Indigenous Iwaidja people and the uninvited colonists resonates throughout the Port Essington story. It is in stark contrast to the history of dispossession, violence, and human rights violations in the subsequent decades as land across Australia was progressively usurped by the immigrants and their descendants. The Iwaidja were evidently healthy, reflecting a hunter gatherer lifestyle in balance for millennia with a natural environment abundant in marine and terrestrial wildlife and other bush tucker.

In 1847 the Iwaidja experienced a classic epidemic of influenza. The majority of the Iwaidja population were sick, with many deaths. The Europeans were apparently much less affected. This infection would have come from one of the ships visiting the settlement in the days prior to the onset of the outbreak*.

Several legacies of Victoria settlement over its 11 torrid years stand out. For instance, the additions to the early taxonomical classifications of Australia's unique flora and fauna, with even then, albeit very limited, some recognition of and respect for Indigenous knowledge. It is refreshing to learn the enthusiasm for natural history of many of the settlement and ship officers of that era. The naturalist John Gilbert and the botanist John Armstrong provided many bird and plant specimens for collections to John Gould, the Kew Gardens, and museums overseas. The settlement was also a refuge for mariners shipwrecked off the Queensland coast and for Ludwig Leichhardt after his 4,800km overland expedition from Moreton Bay, Queensland. Plus, it was also a stopping off point for expeditions and surveys further afield, notably the *Beagle* in 1839, when surveyor John Lort Stokes named Port Darwin after his former *Beagle* ship mate.

Finally, there are certainly elements of mutual respect in those early years between colonisers, the traditional owners of the lands and the visitors from northern neighbour countries. While difficult to reconcile with much of the subsequent 150 years of the Australian story, these snippets from history can provide lessons for ongoing reconciliation.

Professor Bart Currie
Menzies School of Health Research,
Charles Darwin University and Royal Darwin Hospital

---

* Studies of the 2009 H1N1 influenza pandemic demonstrated increased susceptibility to influenza in otherwise healthy First Nations individuals in various countries, postulated to reflect that centuries of exposure to waves of influenza resulted in levels of innate and acquired immunity in Europeans which was not seen in those populations without such historical exposure.

The British in North Australia: Port Essington

Timeline
Victoria settlement

Since the beginning	The land is owned by the Iwaidja and their forebears since the Dreamtime.
1606	Willem Janszoon first sights the coast in the *Duyfken*, in 1606.
Approx 1783	Macassan trepangers start to visit the Arnhem Land coast annually.
1802	Matthew Flinders maps sections of the coast. He meets Macassan trepangers and calls Aborigines 'Australians' for the first time.
1819	Phillip Parker King maps the coast of Arnhem Land and names Port Essington.
1 January 1824	The name 'New Holland' is changed to 'Australia'.
1824–29	Fort Dundas garrison, Melville Island.
1827–29	Fort Wellington garrison, Raffles Bay.
19 February 1838	HMS *Alligator* under Captain Bremer and HMS *Britomart* under Captain Stanley, R.N. depart England. When they arrive in Adelaide, they collect a number of Royal Marines who will serve at Victoria settlement. They arrive in Sydney on 23 July 1838.
17 September 1838	The *Alligator* and transport ship *Orontes*, sail from Sydney. *Britomart* is delayed several days, but *Essington* leaves a few days earlier.

13 October 1838	Schooner *Essington* arrives, transporting a church building. She moors off Point Record to await the fleet.
27 October 1838	The *Alligator* and *Orontes* arrive in Port Essington.
1 November 1838	Schooner *Essington* is chartered by Bremer and departs for Timor to buy buffaloes etc with George Windsor Earl on board. Brig *Britomart* arrives.
15 December 1838	*Essington* returns with buffaloes, pigs, sheep, banana suckers, etc. Later goes to Coepang (aka Koepang, Kupang), Timor for more.
17 December 1838	*Orontes* is wrecked on a previously unknown reef about 5 km NW of the harbour. She manages to beach on Vashon Head.
13 February 1839	Bremer sails in the *Britomart* to Timor, Kissa and Moa, and returns on 11 March.
11 March 1839	*Essington* returns from Coepang with buffaloes and pigs.
27 March 1839	Schooner *Essington* departs.
1 April 1839	Captain Watson, of the *Essington*, rescues Joseph Forbes, who has survived 14 years as a slave in Louron, Timor Laut.
5 April 1839	Dumont d'Urville, and his two corvettes *d'Astrolabe* and *Zélée*, visit.
3 June 1839	*Alligator* departs Port Essington with Captain Bremer, bound for Sydney. Crew on board suffer from scurvy during the journey. Garrison at Port Essington (99 people) mainly healthy, but short of food. John McArthur left in charge as 'acting' commandant. His lack of confirmation in the role causes problems with other captains over the next few years.
17 July 1839	HMS *Beagle,* under Captain John Clements Wickham, and John Lort Stokes, arrives in the port. They depart on 24 July to search for the great inland river. They soon discover the Adelaide River and Port Darwin.

Timeline

24 August 1839	The only theatre production performed in the settlement, the play *Cheap Living*, by Frederick Reynolds is staged (in 2010 it is re-enacted).
25 November 1839	The *Pelorus* and *Maria* arrive in the port with much-needed supplies.
25 November 1839	A cyclone destroys the settlement. The brig *Pelorus* is driven ashore with the loss of eight lives.
10 January 1840	*Ondenemer* arrives from Kissa with fruit and vegetables and 50 buffaloes.
6 February 1840	Schooner *Lulworth* arrives with a cargo of buffaloes.
12 February 1840	HMS *Britomart* heads to Sydney for supplies and to inform the government of the cyclone disaster.
25 February 1840	Captain Augustus Kuper rights *Pelorus* and refloats her after 186 days on her side in the mud.
3 March 1840	HMS *Alligator* returns under Captain Chambers. He has been ordered to swap commands with Captain Kuper of the *Pelorus*.
4 March 1840	Captain Chambers takes command of the *Pelorus*.
18 March 1840	Captain Kuper and the *Alligator* depart Port Essington for China.
24 March 1840	First praus of the trepang fishing season arrive.
12 July 1840	HMS *Gilmore* arrives with timber and food supplies, and naturalist John Gilbert, who is collecting for John Gould.
22 February 1841	*Heroine* arrives from Timor with 65 buffaloes.
17 March 1841	Captain Chambers and *Pelorus* depart for Singapore, leaving the settlement undefended. Naturalist John Gilbert, with a collection of animals and plants, is on board. He returns to England.
19 March 1841	Five Macassan praus arrive for the new season—about 30 come during 1841.
5 June 1841	HMS *Britomart* and Captain Stanley return with a supply ship, *Sesostri*, stays a few days, then travels for 8 weeks through the 'Indian Archipelago' with G.W. Earl, and a number of 'convalescents' seeking good health.

15 June 1841	*Montreal* is wrecked in Torres Strait. Two boatloads of survivors arrive in Port Essington.
14 August 1841	*Britomart* returns with all who were sick now restored to health.
20 August 1841	HMS *Beagle* returns. McArthur declares a holiday and a sports carnival.
22 August 1841	*Britomart* leaves for Singapore, taking the shipwrecked crew of the *Montreal*. *Britomart* is later condemned in Moulmein (Burma) and never returns to Port Essington.
1 March 1842	Earl purchases 50 head of cattle and sails for Port Essington with them in the *Heroine*. Mr Antonio d'Almeida, a merchant, applies to live in Victoria.
29 May 1842	The *Lord Auckland* hits a rock near Vashon Head. Over six days, George Earl and a team manage to refloat her and help her back to Victoria to repair her keel. It takes three weeks.
22 June 1842	McArthur reports that only 17 Macassan praus visited this season, blaming contrary monsoon winds.
2 September 1842	HMS *Chameleon*, a 10-gun brig-sloop, under Lieutenant M. Hunter arrives to replace *Pelorus*.
21 September 1842	The chartered Schooner *Lynheer* arrives from Sydney with cattle.
12 January 1843	The *Chameleon* travels to the islands, especially Macassar. George Earl reports on the visit.
1 February 1843	*Manlius*, with a cargo of cotton, calls in for shelter against the monsoon. Eleven of her crew of 36 were admitted to hospital with scurvy.
3 February 1843	A Royal Marine, probably Private John Durwood, dies of congestive fever, the first death since James Meldrum in March 1840.
February 1843	The *Heroine* arrives with 49 buffaloes, some pigs, and George Windsor Earl.
February 1843	Cases of malaria appear for the first time—six more marines or sailors die during 1843.

Timeline

March 1843	The *Alligator,* now a troop carrier, and the *North Star* under Captain Sir Everard Home, arrive in port. Captain Home reports on the progress of the settlement. The *Alligator* delivers stores, which were left over after the war in China ended the previous August.
March 1843	Six marines are invalided home to England on the *Alligator.* Lt Phineas Priest R.M. goes with them. He is 'suspended from duties'.
22 April 1843	Captain Home in the *North Star* departs for Sydney, taking some of the sick, including George Windsor Earl.
19 July 1843	HMS *Royalist*, under Captain Phillip Chetwode, arrives to relieve *Chameleon,* which then sets off directly to England.
August 1843	Three crewmembers of the *Royalist* die of fever, probably malaria.
15 September 1843	Captain Chetwode dies of fever, as does Private Henry Brown.
5 October 1843	The *Royalist* leaves and is not replaced. Naval ships in Port Essington from now on are mainly survey ships such as *Beagle, Fly, Bramble* and *Rattlesnake*.
19 August 1843	The *Fly* and the *Bramble* arrive on survey trips. Twelve convicts, including trained masons and quarry men, from the *Fly* and 7 more from the *Bramble*, are 'borrowed' to work in the settlement.
19 August 1843	Surgeon Archibald Sibbald arrives on the *Fly* and exchanges with Assistant Surgeon Whipple.
9 April 1844	The *Cadet* departs Ireland bound for Hobart with a relief detachment for Port Essington.
9 November 1844	The *Cadet* arrives to relieve the surviving marines and replace them with 44 fresh marines under Lieutenants George Lambrick and W.A.G. Wright. Dr Tilston replaces Dr Sibbald.
28 January 1845	HMS *Fly* and the *Bramble* return from Sourabaya [sic] and stay a week. MacGillivray re-joins the *Bramble* after a 4 month stay at Victoria.

May 1845	Seventy survivors of two Torres Strait shipwrecks arrive: the *Coringa Packet* and the *Hyderabad*.
June 1845	HMS *Fly* and HMS *Prince George* arrive on the same day.
17 December 1845	Dr Ludwig Leichhardt and companions arrive after a 4,800 km journey, travelling overland. They stay a month, then return to Sydney on the *Heroine*.
4 April 1846	The *Heroine* is wrecked on her return to Port Essington with the loss of eight people. There are five Iwaidja men on board, they survive and return to Port Essington.
13 April 1846	*Enchantress* arrives with 40 survivors from the wreck of the *Heroine*. Passengers include Father Angelo Confalonieri, an Italian missionary, and the 5 Iwaidja men.
17 June 1846	HMS *Bramble* under Lieutenant Yule arrives for a 3-week stay. On board is the accountant and diarist, John Sweatman. They stay 3 months, during which the *Bramble* is deliberately scuttled and flooded to kill a cockroach infestation. The crew lives on Point Record.
August 1846	Sergeant Masland shoots dead an Iwaidja man who is escaping custody. Payback is soon paid by the murder of Neinmal.
1 October 1847	The brig *Freak* arrives with Surgeon John Irwin Crawford R.M. on board and six Royal Marines, under Lt. George Sheddan Dunbar. The *Freak* stays until 16 October and takes four Royal Marine invalids to England when she leaves.
20 November 1847	Strong 'undulating' earthquake hits amid an early wet season. Most buildings now leak through cracks or rotten roofs.
9 June 1848	Confalonieri dies of fever.
9 November 1848	HMS *Rattlesnake* visits. On board are Huxley and MacGillivray, who keep detailed journals.
12 November 1849	HMS *Meander* arrives to close the settlement and transfer the marines to Sydney.
1 December 1849	The garrison sails away and abandons Victoria.

Timeline

5 February 1850	John McArthur steps ashore in Sydney, after 11 years at Port Essington.
14 February 1850	Death of Sir Gordon Bremer, aged 63, dies of diabetes in England.
9 November 1850	McArthur arrives back in England after a 12-year posting, aged 59.
28 July 1862	John McArthur dies, aged 71, in Buckinghamshire, England.
1873–4	John Lewis takes out a lease on Cobourg Peninsula to harvest buffaloes and cattle. He builds a homestead on the beach below Victoria.
1875+	Port Essington is used for trepang fishing and as a base by E.O. Robinson, and then as a customs base by Alfred Searcy to monitor the annual Macassan trepang fishermen.
1887–1930s	Ships are wrecked on the Orontes Shoal and other reefs off Vashon Head: *Red Gauntlet* Sept 1887, *Calcutta* 1894, *SS Australian* 1906. Also, several pearling luggers are lost during the 1920s and 30s.
1916	A Methodist mission is established on nearby Croker Island.
1924	Cobourg Peninsula is gazetted as a Native Flora and Fauna Reserve.
1931	Arnhem Land declared an Aboriginal Reserve.
1976	Fort Wellington area in Raffles Bay proclaimed an Historic Reserve.
1981	Cobourg Peninsula is the first land granted back to its Aboriginal traditional owners by the Northern Territory Government.
2010	Peter Dermoudy and team use a ground penetrating radar to count the graves in Victoria Cemetery. There are 54.
2010	The Northern Territory Administrator, the Hon. Tom Pauling, narrates *Cheap Living* with script-reading actors, to an audience in the hospital ruins, Victoria, its first production in Australia, since 1839.

The British in North Australia: Port Essington

Victoria, Port Essington

Not a place in the world like this can be found,
If you search from the Poles the whole earth around,
If to grumble and growl for ever's your wish,
Why come, and reside in a place like this,
If living you'd call't, from the world quite shut out,
Why you'd do well, there is not the least doubt,
And should you not know, how the time you would spend,
I'll soon tell you how if attention you'll lend—
You'd get up at six, walk, breakfast at nine,
And then you might write, read, or sleep till you dine,
That is, if a few thousand flies, and the heat,
Would allow your poor body or mind such a treat.
At three you'd perhaps dine off (such exquisite stuff)
A slice of <u>Queen's Own</u>, (which she's not known to touch),
After which, if digestion to help was your plan,
You'd go shooting, or riding, (that is if you can),
Or if liking it better, you'd sail on the sea,
You might spend your time thus till you came home to tea.

Figure 1: Victoria, Port Essington (Thomas Hatfield SLNSW FL3233570).

> The tea being over, it brings on the night,
> The flies go to rest—the musquitoes [sic] they bite.
> Then three or four hours, spent as you best like,
> Brings time for your bed, whence you'd rise with the light,
> Thus, having explained the routine for a day,
> It'll answer for most of the year I may say—
> Unless p'rhaps a ship, some diversion entails,
> By arriving at times with the papers and mails -
> And if to find out where this place is, you're striving,
> You'll find it in two lines the problem divining,
> To the shape of a rat had this world been subjected,
> At the tip of the tail 'Victoria's erected—
> Or if like a bullock it had been in form,
> I might have wrote this from the tip of a horn—
> That's as much as to say (if you're not clear in mind)
> At the end of the world 'Victoria' you'll find.

By John McArthur, c. 1847

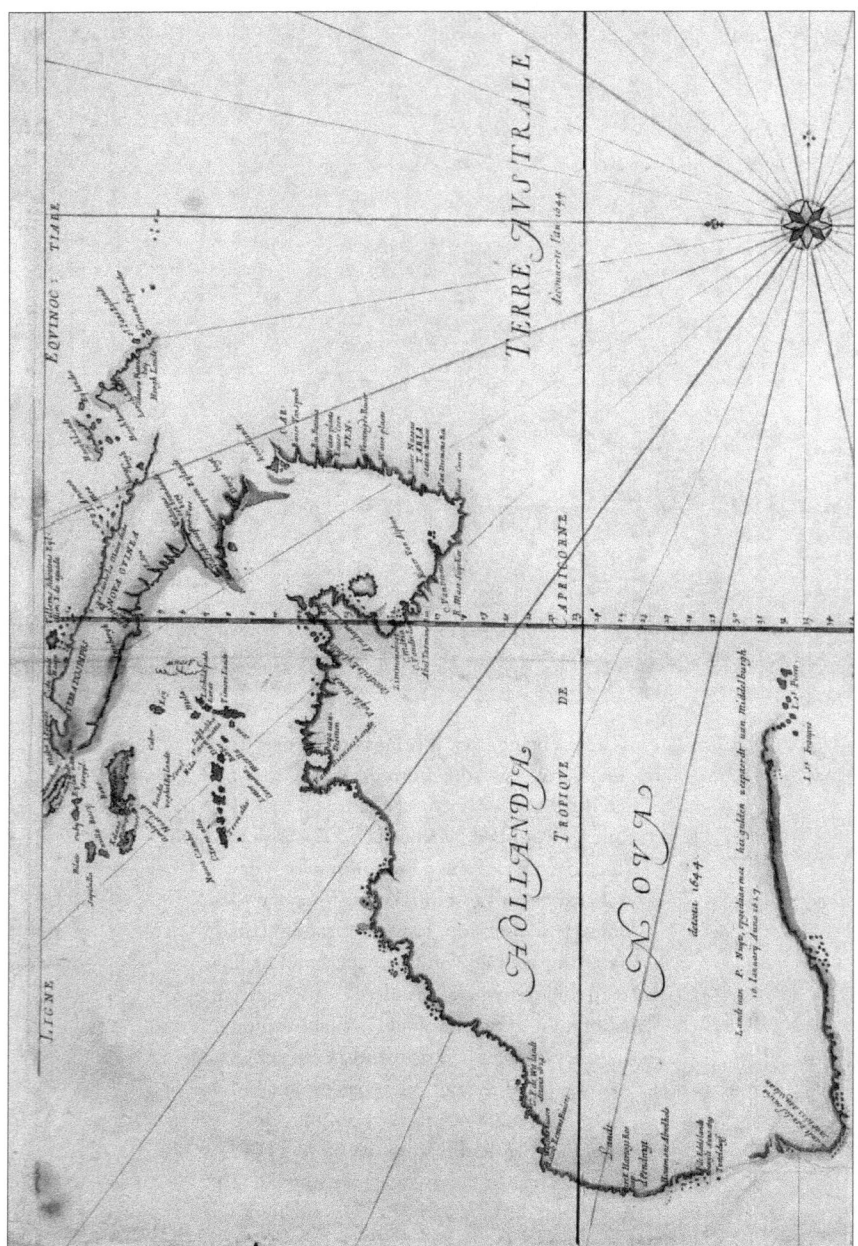

Map 1: The composite map drawn by Joan Blaeu, a Dutch cartographer, in 1659 (http://www.map.net.au/).

PREFACE

> ... The British consider themselves the owners of the whole of New Holland. It is mainly to indicate that assumption of ownership and to secure this vast territory that they are so persistent about establishing an outpost on these inhospitable shores ... (d'Urville, 1839).

The nineteenth century was Australia's first full century after European settlement, and it was a busy time. The First Fleet had arrived in New South Wales only 12 years before the century began, in 1788, so everything was still new for the British. Only the people who had lived for hundreds of generations in every part of Australia, the Aborigines, knew very much about the continent at all. The British called it *New Holland* because the Dutch had named it *Hollandia Nova*, and they mainly lived on the east coast, where most Australians still live.

The rest of the country was ripe for exploring. The country's interior was a complete mystery and most people expected that there would be a huge inland sea in the middle of the continent. What riches were out there to be found?

The Dutch knew the coast of Australia better than anyone. Dutch ships had visited numerous times since Willem Janszoon first sighted the coast in the *Duyfken* in 1606, but they found no trade goods on offer and an inhospitable coast, so they thought it worthless, and mostly left it alone. Nevertheless, by 1659, the Dutch had a composite map of the western half of the continent, from Cape York right round to the Great Australian Bight.*

---

* Incidentally, Janszoon named the continent Zeelandia Nova, but Abel Tasman's name of Hollandia Nova/New Holland, was the one that stuck. Tasman used the name Zeelandia Nova for another island further east.

The British in North Australia: Port Essington

The British needed to gather their own information, of course, and they were masters of subterfuge. The Admiralty routinely kept new discoveries a secret, such as King George the Third Island, which was plotted on 1767 maps in the wrong position. Even Lieutenant James Cook kept secrets. Cook knew of Bass Strait without ever seeing it, for example, because the strength of the waves that pass through it told him it was there. Nevertheless, his map showed land all the way to Tasmania. Also, Governor Arthur Phillip knew he need not settle at Botany Bay in 1788, because Cook's secret information told him Port Jackson—a harbour Cook passed but never entered—was a little further north (Short, 2020).

Once settled, the British, of course, expected foreign powers would be as circumspect as they were, so they sent their own explorers out to examine the Australian coast in detail. They looked especially for the rivers that would connect the inland sea with the oceans. In 1802, Captain Matthew Flinders—perhaps the most famous of these British coastal explorers—took a cat named Trim and commanded a little survey ship named *Investigator*. With him was Bungaree—a *Kuringgai* Aborigine from the Broken Bay area near Sydney. Bungaree's skills in communication with other Aborigines, even without shared languages, were integral to the success of their survey expedition.

Some of Flinders' best maps were of the coast of Arnhem Land[*] in the Northern Territory, where he met Macassan trepang fishermen and local Aborigines. The latter he called 'Australians'. In fact, it was Flinders who first called the continent *Australia*, a name that was formally recognised in 1824.[†]

Captain Phillip Parker King, the next explorer to come by ship to Northern Territory waters, came in the *Mermaid* in 1819. King was Australian born, from Norfolk Island, and the son of the third

---

[*] Arnhem Land was named after the Dutch East Indiaman, *Arnhem* (or *Aernem*), that visited the coast in 1623. This little ship was wrecked near Mauritius in 1662 and her crew are thought to be the last people to have seen (and eaten) a live dodo.

[†] The name 'New Holland' was changed to 'Australia' on January 1, 1824, as recommended by Governor Lachlan Macquarie in 1817.

governor of New South Wales, Captain Philip Gidley King R.N. Like Flinders before him, King also employed Bungaree as a liaison officer, to work with all the tribes of the coast they had contact with.

King's charts filled in some of the gaps left by Flinders and provided information to the navy about possible settlement sites. Using them, it was just a few years later that the British government sent out military settlement parties, with workforces made up of convicts, to set up garrison settlements that would protect the north coast.

Despite the Dutch apparently never having any interest in settling along the north coast, the British had little trust in them. It was the same with the French. In fact, a number of French 'scientific' expeditions had already nosed around, and some in the British government were worried that they would lose any tenuous claim they might have on the north coast, if they did not act soon. The British needed a settlement on the coast, the argument went, in order to ensure they retained the whole continent as British, and, almost as an aside, they were also hoping to begin trading with the islands of the East Indies.

The first garrisons were Fort Dundas on Melville Island (1824–29), and Fort Wellington, built on the mainland coast in Raffles Bay on Cobourg Peninsula (1827–29). The latter was constructed only when it was clear that Fort Dundas was failing, and many of the stores and some of the men were transferred there. Unfortunately, Fort Wellington did little better than its predecessor.

The main problems facing these settlements were that no-one knew anything about the tropics and how to survive in them and resources were hard to find. Worse than that, few ships ever visited them: they were just too far away, and isolated.

People died of scurvy and malaria, and meetings with the local Australians often ended in violence. A number of the Tiwi on Melville Island were killed by the settlers, and they responded by murdering several of the settlers, including the doctor, John Gold. At the same time, Captain Smyth, the first commandant of Fort Wellington, put in a shoot-first policy, after the local Iwaidja visited the settlement in

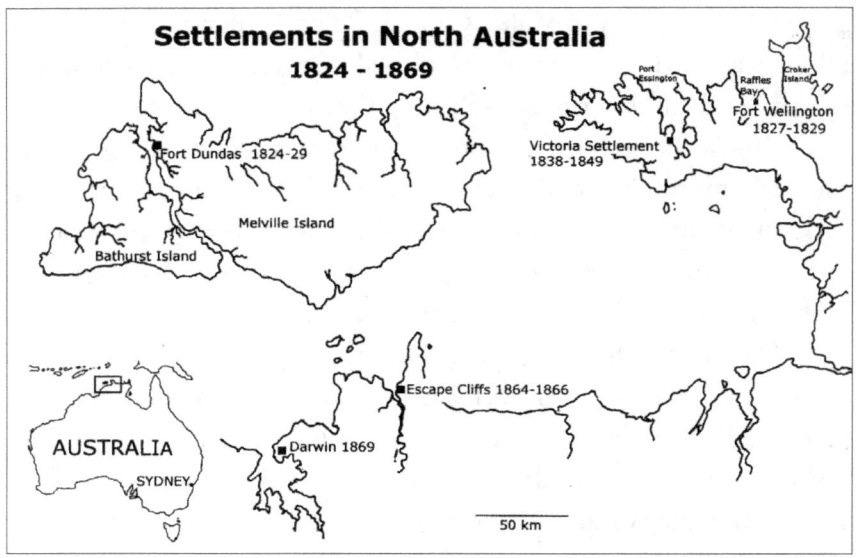

Map 2: Settlements in North Australia 1824–69 (Pugh 2016).

the dark of the night to steal the nails from a dinghy, axes, and even a pile of hammocks.

Later, deciding he needed to capture an Aborigine and teach him or her English, so he could then communicate with the tribe, Smyth sent out a hunting party of soldiers and convicts to capture one. Several Australians were savagely killed, including by bayoneting a mother and her baby during a late-night attack on a large party camped on a beach. The hunters were rewarded five pounds for returning with a wounded six-year-old girl, named Reveral. Remarkably, Governor Darling did little more than 'tut-tut' and wave a finger of reproach to this atrocity.

Fort Wellington stumbled on for two years. The second year was better. Everything improved under Captain Collet Barker: relationships with the Iwaidja were repaired; Macassan trepang fishermen came in larger numbers; and the health of the men improved. However, it was too late—the government had had enough, and Fort Wellington was abandoned in late 1829.

The stories of Fort Dundas and Fort Wellington are presented in earlier books in this series. This book tells the history of the

Figure 2: Adam Head, Port Essington.

establishment and life of the third military settlement on the north coast, started about a decade later, in 1838. Called Victoria* after the new queen, it was built in a port that had long been recommended by maritime surveyors and ships' captains: Port Essington†. This huge natural harbour cuts into Cobourg Peninsula and it is so big it outstrips Sydney's Port Jackson in terms of navigable waterways:

> … the deep-water anchorage under Point Record would contain twenty-five sail of the line, and in and about the anchorage off Victoria five hundred sail of merchantmen might lie. The outer anchorage or roads would contain the whole navy (*Colonist*, 25 August 1838).

For most of its existence, Victoria was managed by a captain of the Royal Marines named John McArthur, and the settlement lasted nearly 12 years before being abandoned. It is now mostly forgotten. However, its existence was timely for one of Australian history's household names, Ludwig Leichhardt. He and his small party travelled by horseback and foot across Queensland from Brisbane in 1844.

---

* The Colony of Victoria was declared in 1851, after Victoria settlement was abandoned. The first settlement in that part of the country was Portland in 1834. Victoria became a state in 1901.

† Leichhardt recorded the area as already having the Iwaidja name Limbo Cardia (Leichhardt, 1847).

He arrived in Victoria Settlement the next year, after 4,800 gruelling kilometres and the death of one of his party. Exhausted and starving, he was lucky to make it alive (his luck ran out in 1848—he and his companions disappeared in the bush and were never seen again).

The story of Victoria settlement starts with a recently knighted naval commander who had been in these waters before: Captain Sir John James Gordon Bremer.

Figure 3: Sir Gordon Bremer.

Chapter 1
Captain Sir John James Gordon Bremer, RN (1786–1850)

> We soon met Commodore Bremer … a man about fifty-five years old; his expression is pleasant and kindly, and his manner civil and engaging (d'Urville, 1839).

Gordon Bremer first came to be noticed, as a lieutenant, after his role in the capture of the French ship *De Weser* at the Battle of Trafalgar, in 1805. At 19, he was already a veteran, having first joined the navy as a volunteer on the *Sandwich*, in 1794 at the age of eight. Bremer's family tree reads like a *Who's Who?* of eighteenth-century naval officers, with a half dozen or more lieutenants, captains, and commanders in his lineage (O'Byrne, 1849), so he clearly had all the right connections—but he was also talented. He was promoted to full lieutenant on HMS *Captain*, and later, in command of the 10-gun *Bermuda*, he captured 60 men and the 60-gun *Bon Genie* from the French off Bologna. By 1814, by then a captain, he had fought in battles from France to Newfoundland, Burma, India, and China. In 1816, his command, HMS *Comus*, was wrecked on the rocks off St Shotts, Newfoundland—with no loss of life—during an anti-African-slavery mission. It was the only time Bremer lost a ship in his long career. In the automatic court-martial, he was warned by the court to be more careful in the future. The court found that he had been overconfident in his navigation and had failed to take frequent depth soundings (Hepper, 1994). However, Bremer and his officers were also praised 'for their arduous exertions in their endeavours to save her, and also for their good and steady conduct throughout the business, both in the boats and on shore' (*Naval Chronicle*, Vol.36, p. 511). Bremer's career could continue.

By February 1824, the thirty-eight-year-old was one of the most experienced officers in the navy. The Colonial Secretary in London, Earl Bathurst, recruited him to take command of an expedition tasked with establishing *two* military settlements on the north coast of Australia, using his discretion to choose suitable sites. The two Tiwi Islands, the mouth of the Liverpool River, and Port Essington on the Cobourg Peninsula, were all candidates.

Bremer, in command of the *Tamar*, carried Earl Bathurst's orders to Governor Thomas Brisbane in Sydney:

> My Lords, I am commanded to signify to you His Majesty's pleasure that a Ship of War should be dispatched without delay to the North West Coast of New Holland, for the purpose of taking formal possession, in the name of His Majesty, of that part of the said Coast contained between the western Shore of Bathurst Island and the eastern side of Cobourg Peninsula, including the whole of Bathurst and Melville Islands, and the said Peninsula.
> (Earl Bathurst, Feb. 1824).

Bremer spent a few weeks in Sydney in preparation for the northern settlement. Convict labour was needed, but for legal reasons, because the new settlement was outside the longitude mentioned in the act that established New South Wales as a penal colony, any convicts sent had to be volunteers. Skilled workers of use to a new settlement were wanted, and advertisements went up around the colony. Their inducement was the possibility of earning tickets-of-leave after only a year's service in the north, which was a valuable prize indeed!

Bremer hurried the preparations because the winds shift eastwards late in each year, and he was to sail on to India once the fort was established. Forty-five skilled convicts were accepted, among them carpenters, stonemasons, brick makers, bricklayers, plasterers, nail-makers, a plumber, servants, and a glazier. Thirteen of the convicts that served at the settlement over the years were of African descent, because many Europeans of the time thought that Africans were more suited to a tropical climate compared to other races. (Frederickson 2001).

Bremer also wanted free settlers, and he placed advertisements in the *NSW Gazette* to attract them:

> ... passage and Provisions found them by the Government and be allowed Rations for six months after their arrival, provided for the half of that period they devote their Services to the Crown (HRA, Series III, Vol VI: 643, 1824).

Only three skilled 'mechanics' signed up: William Potter, nail-maker and blacksmith, Henry Feathers, a bricklayer, and Edward Chapman, a sawyer. They would receive double pay for their efforts.

Bremer's orders allowed him to secure a convict transport ship, the *Countess of Harcourt*, and an ex-survey cutter, the elderly *Lady Nelson*, which would remain at the new settlement to trade for supplies in the East Indies.

The *Countess of Harcourt* had started life as a merchant ship, and was launched at Prince of Wales Island, near Penang, Malaysia, in 1812. The *Countess* made five trips to Australia, transporting convicts under the command of George Bunn, starting in 1821. On her first trip, she sailed from Portsmouth on 19 April 1821, and arrived in Hobart on 27 July with 172 male convicts—a journey of 99 days. This remained a speed record until 1837—the First Fleet had taken 252 days).

The *Countess* was back in Sydney on a third trip transporting convicts plus soldiers of the 3rd Regiment of Foot (the 'Buffs'), when she was ordered to accompany the *Tamar* to northern Australia. Whilst the *Tamar* carried the officers, the *Countess of Harcourt* transported the convict volunteers and most of the soldiers and marines, plus 12–18 months' supplies for the commissariat. The smaller *Lady Nelson* was also laden with supplies. The little fleet set off on 24 August 1824 under Bremer's command, and headed north to Torres Strait, before turning west towards Port Essington, reaching there on 20 September. According to *The Monthly Magazine,* the *Tamar* was the largest warship yet to navigate the dangerous shoals of northern Australia (*Monthly,* 1825).

Bremer had not been given enough resources to establish two settlements, so he changed his planning for just one. The fleet sailed first to Port Essington, and he formally unfurled the Union Jack, and took possession of all the land stretching west from Cape York to 129°E longitude, in the name of King George IV*. Lieutenant John Septimus Roe scattered some coins and buried a bottle containing a copy of the possession documents, calling the spit of land they were on 'Point Record'. The bottle, incidentally, has never been located.

Whilst there, someone found a brackish well containing a small quantity of thick water that had been built by 'Malays', but there was not enough to be a source for a new settlement. Bremer sent parties out in small boats, and on foot, to search for a fresh water creek or billabong that would be more useful, but after a few days without luck, he moved the fleet further west to Melville Island. When they set about searching for water there, Bremer himself found a permanent billabong by falling into it whilst stalking a duck. There was also a stream inland from a beach in the Apsley Straits:

> ... Tuesday 28th: Captain Bremer, while shooting in marshy ground, fell up to his middle in water, which upon tasting, he found fresh, and a running stream: weighed anchor about three o'clock and went further down the bay, to a place where Captain Bremer had found the fresh water, and where he now determined to fix the settlement: anchored then in a well sheltered bay, with deep water almost to the shore.
> (Anonymous officer: *The Sydney Gazette,* 10 March 1825).

Within a few days, the construction of a fort was well underway. Three weeks later, on the anniversary of the Battle of Trafalgar, 21 October 1824, one bastion of the fort was complete and Bremer, in a commemorative mood, lined up the soldiers and convicts, ordered the marines to hoist the Union Jack and fire a Royal Salute

---

* This moved the border of New South Wales a full three degrees west, to 129°E (where it remains as the Western Australia–Northern Territory border).

with the two 9-pounder cannons. He then formally named the fort, Fort Dundas. He could then happily relinquish command of the fort to Captain Maurice Barlow of the 3rd Regiment, and sail on to India:

> ... On the 13th of November, the fort, wharf, soldiers' huts, officers' houses, and commissariat store being completed, also an excellent well, thirty feet deep and six in diameter, and the provisions all landed, Captain Bremer took his departure for India, leaving an officer and thirty marines to assist in the protection of the settlement. The establishment at this time was as follows: Captain Barlow and Lieutenant Everard, 3rd Regiment; Lieutenant Williamson, Royal Marines; Assistant-Surgeon Turner, Royal Artillery; Mr Miller, Commissariat Department; Mr. Tollemache, Commissariat Storekeeper; thirty soldiers of the Royal Marines; fifty of 3rd Regiment; and forty-five convicts. One small vessel of about sixty tons (the *Lady Nelson*) was also left for the purpose of fetching supplies from the Island of Timor (Campbell, 1834).

He had stayed long enough to see the initial settlement established, and his reports to London were in such glowing terms that the Admiralty was encouraged. His career continued brightly. Sir John J Gordon Bremer was awarded a knighthood. His role in the failure of Fort Dundas was forgotten. He had enthusiastically sited the new fort where it could never have been a success, but, nevertheless, in 1838, he was chosen again to return to Port Essington and establish another new settlement.

In fact, when he returned to Sydney for a second time, he was welcomed with excitement. The merchants and gentlemen of Sydney expressed their admiration of Sir Gordon and the 'zeal and enterprise which have induced you, under many trying circumstances, to undertake this arduous adventure' (*Colonist*, 25 August 1838).

Bremer's reply to such laudation and flattery was low key but promised great things:

> ... Having long been of opinion that a British settlement on the north coast of this wonderful country had become an object of the utmost importance in every point of view, it was with peculiar gratification that I accepted the command of the

little expedition Her Majesty's Government has entrusted to me. There are many difficulties and privations inseparable from a position so peculiar as ours will be—yet I entertain a hope that we shall conquer them ... (*Colonist*, 25 August 1838).

Bremer may have then claimed a long interest in a new settlement, but it was others who pushed for it. He named the new settlement Victoria, after the new Queen, and, like Fort Dundas, it also appeared to him as a settlement of boundless opportunity. He advocated the selling of land to permanent settlers, envisioned a flourishing British trade colony to rival all others. Indeed, Victoria did last much longer than Fort Dundas and its concurrent replacement— Fort Wellington—but once again Bremer's optimism was misplaced.

There had been calls to try again soon after the northern forts were abandoned, particularly after Commandant Barker's favourable reports of Fort Wellington were disseminated. The closure of the forts may well have saved the British government £761 per annum (Goderich, 29 September 1831), but the idea of a northern settlement would not die.

In 1832, the Secretary of State, Robert W. Hay, wrote to Governor Richard Bourke, blaming Governor Ralph Darling for jumping too early in his closure of Fort Wellington (Hay, 21 Jan 1832). Then in 1834, Major John Campbell, who had been the second commandant at Fort Dundas after Barlow, presented a long and enthusiastic paper on Melville Island and Port Essington to the Royal Geographical Society. He encouraged further settlement. 'Port Essington', Campbell wrote:

> ... is as the friendly hand of Australia, stretched out towards the north, openly inviting the scattered islands of the Javanese, Malayan, Celebean, and Chinese seas, to take shelter and rest in its secure, extensive and placid harbour, where they may deposit the productions of their native inter-tropical isles, and receive in exchange the more improved manufactures of the temperate zone (Campbell, 1834).

The trader, William Barnes, who had been instrumental in the original settlement of Fort Dundas, wrote to the *Colonist* during

1836, declaring that Port Essington was always the best choice for a settlement. Moreover, Barnes was not short of his criticism of Bremer:

> SIR,—Some short time back, an account appeared of the cause of the abandonment of the settlement on the North Coast of this Island. I am surprised any person of common sense should have sent forth such a bantling to the world. The settlement on the North Coast was not undertaken by H. M. Government in England without great deliberations …
>
> After a very long conference, charts, papers &c. were examined. I was then called on to explain the nature of the trade, which I did to the satisfaction of all present. Earl Bathurst stated His Majesty's Government and himself were perfectly satisfied on the point, and that the Lords of the Admiralty, would be ordered to despatch a vessel forthwith, and offered me a passage out, free of any expense. I am sorry I did not accept of it, had I done so the settlement would never have been formed at Melville Island, but the spot originally intended, Port Essington. I would point out the cause of failure, but as the parties are not here it might be said, I can write what I please without fear of contradiction.
>
> Thus far I will add, Capt. Bremer was in a hurry to get on the Indian station, where he received Company's allowance with other chances of making money. Captain Barlow, a young man, vain with the idea of being called a Governor, if you attempted to talk to him about trade, the only answer would be, I am commandant, I shall do as I like …
>
> Yours obediently,
>
> W. M. BARNES. (Barnes, August 5th, 1836).

Captain John M. Laws R.N., commander of HMS *Satellite*, had visited both Fort Dundas and Fort Wellington in September 1828 and July 1829. He wrote a positive full account of both settlements, particularly Fort Wellington, at a time when all the other reports on the settlements the government was receiving were damning. Unfortunately, Laws' reports arrived too late to influence any decisions about the settlements' futures, and they were abandoned. His report on Raffles Bay, however, did provide important evidence that was drawn upon by proponents of a new attempt at settling the north (Cameron, 2016). Laws even made suggestions about how the settlement could be staffed:

> … Port Essington should be the penal settlement for the British possessions in the Indian seas; and every encouragement should be given to emigration from Calcutta and Madras, (in the miserable avenues of which hundreds are dying daily,) and at once a garrison should be formed, with two companies of the Ceylon regiment, with all their attendants; any of whom, by walking half a mile from the camp, would find plenty of the vegetables they had been accustomed to eat all their lives, which vegetables the English soldier (who thinks of no other resource than the commissariat) looked upon as poison … (Wilson, 1835, p. 156).

The *Colonist* continued to encourage a new northern settlement several times during 1836. The newspaper was also critical of Bremer:

> … In short, instead of merely looking in at Port Essington and then posting on for some other locality, the naval officers entrusted with the selection of a suitable locality for a settlement on the north coast should have spent weeks and even months in examining every nook and corner in Port Essington and in exploring the surrounding country in every direction, before they had turned their backs upon one of the most suitable localities for a British settlement that could possibly be desired. In a word, had a British settlement been formed in the first instance at Port Essington instead of Melville Island, or Raffles Bay, and a few gadongs [sic] established by our colonial merchants for trading with the natives of the Eastern Archipelago, we are confident that a flourishing commercial colony would have been at this moment in existence on the north coast of this continent, teeming with enterprising Malays, with industrious and plodding Chinamen, and with patient and laborious Hindoos and Cingalese (*Colonist*, 25 August 1838).

The idea of stopping the supply of convicts, which were still being sent out from England to the established colonies, was growing. 'The north is the place for convict settlements … somewhere near Port

Essington' trumpeted the *Colonist* (26 May 1836) and in 1837, J.D. Lang published an argument that Port Essington would be the best place to send convicts. It was surely fitting and reasonable' he wrote, that 'these hardships, difficulties and diseases should be encountered and surmounted by transported felons, rather than a free emigrant population' (Lang, 1837).

There was interest in Northern Australia from across the British Empire. Even the *Oriental Herald* published letters about it:

> ... the settlement of a colony on the north-west coast of Australia is an object of such vast importance to the commercial interests of Great Britain, that too frequent opportunities cannot be taken to acquaint the public with the advantages derivable of it ... the soil and climate of the country in the vicinity of Raffles Bay, are stated to be well adapted to the growth of cotton and pepper ... tobacco, the castor oil plant, sugar-cane and even spices ... Any number of emigrants may be obtained from China, and from many of the islands in the Archipelago ... (Roberts, 1839).

By 1838, however, the most influential proponent and principal instigator of a new settlement was a 25-year-old civilian adventurer named George Samuel Windsor Earl (1813–65). Earl had emigrated to the Swan River Colony when he was 16 years old, but within two years, he was working at sea throughout Asia, working his way up to captain of the *Stamford*, in Singapore by 1834. After he published several books on the East Indies, he was recognised as an authority on them. He also had a talent for learning languages, and established a reputation as a linguist, speaking and writing at least four European languages and four Malayan languages (Malay, Bugis, Bajau and Macassarese) (Allen, 1973).

During 1834, Earl was in Singapore and several Chinese merchants tried to employ him to run trepang and turtle shell collecting expeditions to Australia. Earl was aware, however, that without the protection of a government settlement on the coast, his chances of success were low.

Back in England, two years later, Earl approached the Colonial Office to discover what was planned for the north coast. 'Nothing', he was told. So he went directly to the Colonial Secretary, Lord Glenelg, and outlined a plan to restart a British trepang industry in Australia via a settlement that would initially trade with the nearest islands, and eventually become the dominant player in the region.

Earl had some powerful friends to help. Sir John Barrow, the Second Under-Secretary to the Admiralty, was already interested in Australia and supported the new proposal. With him was Captain (later Rear-Admiral) Francis Beaufort, the Hydrographer of the Navy based at the British Admiralty. Together they pressed Lord Glenelg for a decision, arguing that a settlement would not only be a strategic asset, but a refuge for shipwrecked sailors, a 'resort' for English whalers, and a trading port for the products of the region: trepang, tortoise shell, sago and timber. Cheap labour would come from the nearby Indies, and no doubt, Buginese and Chinese settlers would soon find their way to the port.

John Barrow had been instrumental in the establishment of Fort Dundas, in 1824. Then, he had been concerned about Britain's tenuous claim to the north. In a letter to the Under-Secretary of State for War and the Colonies, Sir Robert Wilmot Horton, he explained:

> ... From the neighbouring island of Timor, it is but a step to the northern parts of New Holland; and it would be well to bear in mind that they [the Dutch] would have a justifiable plea, in planting an establishment on any part of the Northern Coast of the latter, in our own example of taking possession of the Eastern Coast and Island of Van Diemen, the original discovery of which by the Dutch is not disputed. Indeed I believe it is admitted... that Occupancy is a stronger title than priority of discovery: but be this as it may, in the present instance our own conduct may be quoted against us ...
> (Barrow, 1824).

More than a decade later, Lord Glenelg was also convinced by the old argument of the north coast's vulnerability to claim by foreigners. It would, said Barrow, be a 'most humiliating mortification to witness the tri-colour flag or that of the stripes and stars waving on Dampier's land' (Barrow, 13 Dec 1836).

The Netherlands had discovered and mapped the coast long before the British arrived, and the French always seemed to be poking around. Even the Americans were considered a potential risk*. Glenelg agreed to a new settlement being established, on the condition it remain a naval base until it could prove itself as a viable trading centre.

During the 1830s there was also anger among England's shipping elite, regarding the number of ships being wrecked in Torres Strait. The stories of two high profile wrecks, the *Charles Eaton* in 1834, and the *Stirling Castle* in 1836, were of huge public interest, producing a myriad of articles and books. When Eliza Fraser and three companions were rescued from the 'captivity' of Badtjala people in far north Queensland, the protest that something must be done about travellers' safety reached a crescendo.

The Colonial Office was pressured to do something about the danger to property and people, noting that a settlement in the north might just do it, and it would provide a destination for shipwrecked mariners seeking salvation. Glenelg agreed. It would also be a place of trade and immigration, and a foil for the Dutch settlements spread throughout the East Indies.

The use of convict labour was abhorrent to Earl†: 'I do not think that any mechanics will be taken with us, which I am much rejoiced at for I am convinced that the less we have to do with this hot-bed of vice, the better it will be for us' (Earl, 16 August 1830) and 'Sufficient sin and misery have already been created by Britain vomiting forth her outcasts to people a country well deserving a better system of colonization' (Earl, 1837).

---

* Henry Wilkes, an American, had arrived in Sydney Harbour, unannounced, with two exploration ships, *Vincennes*, and *Peacock*, but he was more interested in Antarctica. There were also more than 150 American whaling vessels in Australian waters in the 1840s (Powell, 2016).

† Nineteen convicts were later 'loaned' to the settlement for a few months in 1844–5.

Earl had the support of enthusiastic merchant men who promised support, and possibly would even settle at the new colony and start businesses. Several of these men also approached Bremer in Sydney before he left for the north.

William Barnes again joined the push for a new settlement by writing to the *Sydney Monitor* and providing his original correspondence with Earl Bathurst. It was Barnes's ship, *Stedcombe*, which had been taken by pirates in the Banda Islands, with all but the two cabin boys beheaded. Barnes claimed he had always advocated that the settlement should be *east* of Melville Island, where the Malays fished for trepang. If only Captain Bremer had listened to him, in 1823 …

During the 1830s, Barnes was still advocating trading with the Malays, and put himself forward as an expert in how to do it. He also warned that it was better to be friendly with them than otherwise:

> … as the Malays are, when known, not that dangerous sort of people, which some travellers have attempted to make them— but on the contrary are friendly disposed, but like all "demi- savages", they never forgive an injury (Barnes, 3 Sept 1838).

Spiteful demi-savages notwithstanding, the settlement was allocated a man-of-war for its defence, and Sir Gordon Bremer[*], once again, was given overall command. The ship was the 28-gun HMS *Alligator*. She was to be accompanied by the *Britomart*, a brig under Captain Owen Stanley, R.N. The ships departed England bound for Australia's north coast, via Sydney, on 19 February 1838. On board the *Alligator* was a contingent of 24 Royal Marines under Captain John McArthur and Lieutenant Phineas Priest, as well as three civilians: McArthur's son, James, who was to be storekeeper; John Armstrong, gardener and botanist; and George Windsor Earl, who was appointed as linguist and draftsman. The latter would be paid £50 per month (Stephen, 30 Nov 1841).

The *Alligator* did not get far. She was damaged with a split bowsprit in a storm whilst still in the English Channel and had

---

[*] Owen Stanley returns later in this story, as commander of the *Rattlesnake*. He is remembered in the name of the Owen Stanley Ranges in New Guinea.

to return to England for repairs. That took a number of weeks. Leaving again on 8 March, Bremer managed to catch up with the *Britomart* in Tenerife, and then travelled with her to Rio de Janeiro and Sydney, via South Africa and Glenelg Roads near Adelaide. In Adelaide, Bremer collected a further detachment of 20 Royal Marines, including some with families, who had been acting as South Australia's police force since the previous year. A dozen of them, many still teenagers, plus Dr Frederick Whipple, a surgeon, volunteered to join the settlement party*. The privates were mostly illiterate†, but healthy and strong enough to 'hold a musket and march', which seemed to be about the only prerequisite for service (Powell, 2016).

At the end of July 1838, the ships arrived in Sydney for an eight-week stay. Bremer immediately visited Governor Sir George Gipps, to present his orders from Lord Glenelg:

LORD GLENELG TO SIR GEORGE GIPPS.
(Despatch No. 66, per ship Maria.)
Downing Street, 25 January 1838.
Sir,
This Despatch will be presented to you by Captain Sir James Gordon Bremer, R.N., who has been appointed by the Lords Commissioners of the Admiralty to proceed in Command of HMS Alligator to establish a Post on the Northern Coast

---

* Three women, Margaret Mew, Susan Seagar, and Kaziah Davis, joined their men as pioneers. The latter two were pregnant, though Seagar's baby died at birth. They were the first of 10 women who would eventually live in the settlement (Spillett, 1972). Corporal Richard Mew and Margaret Mew brought their two little girls, Mary, and Eliza, along for the adventure, and they had a third child (Margaret) in the settlement fourteen months later (on 7 January 1841). Private Joseph Davis and Mrs Kaziah Davis also had a child, the only boy in the settlement in the early days, Josiah was born on 7 February 1841.

† Peter Spillett's research in England in 1970, managed to find some of the attestation records for marines who served at Port Essington, and from them and other sources, create a roll for the garrison. Men came and went, but Spillett listed 108 Royal Marines stationed at Victoria; 48 of them arrived with Bremer in 1838, and 60 more in 1844, when the first garrison was relieved and went home (Spillett, 1972). (See Appendix 1.)

of Australia, for the purpose of giving protection to British Australia. Commerce carried on thro' Torres Straits with China and India and with the Islands of the Indian Archipelago, and of affording an Asylum for those who may be shipwrecked on that Coast. Sir J. Bremer will Communicate to you the Instructions which he has received, and you will afford him every assistance in your power in carrying into effect the objects of the Expedition. You will issue a Commission under the Seal of the Colony commission to appointing Captain Sir J. G. Bremer, or in his absence the senior Officer in Command of the Marines, to act as Commandant with such powers as may be necessary for the order and good Government of the Post to be formed, as it is within the limits of your Government.

I have, &c, GLENELG (Glenelg, 25 Jan 1838).

Gipps may have been surprised by the news that once again the Governor of New South Wales was expected to support a new attempt on the hell that was the north coast of Australia, but at least, this time, the costs were to the navy, rather than the NSW treasury, and there were no orders to send convicts.

Huge amounts of stores were needed—everything from houses to farming equipment, cattle to chickens and kangaroo dogs (greyhounds). Packed into the *Alligator,* the *Britomart,* and a third ship, the *Orontes*—hired to transport stores at the cost of 14s 11d per ton per month—were six houses, five months' worth of salted foods, and eight months' supply of everything else for the settlers. Bremer listed what came aboard on 16 September in the *Alligator*'s log:

... Recd During our stay in Port Jackson (by purchase) Bread 102660 lbs, Rum 3345-Gals, Salt Beef 26600 lbs, Salt Pork 6300 lbs, Flour 29385 lbs, Suet 2007 lbs, Sugar 12547 lbs, Tea 4517? Pease 336 bushels, Oatmeal 7000 lbs, Lemon Juice 3402 gals, Tobacco 4701 lbs, Soap 2228 lbs, Vinegar 1105 Gals, Rice 2540 lbs, Shoes 466 pairs, Guernsey Frocks 250, Duck 400 trowsers 400, Paramatta Cloth [?], Beds 50, Blankets 140, 960 yds calico, Blue Cotton 49 ¾ yds, Shawls 72, Cotton handkerchiefs 136, 3 Pieces of Print and 8 lbs blue bead ... (Bremer, 1838).

The Customs Office, which did not record government supplies, listed a few extra treats on the *Orontes*, perhaps for the officers: '3 casks preserved provisions and 4 casks herrings' (Herald, 17 September 1838). Also on board were 34 iron ships' tanks that were to be used as rat-proof larders (Pearson, 1992), and several timber framed weatherboard pre-fabricated buildings, including houses, two barrack rooms, a kitchen, storehouse, and a hospital.

The *Alligator* and *Britomart* also carried four months' supply on board for their own use, but as other ships, such as the *Beagle*, under Captain Wickham, were expecting to use the port as a revictualling base, the commissariat had to be prepared for them also. There was too much for the three ships to carry, so a fourth, a private schooner (renamed *Essington* from *Isabella*) was chartered and paid £150 to help. She was owned by a Sydney local 'pilot', Captain Thomas Watson, who had bought her in the hope of regular business with the new settlement. The *Essington*'s major contribution was transporting a church that had been donated by the Lord Bishop of Australia. The church was a prefabricated, wooden-framed, weatherboard kit that had cost £300. When constructed, it would hold up to 300 people.

The *Essington* was especially needed after difficulties arose loading the *Orontes*:

> … A large punt, containing a quantity of building materials intended to be used in erecting a Church at Port Essington sunk in the Cove, on Tuesday, whilst being towed off to the *Orontes*, and has not yet been recovered. The loss of the materials will, if not recovered, cause a detention of a few days to the ships going on that expedition (*Monitor*, 7 Sept 1838).

Captain Watson's holds and deck space were loaded, and the ship was ready to depart earlier than the others, on 11 September, so the *Essington* headed north alone*. She arrived in Port Essington 10 days before Bremer and the *Alligator*.

---

* For the complete log of the *Essington*'s journey to Port Essington, see acms.sl.nsw. gov.au/_transcript/2010/D04420/a1490.htm.

The British in North Australia: Port Essington

Bremer's little fleet finally was ready on 17 September. It was joined by two other ships, the *Canton,* and the *Lady Kennaway,* because the captains wished to sail the dangerous passage through Torres Strait in company. The *Canton* carried Bremer's personal launch that would be useful for exploring the harbour, and the *Britomart* towed a small sailing vessel named *Lizard**. A delay at the last moment saw the *Britomart* spending a few days waiting for the *Canton*, whilst the *Alligator, Orontes,* and *Lady Kennaway* sailed north.

Governor Gipps watched the settlers sail out of Port Jackson and wished them well. He wrote almost immediately to Lord Glenelg to tell him they were on their way. Whatever he thought of the venture is lost in the platitudes of his politically correct letter:

> ... I cannot, My Lord, close this Despatch without congratulating your Lordship on the prospects which are opened, not only to this Colony but to the British Merchants in general, by the Establishment of this Settlement on the Northern Coast of Australia ... (Gipps, 23 Sept 1838) (see Appendix 2 for the full letter).

Sailing up the eastern coast of Australia was not without its challenges, but it became increasingly more dangerous the further north a ship travelled. Crossing the Great Barrier Reef at its northern end to enter Torres Strait was a nerve-wracking experience—and not just because of the hidden reefs and shoals:

> ... entered the Great Barrier and steering W½S under all sail, made the best of our way for Murrays Island. On entering the Barrier we passed through an exceedingly Narrow passage with broken water on both sides; the Navigation here is at all times one of great danger, more especially to those who are unacquainted with the Barrier (Watson, 1838).

The *Essington* was approaching Murray Island, and Watson was expecting to be able to trade for the island's products, particularly

---

* It is possible that Bremer's 'launch' and the *Lizard* are the same boat, and as the *Canton* did not enter Port Essington, the launch was unloaded and towed by the *Britomart*. A confusion arises where another 'decked boat' called the *Lady Jane* is mentioned in letters.

turtle shell, in exchange for knives and hatchets. It was wise to be prepared for treachery:

> ... All our Guns were now run out, and a round of blank cartridges fired to clear them, and each of the boat crews (being in all 12 Men) were served out a Musket Bayonet, and Cutlass. To the remainder of the crew a Musket each, with six rounds of ball Cartridges, were distributed; and at the same time we endeavoured to impress upon their minds the necessity of always having them in readiness should any emergencies call for the use of them, but by no means to attempt the use of them under any other circumstances (Watson, 1838).

However, the islanders were peaceful and friendly, and the trading was good. Watson had also been charged to enquire about possible survivors from the wreck of the *Charles Eaton* that had been wrecked nearby, on 19 July 1834. Then, the ship had capsized and destroyed or swamped all its lifeboats except one. That was quickly seized by Third Mate George Piggott and four seamen, who then abandoned the others and made their escape*.

Captain George d'Orley and his wife Charlotte, their two children, several other passengers, and 17 seamen, made rafts from the wreckage. They managed to beach them on nearby islands, only to be immediately murdered by the islanders, except three-year-old William d'Orley and the ship's boy, John Ireland. Charlotte was clubbed so hard over her head that she was recognised—long after her flesh had gone—by remnants of her long blond hair that still ran through the holes in her caved-in skull. The European skulls of seventeen of the crew were identified among 45 skulls collected by Captain Lewis in the *Isabella*.

---

* Piggott and his companions sailed west for two weeks, towards Timor, and reached the island of Timor Laut. They were immediately attacked by villagers. However, they managed to survive and recuperate, and waited there 13 months before being rescued, in December 1835. Whilst there, they heard stories of another European in the neighbouring village of Laoura. This was Joseph Forbes, a cabin boy of the *Stedcombe* from Fort Dundas, taken as a slave by pirates, in 1825. Forbes was eventually rescued by Captain Watson in the *Essington*, in 1839 (Pugh, 2016).

Figure 4: The rescue of William d'Orley by the *Isabella* (*Essington*), from Murray Island, Torres Strait, J.W. Carmichael (silentworldfoundation.org.au).

A Murray Islander, named Duppar, took pity on the two living boys, and he managed to rescue them by exchanging them for a bunch of bananas. Duppar 'adopted' the boys and treated them kindly, called them Wak and Nass, and raised them quietly for the next fourteen months. Then, the convict transport ship *Mangles* called into Murray Island to trade, and John Ireland was spotted in one of the canoes that came out to meet the ship, and four-year-old William was seen on the shore. It took nine months for a rescue to be organised, and it was Captain Lewis, in the schooner *Isabella*, who picked the children up. William d'Orley, who spoke no English, wept for days after being parted from his Murray family, but both boys were returned to their families in England. William was then raised by his uncle.

When the *Essington* came to in the waters off Murray Island in 1838, the islanders no doubt recognised her as the formerly named *Isabella* because she had been there before, under Captain Lewis. Trade was initially brisk and, as the people warmed to each other, Watson enquired about George d'Orley and the ship's boy, Saxon, the only two from the *Charles Eaton* yet to be accounted for. He was told that they had been taken to Darnley Island and murdered there.

When Watson met Duppar, a 'tall and powerful' man of middle age, he told him that he had brought presents from Wak and Nass:

> ... for the kind manner in which they had treated those youths during the time they were resident upon Murrays Island, and I told them if they always behaved well to white people, they would be rewarded for it with many presents. I then distributed the presents I had received from Mrs Slade in the name of Wak [John] and Nass [William], viz 6 Tomahawks, 1 Bundle of Fish hooks, and a box of rings, together with other small articles; they appeared highly delighted with what they had received, more particularly since they came from their white protegees, about whom they made many anxious enquiries ... (Watson, 1838).

The next day, Duppar visited the ship again, and:

> ... brought with him a small Image, cut out of white wood, and which he said was a representation of his absent friend Nass; this he brought as a present for me, and I also gave him something in return. The Natives all appeared very anxious that we should pay them a visit on shore and being desirous as far as I could to gratify their wishes I lowered the two quarter boats, mounting a swivel Gun in the bow of each, and every man carrying his Arms with him. In this manner we pulled for the beach, and no sooner had we arrived there than we were surrounded by Natives expressing in various ways their delight on seeing us on shore; they came about one hugging and caressing me, as if they could not show me sufficient attention, and at length took me out of the boat, and carried me for some distance upon their shoulders. When I mentioned my intention of leaving them tomorrow, many of them wished to come away with me that they might see Wak and Nass, the Native Duppar crying and kissing the wooden representation of the little D'Oyley whom he denominated his absent friend (Watson, 1838).

Watson continued trading among the islands for a few more days, then set a course to Arnhem Land and Port Essington across the Gulf of Carpentaria. They arrived there on 13 October 1838. Watson was hoping that the *Alligator* and the *Orontes* would already be in the harbour, but 'to our disappointment found ourselves the sole Master of the Harbour, not even a Native to be seen' (Watson, 1838). The crew spent a few days searching for water and exploring the coast whilst hunting for wild game. Watson mentioned seeing large crocodiles, pigeons, wild ducks, cockatoos, pelicans, and several large snakes, both in the water and on land. He collected a number of bush fruits, such as a cucumber on a vine, and the native nutmeg (*Myristica insipida*), which he expected would 'become an article of great value to the Colony'.

After several days waiting, Watson became impatient. The *Essington* had caressed a reef on the journey through the Torres Strait, and he needed to inspect her bottom for signs of damage. This could not be done with the church still loaded onto her decks, so he moved the *Essington* to Point Record, and the crew unloaded it.

On 24 October, Watson met his first Iwaidja men: the Aborigines of Port Essington:

> ... This morning we observed a Canoe push off from Middle Point with three natives, they landed about ½ Mile from us, and then walked along the beach to where our people were employed. Each of them carried a Spear, they also had with them some small pieces of Tortoise Shell, which I purchased off them. After having been with them some time on Shore I got them to pull me in their Canoe to the Vessel, where after remaining some time, and partaking of something to Eat [etc] they again embarked for Middle point ... (Watson, 1838).*

On 27 October, the ship was light enough to beach so Watson could inspect it for damage and found—as he had suspected—that the ship had lost copper sheeting off the stern post. In the meantime:

> ... At 2h-30m P.M. we discovered a ship at a distance in the offing which we supposed to be the long looked for *Alligator* and shortly after a second ship was seen. Made them out to be the *Alligator* and the *Orontos*, Merchantman, with stores for the settlement. Lowered a boat and went on board the *Alligator*, found she had left Sydney on Sept'r 17th Ult. ... (Watson, 1838).

---

* See Appendix 3 for more of the Essington's log.

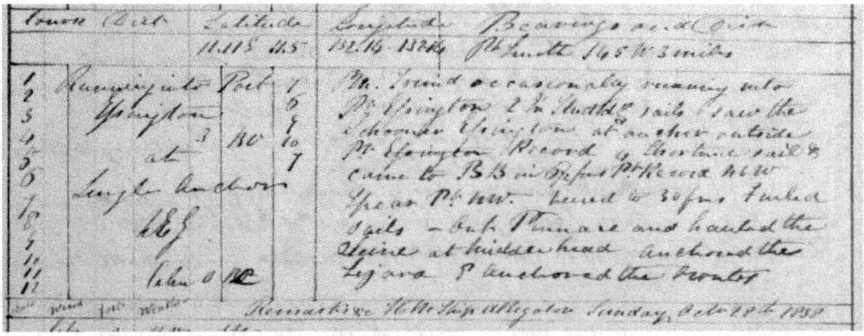

Figure 5: HMS *Alligator* log, 28 October 1838 (Bremer (2), 1838).

The *Alligator* and the *Orontes* had had an easy trip north without any major problems, with plain sailing, albeit mostly with slow winds. The *Lady Kennaway* had separated on the first night, and never managed to find the fleet again, but Bremer and Captain Joseph Short remained in sight of each other.

Bremer had an important duty to perform on the way. On 19 October, the ships came to in deep water, just off the coast of Cape York, and dropped anchor. Boats were lowered, and Bremer, the ships' officers, and the Royal Marines, were rowed to the nearest beach. From there, they climbed a nearby headland and raised the Union Jack. Sir Gordon Bremer then took formal possession of Cape York and the adjacent islands in the name of Queen Victoria. The Royal Marines fired a salute with their muskets and gave three hearty cheers, and the *Alligator* replied with cannon. The local Aborigines and Torres Strait Islanders didn't know it, but they had just become British subjects.

From Cape York, the ships went straight to the uninhabited Booby Island, a half day's sail away. Booby Island[*] was an important staging post for nineteenth century mariners. Near its centre there was a small cave containing a large chest, covered with a tarpaulin, labelled 'Post Office':

---

[*] Booby Island was named by Lt James Cook after the large numbers of Boobies, the sea birds, living there. The Kuarareg people of the western Torres Strait call the island Ngiangu.

> ... on opening this box we remarked that it was fitted with every convenience and requisite for writing Viz Pens, Ink, Paper, Pencils and Indian Rubber, As well as a blank book for the entry of the names of all Ships which may at any time call. From Memorandums made in the book, it appears that all these requisites for conveying useful information were placed there, by a Colonel who was on his way to India to join his Regiment, in the HMS *Rattlesnake* ... (Watson, 1838).

Here were also left letters destined for other ports, and—in later years—emergency provisions for ship-wrecked sailors. Bremer learned that Watson and the *Essington* had been there two weeks before them. Watson:

> ... left an account of our passage through the Straits, and also a Chart of the route the Schooner had taken in search of the supposed survivors of the *Charles Eaton*. Finding no account of HMS *Alligator* and Brig *Britomart* having passed through the Straits, on their way to Port Essington, we returned on board and bore away under all sail for Port Essington, Steering W by N. ... (Watson, 1838).

From the Record Book, Watson also learned the fate of a ship he had sold before purchasing the *Essington*:

> ... Amongst other papers I found one giving the account of the loss of the Brig *William* of Sydney, Kronger[?], Master, which was wrecked on Cockburn Reef on Sept'r 8 Ult: Crew all saved Ship *Trusty Jammison*[?], which called at Booby Island on the 12th Ult: on her passage to Lombock. The Brig *William* had belonged to me, and only last voyage I commanded her, but afterwards sold her; it appears singular that I should be first to discover her loss ... (Watson, 1838).

From Booby Island it was a straight sail of about 1100 kilometres to Port Essington. It took them six days to reach Croker Island. Then, early on 27 October, they had their first view of Point Smith and the entrance to Port Essington. Bremer had last entered the port fourteen years previously.

The *Alligator*'s log recorded their arrival in Port Essington:

> ... Saw the schooner *Essington* at anchor outside Pt Essington

Record & shortened sails & came to BB in 6☒2 fms [fathoms] Pt Record NW. Spear Pt NW ... to 30 fms Furled sails—Out Pinnace and hauled the seine at Middle head Anchored the *Lizard* & anchored the *Orontes* (Bremer, 1838).

Although not noted in Watson's journal, Earl recorded that as he arrived on board the *Britomart*, at Point Record, there were natives on the deck of the *Essington*, 'dressed up in all sorts of fantastic finery which they had obtained from the crew' (Earl, 1846). There was also a group camping on the nearby beach. Watson and his crew clearly had begun positive cross-cultural relationships. He found the natives to be 'very friendly' and they had even helped him unload the church.

Captain Owen Stanley and the *Britomart* took several more weeks to arrive. The brig entered the harbour on 1 November, towing Bremer's launch, which had been carried on the deck of the *Canton*. She had been unlucky, as she had run aground on a reef in the Torres Strait, but she was undamaged, although the crew had spent an anxious few hours waiting for the tide to rise enough to float them free.

By the time the *Britomart* arrived in Port Essington, Bremer and Captain McArthur had explored the inner harbour and chosen the best site for a settlement. It was on the western side of the harbour, on a plateau above white cliffs, 15–20 metres above the high tide mark. There was a white sandy beach on the southern side, and deep enough water for the mooring of any number of ships within rowing distance.

Two other ships are listed in James Teggs' *New South Wales Pocket Almanac and Remembrancer* (Teggs, 1 January 1839), as well as in the 'Shipping Intelligence' section of several newspapers, such as the *Sydney Herald*, as departing for Port Essington during September and October 1838. They provide a reminder to take care with what is written in newspapers, even in 1838. One was the barque *Regia*, under Captain Thomas Johnson, on 23 October, which, according to *The Australian*, was carrying a gentleman with perfect knowledge of the Malay language to Port Essington to begin trade talks with the islands. They clearly meant George Windsor Earl, but he had already departed on the *Alligator*, and, anyway, the *Regia* sailed south to Port Phillip. The other ship was the *Bright Planet*, under Captain Moore. She was a 22-year-old merchant's barque that left three days after Bremer's fleet, apparently for Port Essington. Records show, however, that she arrived in the Swan River Colony, on 10 November. There is no record of her arriving in Victoria at all—even though the Customs Office listed her load as supplies for Port Essington! The supplies ended up in Perth instead, and perhaps were always meant to. Nevertheless, the list is included here because it gives an interesting snapshot of a remote settler's diet in 1838:

> September 15—*BRIGHT PLANET*, 180 tons, Moore, Master, For Port Essington: 54 boxes candles, 4 crates bacon, 2 crates ham and cheese, 3 crates 4 casks 3 cases cheese, 2 crates crockery, 3 casks glass, 1 pipe vinegar, 3 casks tongues, 31 tierees [sic] pork, 54 casks beef, 10 hogsheads 30 casks ale, 10 hogsheads porter, 3 pipes 8 quarter-pipes 10 half-pipes 10 casks 15 casks wine, 2 hogsheads oatmeal, 75 hogsheads beer, 10 casks lard, 31 baskets 70 bags sugar, 6 bags saltpetre, 1 case drapery, 1 case haberdashery, 1 case hosiery, 1 case stays, trunks 1 cask 2 cases shoes, 4 bales 1 case slops, 6 cases hats, 2 bales woolbagging, 35 packages spades, 137 bags barley, 12 cases cigars, 2 pipes brandy, 1 hogshead 49 cases gin, 5 puncheons 2 hogsheads rum, 7 pipes arrack, 12 packages tinware, 334 bags flour, 167 bags maize, 3 cases bonnets (Herald, 17 September 1838).

In Port Essington, the *Alligator* and *Orontes* were moved to the cliffs on November 3, and work parties were sent ashore to start building access paths up to the plateau from the landing site.

Soon after, two Aborigines, Langari and Wanji-Wanji, paddled out to the *Alligator* and were welcomed aboard. The British could not understand their language, of course, but they used the word 'commandant' several times, pointing towards Raffles Bay. The last commandant of Fort Wellington, abandoned in 1829, was

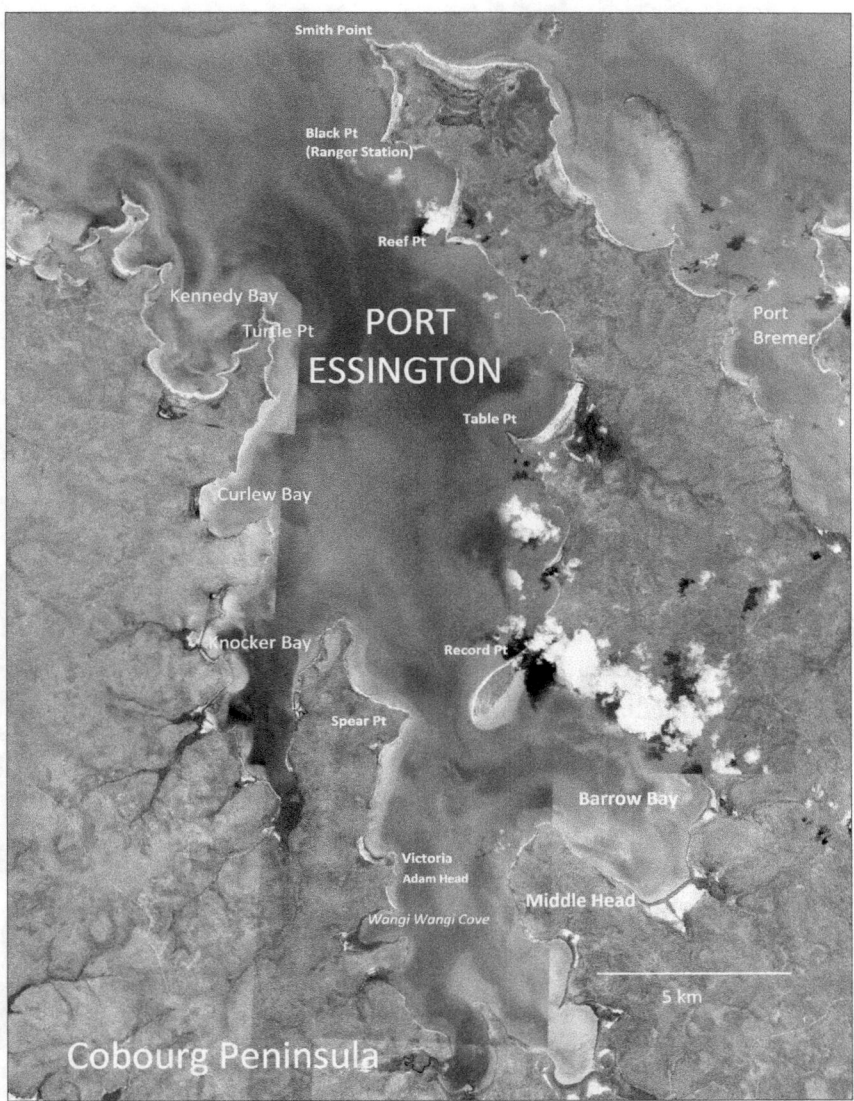

Map 3: Port Essington 'This fine Port must ere long, become one of very great importance, to all Ships bound from Sydney and Van Diemen's Land and from India' (Watson, 1838). (Google Earth, 2020).

Captain Collet Barker. He was an extraordinary man who seemed to instinctively understand how to develop positive relationships with the Iwaidja.

> ... Langari delivered a long address, shedding many tears, and frequently touching his shoulders with both hands in a sort of half embrace (Earl, 1846).

Langari was at ease on the *Alligator* and seemed to have mistaken Commandant Bremer for Commandant Barker. Wanji-Wanji was a much younger man who may not have experienced European men before. He was terrified. His 'teeth chattered, and his eyes rolled about in an agony of alarm and apprehension', but soon after, wrote Earl, Wanji-Wanji developed more confidence, and became a regular—and useful—visitor to the settlement*.

Captain Barker had left behind many Iwaidja contacts and friends in 1829. Two of the most memorable were Mariac and Iacama, who were nicknamed Wellington and Waterloo by Commandant Smyth. Bremer was keen to meet them, and asked after them, but was told they had died of smallpox (known to the Iwaidja as 'mea-mea' or 'oie-boie') several years before. Nevertheless, it seems the relationships that Barker had built a decade before, were remembered by the Iwaidja, and they were immediately willing to remain on friendly and welcoming terms with their new British guests. Two men were so keen to please, they pretended to be Wellington and Waterloo—despite looking nothing like the description Bremer had of the originals. Bremer was happy to report on the early success with the Iwaidja:

> ... It affords me the highest gratification in being enabled to acquaint their Lordships that the most satisfactory understanding had been established to entertain a hope that something like civilisation may spring up amongst them (Bremer, 9 February 1839).

Almost as soon as the anchors dropped below Adam Head, work parties climbed to the tableland and started clearing the scrub and constructing holding yards for the animals. The vegetation was open sclerophyll forest, dominated by *Eucalyptus tetradonta*, with vast numbers of *Livistona* sand palms, cycads, and Acacia.

---

* Other Iwaidja who were known to Collet Barker at Fort Wellington also visited: 'One-eye', Miro, Mingo, and Yamaloo. These men, as McKenna points out, knew far more about the British than the new arrivals knew about them (McKenna, 2016).

Other marines started clearing for the gardens, under the direction of the botanist, John Armstrong. In October, the bush is dry in the north, so they were able to use fire to do much of the work, burning off all the grass and deadwood, prior to felling trees and tilling the soil. The settlers had collected seeds and seedlings in Rio de Janeiro, Sydney, and Cape York, and they were keen to plant them before the rains started in November.

The tableland extends over about 35 hectares. The cliffs run between two headlands on the eastern side: the 23-metre-high Minto Head* in the north; and the 17-metre-high Adam Head in the south. Its western edge runs down to mangrove swamps and mud flats in an inlet. To the south lie almost limitless expanses of forest, unknown and unexplored by the new British arrivals—although they could see two flat-topped mountains in the distance, named Mount Bedwell and Mount Rose, by Phillip Parker King. Stokes estimated their heights at about 120 metres (400 feet).

Wanji-Wanji took his new guests a little along the bay to the south to show them a freshwater spring running into a cove, which was subsequently named after him. It was inconveniently far, so Bremer ordered the digging of a well behind the beach to the south of Adam Head. When that was successful with sweet water at six metres, several more wells were dug up on the tableland. Wanji-Wanji Cove was more useful later, however, as a source for lime from coral, and clay for brickmaking. Private William Handy, a master brick-maker, made the first bricks and taught other marines the trade.

The crew of the *Alligator* also dug wells on Point Record, where Bremer's men had discovered the bamboo walls of Macassan wells in 1824. The crews of the *Britomart* and the *Orontes* found water at Spear Point† for their use, and then Captain McArthur and his son,

---

* Minto Head was named after Lord Minto, First Lord of the Admiralty.
† 'Spear Point' was so named by P.P. King in 1819, after Iwaidja men threw spears at him here.

James, discovered several pools of fresh water three kilometres south of the settlement (Earl, 1846).

The well near the beach may have been a little too close to the sea for safety. One of the well-diggers hung his hammock in the trees on the beach and slept there. He was woken by his blanket being pulled off. He looked down to see a large crocodile happily munching on the cloth. His shouts brought his mates, but the crocodile was long gone by the time they arrived, and:

> ... For some time this story was not believed*, but when afterwards the huge reptile, on a similar excursion, was shot, a portion of the blanket was found in his stomach with the paw of a favourite spaniel, taken when swimming off the pier head (Stokes, 1846).

Like fisherman's tales, a good crocodile story improves with the telling. Fanny, the spaniel, had been swimming off the pier when she disappeared, and Stokes' story had the marines 'thirsting for revenge' and baiting a large hook to catch the beast. The crocodile was eventually shot in the head and died, with its brains exposed, after 'a violent struggle of many minutes', and:

> ... some of the men returned the compliment he was supposed to have intended for their companion, by eating a considerable portion of his remains (Earl, 1846).

All the marines initially lived in tents on the tableland, and a large officers' tent was put up on Adam Head for Bremer and McArthur, whilst Lieutenant Phineas Priest and Dr Whipple raised their tents nearby. The marines put the prefabricated storerooms together quickly, so that perishable stores could be unloaded, and then the barracks, which Earl says were 'each forty feet long by sixteen wide' (12m X 5m). Married men started to construct huts for their wives and children. One or more of the Royal Marines may have been Cornish stonemasons, as a row of 'Cornish chimneys' was built for the married quarters. Like most newcomers to the north, everyone

---

* This behaviour might seem unlikely, but it happened again in almost the same place, 30 years later! John Lewis tells the story of shooting an 'alligator' which lay under his mate's hammock. It managed to escape into the harbour (Lewis, 1922).

Figure 6: Government House from the battery on the Queen's birthday
(Stanley, SLNSW).

suffered from the bites of sand-flies and mosquitoes, and the October-November heat was debilitating, and a constant topic of conversation.

Bremer enjoyed meeting the Iwaidja:

It is very great gratification to me to be able to acquaint their Lordships that I have established a most friendly intercourse with the natives ... By kindness and conciliation, the occasional donation of an axe or a knife, a few beads and coloured calico, and biscuit, the only food they desire, they have become greatly domesticated, many of them living constantly with us... (Bremer, 13 December 1838).

Soon after work on constructing the settlement had started, and because Bremer knew that he would need farm stock, such as cattle, buffaloes, pigs and chickens, and fresh food for the garrison, he hired Captain Watson and the *Essington* to travel to the islands north-west of the port, to get them. George Windsor Earl was sent with him to do the purchasing, using his knowledge of the Malay languages. They sailed on November 1, the same day the *Britomart* arrived, although a few hours later than planned because, when the captain and Earl returned to the schooner at 5 P.M. the evening before, ready to sail, they found the men 'intoxicated by spirits given to them on board the *Orontos* [sic]'. It was not until midnight that the crew had recovered enough to weigh anchor and make sail, amid 'light Airs and variable'. Alcohol remained a continuing problem for the whole of their journey.

The *Essington*'s colours were hoisted to salute the *Britomart* as she left the harbour and turned nor-nor-west for the six-days sail to the 'Coast of Kisha' (Kissa or Kisser), an island about 30 kilometres off the eastern end of Timor. In 1838, its Calvinist Christian community of more than 8000 people had become the 'resort of traders' for the region (Earl, 1841). It was ruled by two brothers—rajahs—one of whom ruled the Dutch residents, the other the island's natives.

George Earl went ashore to visit a German missionary he knew of, a Mr Bier, who was willing to help as much as he could, and they began to gather together a herd of buffaloes and other livestock, for transport from Kissa and the smaller island of Moa. In the meantime, Captain Watson opened his own trading on November 8:

> … At 8 AM went on shore to commence my trade and then found … the Rajah (Zacharias Frederick Baker) and Orang Kaire*, Our business was carried on under the cover of a spacious boat shed, which formed an excellent substitute for our more elegant and substantial Market Stalls; a great number of Natives were in attendance, and also the Missionary Mr Biers, The following are the articles which I purchased, Viz Pigs, Bee's Wax, Tortoise-shell—Sandlewood [sic], Indian Corn, Yams, Pumpkins and other fruits. The Articles most in request amongst the Natives are: Muskets, Powder, Black and White Calicoes, Brass Wire, Bar Iron, Knives, Manufactured Glass [etc]. I here met with a Native Pilot named Glass, and made an agreement with him to Pilot the Schooner among the Islands, At 5 P.M. returned on board with the Rajah and Orang Kaire, and after having given them refreshments, and thanked them for their Kindness and attention, we took an affectionate farewell of them and they embarked for the Shore (Watson, 1838).

---

* Literally a 'rich man': a man in authority, possibly also 'orang kepala', or village head. Earl called them 'chiefs'.

As the days passed, Watson moved on to trade with several other villages along the coast, albeit with some anxiety about the length of time Earl was away from the ship. Earl was certainly busy. He discovered that the descendants of the Dutch settlers who had come with the East India Company, had 'superior intelligence' and a 'well-regulated community' and the Malay village chiefs gave him a highly favourable reception. The Kissa chiefs told Earl to go to Moa for better quality and cheaper buffaloes than they could provide, which was an honesty which astounded Earl.

Earl asked the Kissa chiefs about the *Lady Nelson*, the supply ship that had been taken by pirates on Babar Island in 1824 (Earl, 1841). Captain Samuel Johns, of the *Lady Nelson*, had been tricked into following the Babar villagers from Pulau Leti back to Babar, where Johns and the crew were murdered, and the *Lady Nelson* scuttled. Later, the *Stedcombe* had also been plundered, with less planning, but its two cabin boys survived to become slaves in a village on the island of Timor Laut. There were rumours spread from the survivors of the wreck of the *Charles Eaton* that one of the boys was still alive. His name was Joseph Forbes. He was finally rescued by Captain Watson and the Essington, on 1 April, the next year. Watson took an Orang Kaire hostage until the villagers brought the Englishman to his ship. After 15 years of slavery:

> ... the appearance of the Englishman at the time we received him on board, was in the highest degree remarkable[?] and such as was calculated to draw forth the strongest sympathies from the bosom of any human being, whose composition was not entirely void of compassionate feelings ... (Watson, 1838).

On 15 December, the *Essington* arrived back in Port Essington at midnight and dropped anchor beside the *Alligator* and the *Britomart*. The cargo collected in Kissa and Moa included:

> ... nineteen buffaloes, sixty pigs, more than a hundred sheep, several tons of yams, and a quantity of poultry; with a number of banana stems, cocoa-nuts [sic], and seeds to plant in the garden; the whole having been purchased with goods that cost

at Sydney somewhat less than £30 sterling (Earl, 1846).

A couple of pigs, 'too fat to stand upon their legs', and half the sheep, who were 'wretched, long legged things, not at all fitted for a sea-voyage', died during the journey to Victoria (Earl, 1846). They finally landed '16 Buffalo, 47 Sheep, and 70 Pigs' for the use of the settlement. A grand success were the banana plants, as they started to shoot as soon as they were planted.

On the way into the harbour, the *Essington* passed the *Orontes* at Point Record, empty of her stores and cargo, and preparing to sail to India. News came in, about 24 hours later, that she had left the harbour and ran straight into some rocks at speed—and punched a huge hole in her hull. Captain Joseph Short managed to beach her on Vashon Head without loss of life, but the ship was wrecked beyond repair. The 26 crew members were picked up by the *Britomart* and brought back to Victoria, with as much equipment and stores as possible being salvaged from the wreck. Some of her timbers were used in the construction of the fort in Victoria (d'Urville, 1839).

Captain Short may have been more than a little embarrassed when the salvagers discovered, locked in his cabin, 'full cases of wine, preserved meats, and fruits, and crockeries and sundries' (Lubbock, 1967). He, and his wife Caroline had to wait, like the crew, for transport away from Victoria. They eventually travelled to Timor on the *Essington*, and then on to India the next February, whilst the rest of the crew waited for transport to Sydney (Spillett, 1972).

As the seasons changed, and the winds swung round to come from the west, the settlement was hit by occasional thunderstorms and torrential rain, heavier than that ever experienced before by the young marines. The humidity closed in. The smell of mildew pervaded the storerooms and houses. Layers of mould appeared on clothing and anything left in moist areas. Leather particularly needed regular cleaning, and footwear wore out quickly. The 466 pairs of shoes brought by the *Alligator* were a boon to soft English feet,

Figure 7: 'Situation of the *Orontes* when Abandoned by Her Master and Crew, Port Essington, Decr. 28/38' (Owen Stanley, SLNSW 1837–43 SAFE/PXC 279).

but they were all mostly gone two years later, when the settlement became 'destitute of shoes and shoe leather' (McArthur, 2 November 1840). Eventually a substitute made of wood and canvas was needed (McArthur, 25 February 1841), but many of the men went barefoot much of the time.

By Christmas and New Year 1838, most of the garrison had reasonably comfortable accommodation, with only a few still in their tents. With the supplies brought in from the islands by the *Essington*, there was plenty of good cheer for seasonal parties.

Several friendly Iwaidja regularly visited the settlement during this time, sometimes sleeping on the ground outside the marines' tents, or in a camp on the beach. Iwaidja families started to trade fish, oysters, and crabs, for flour, sugar, biscuits, or old clothing. During this time, a few items went missing—particularly knives and some carpenter's tools, and eventually a man named Mallamay was caught red-handed, stealing a shirt from a clothes line. He was 'arrested' by two burly marines and marched to the officers' tent for an audience with Sir Gordon Bremer. Poor Mallamay was dreadfully frightened, and Earl thought it was because he was expecting to be put to death, as that was what the Macassans would have done, but Bremer forgave him, thinking the fright was sufficient punishment. Then, 'on being released, he walked away for a few yards in as composed a manner as he could assume, and then bounded off through the dark forest like a deer.' The episode had been nothing but a cruel entertainment for the officers.

In a charming letter to his wife, Bremer wrote that he found the people to be 'really amiable':

> ... they evince a great fondness for their children, and in their intercourse with each other display a kindness and attention which would honour a more polished society; nor are they by any means deficient in natural politeness. They never fail to introduce a stranger of their tribe to us, and endeavour to give him our names. They never leave us, when they go into the woods to sleep, without individually saying 'Goodnight' which they utter as plainly as we can. My bald head is a source of infinite delight to them. Those who know it will quickly raise my cap in order to display this wonder to strangers, and then a burst of surprise and merriment comes from the whole party... (Lubbock, 1967).

Counting the settlers and the crews of the three ships moored in the harbour, there were about 300 men, women and children involved in establishing the settlement in the first month or two. They were a healthy lot. Dr Whipple and the ships' surgeons had little to do other than treating infected sand-fly bites, and jellyfish stings.

Within weeks, the storehouse and the officers' quarters were well advanced. A roadway had been cut through the cliff down to the sea, and a stone pier constructed by using the blocks that were cut from it. By mid-December it already extended 15 or 20 metres out from the high-water mark.

Bremer planned that the two headlands—Adam Head and Minto Head—would be armed for defence. Minto Head would have

Figure 8: Battery on Adam Head in front of the fort tower
(Stanley, SLNSW FL1893215).

a battery of six 18-pounder cannons and two mortars, and Adam Head two 18-pounder cannons and a mortar. This would give the marines' cannons complete coverage of the whole inner harbour.

In February, Bremer wrote a brief report to Sir John Barrow, giving him the first information on the new settlement:

Figure 9: The fort on Adam Head with the magazine in the ground beside it
(Stanley 1847, SLNSW f119).

Port Essington, 9th February 1839.

On the 27th October 1838, I reached this place, and, after due consideration, fixed on this spot for the settlement. Our Operations commenced on the 3rd November and have proceeded with so much vigour that we have now a very admirable little town. The position is on a considerable piece of rising ground, midway on the western side of the inner harbour. The soil around is of the finest description; and we have already four wells sunk, which afford abundance of water. A finer harbour is scarcely to be met with in the world; The *Alligator* and *Britomart* lie in 18 feet at the lowest water of springtides, within hail of an excellent pier, which extends 100 feet. On Point Record and Spear Point are wells where ships can water most expeditiously, while around our settlement are large ponds and many running streams, all excellent. The rains have fallen but slightly this season, and our gardens in consequence have not made that progress I had hoped for; nevertheless, the orange, lemon, banana, plantain, and cocoa-nut trees are in beautiful order; while the pumpkins, melons, &c., give ample promise.

As regards climate I have no hesitation in expressing my opinion that it is as fine as any tropical one in the world. We have had very hard labour and been constantly exposed to the sun; occasionally the thermometer in the shade has been 98° and 100°; yet not one serious case of sickness has occurred. Some disposition to scurvy in two individuals had manifested itself, but by timely means it has been overcome. We have now a stock of cattle for a month, and I look for a further supply on the return of the schooner *Essington* from Timor. That vessel sailed in December last for the islands to the northward, for the purpose of opening a trade; and on board her I sent Mr. G. W. Earl, whose interesting account of his voyage is amongst my other reports. He found a considerable Christian population, under the guidance of some intelligent Dutch missionaries, and has given me so much information, and caused such a desire on my part for more, that I purpose proceeding to Little Moa and Kissa in the *Britomart* about the end of this month. My absence will probably not exceed fourteen or sixteen days; and on my return I hope to find the ship from India, by which I trust I shall be able to give a further account of these highly interesting islands (Bremer, 19 February 1839).

Bremer was pleased with the progress. With his optimism was as high as ever, he decided to personally travel to Timor, the nearest European settlement, Moa and Kissa, to personally ensure the new trade possibilities were advertised and promoted at the highest level.

He left in the *Britomart* on February 15, but it was a tedious voyage, taking more than two weeks against the westerly monsoon. He spent five days in Dili, then sailed back via Kissa and Moa. In Moa, he heard the news that he was waiting for—several large Macassan praus had already passed by on their annual journey to Australia to collect trepang. The trepang fishery was seen as an integral part of the future success of the new settlement. In 1829, Collet Barker recorded over a thousand Macassan fishermen, in 36 praus, visiting Raffles Bay during the season. Bremer expected that Victoria would become an important trade centre for European goods and give the Macassans an alternative to the Dutch monopoly in the islands.

Back in Port Essington, Bremer discovered that the praus had sailed right past the port and were busy trepanging in Bowen Strait, without knowing of Victoria's existence. The captains eventually heard of the settlement from local Aborigines, and word passed along that they were intending to visit. Surprisingly, the same source told Bremer that there were two large European ships in Raffles Bay, and that they were building houses on the shore. This seemed unlikely—European ships could not pass through Torres Strait against the westerly winds, so where did they come from?

The very next day five praus arrived, flying Dutch colours, and the crews set up a camp on the sandy beach south of the settlement:

> ... they seemed very much pleased at finding us here, for they rightly conjectured that our presence would prevent the natives from molesting them, which had heretofore been the case to a very considerable extent (Earl, 1837).

Their leader was Bapak Padu. He had been visiting the Australian coast for more than 30 years and had known Captain Barker and the

Fort Wellington settlement well. In fact, he still used the telescope and compass he had bought there, ten years before. Padu held Collet Barker in high esteem and was saddened by the news that Barker was long dead, murdered at the mouth of the Murray River in 1840.

Padu confirmed that there were two European ships in Raffles Bay, so Bremer sent Lieutenant Peter Benson Stewart, in the 'decked boat'*, to see what the French were up to. He met Captain Jules Sébastien César Dumont d'Urville, who was leading a 'scientific expedition'. He found d'Urville's scientists taking mundane astrological measurements, samples of plants and shells, and filling their water tanks (Earl, 1846). They had already made a minute survey of the bay and Bowen Strait, including water depths, resources, and the best sites for settlement. The two French ships—*d'Astrolabe* and *Zélée*—had been in Raffles Bay for eight days, and the scientists had set up an observatory on Second Island, north of the abandoned Fort Wellington (see *Fort Wellington*, Pugh 2020). Historian Alan Powell questions the motives of the French. Captain d'Urville had decided—'for some unstated reason'—to visit the abandoned settlement at Port Raffles. To do this they had to sail through the Torres Strait, the most dangerous waters in the north. They were unlikely to do this this just out of curiosity, so Powell thinks that d'Urville may have had secret orders to explore the bay as a potential naval base (Powell, 2016).

The French were invited to visit the settlement, and they stayed several days from 5 April. The officers were taken on a grand tour of the settlement and d'Urville recorded his impressions in his journal:

> ... Victoria Town is situated on a flat piece of ground about ten to twelve metres above sea level. A wide road with a very gentle slope had been cut in the cliff beside the beach and runs down to the jetty; we followed it. We soon met Commodore Bremer, who, already informed of our arrival, was coming out to receive us. He is a man about fifty-five

---

* Possibly the *Lizard*.

years old; his expression is pleasant and kindly, and his manner civil and engaging. He received us with perfect cordiality and politeness, and we were made to feel as if we were meeting old friends. He led us first to his dwelling; it is placed on the highest point of the plateau and the view extends over the whole roadstead, in the middle of which the vessel, the *Alligator*, lay at anchor. This pleasant situation allowed quick and easy communication between the governor and his vessel. Commodore Bremer, without leaving his house, was able to watch the movements in the harbour and at the same time the work going on shore. The house, completely built of wood, had been made up at Port Jackson, and had every comfort that could be desired. All the rooms were arranged with good sense; drawing room, bedroom, study, washroom, bathroom, office; nothing was lacking.

We had hardly arrived there when the sun began to rise quickly above the horizon, and we hurried to set out on a tour of the settlement. M. Bremer wished to be our guide, and he led us first to the fort placed on the end of a small promontory about thirty metres from his house and about fifteen metres above sea level. It consisted of a single battery placed on top of the cliff overlooking the roadstead. It was built of strong, wooden planks and a few ship's timbers from the wreck of the *Orontes*. The battery is in the shape of a semi-octagon and is pierced by four openings, of which three had cannon. This little fortification was completely open on the landwards side but covered the jetty and roadstead that it was meant to defend against foreign invasion (d'Urville, 1839).

Captain d'Urville's crew included a marine artist, Louis le Breton, who spent a few days painting images of the settlement.[*]

The final event of the Frenchmen's visit was a grand dinner with the settlement leaders:

> ... At four o'clock the officers of the two corvettes and most of the English officers repaired to the governor's house where we sat down for dinner. Nothing was spared to make it a magnificent spread and the most unrestrained merriness was in evidence ... (d'Urville, 1839).

---

[*] Some of le Breton's works are included in this book, and as d'Urville's journal is a useful outsiders' view of the new settlement, more of it is reproduced in Appendix 4.

The British in North Australia: Port Essington

Figure 10: Port Essington, Louis Le Breton, *Voyage au Pôle Sud et dans l'Océanie, 1839.*

The French were good dinner guests and, of course, they were happy to provide their best bottles of Bordeaux wines for the table. The remains of these same bottles were found by Jim Allen and his team of archaeologists, 130 years later, in the rubbish tip behind the site of the commandant's house (Allen, 1973).

Bremer was an excellent host, and his guests were entertained by his eldest son's theatrical antics, performing a 'burlesque', including imitating Iwaidja dances and spear throwing*. By that time, Bremer was in his last few weeks at the settlement, and his optimism about the future success of Victoria remained high. Even D'Urville was impressed by his zeal and enthusiasm, although the Frenchman was not so assured of the future success of the settlement:

> ... I was full of admiration for this white-haired gentleman who had left his country and his family to come to this unpromising spot and undertake a laborious and difficult task. He appeared happy in the midst of the little colony of which he was both founder and father; one thought alone seemed to concern him above all others, to see Victoria prosper, and although we could not entirely concur in the vision of the future that he held for his settlement, none of us had the courage to try and destroy his illusions with which this happy father seemed to surround the cradle of his child (d'Urville, 1839).

When Sir John Barrow received Bremer's dispatch, he was also pleased. Barrow was an enthusiastic supporter of the settlement. He had been actively involved with the two earlier, failed, northern settlements, and he was particularly keen to see Victoria prosper. 'There is no fear' he wrote:

> ... that it will experience the fate of that untimely abandonment which befell the two former infant establishments on the same coast; namely, Melville Island and Raffles Bay; which were hastily broken up from the dislike of the military officers in command, with the single exception of one (Captain Barker), and the misrepresentations made to

---

* There are so few references to Edward Bremer that it is as if he was not there at all, but d'Urville called him 'young M Bremmer' (M = 'Monsieur') and described his theatrics of that night.

the Governor of Sydney. All this was fully substantiated by the reports of Captain Laws, of the Royal Navy. The alleged causes which led to this abandonment were, 1st. The unhealthiness of the climate. 2nd. The hostility of the natives. 3rd. The non-visitation of the Malays. Now every one of these allegations was proved to be utterly without foundation (Barrow, 1839).

Bremer maintained his enthusiasm for the community and, when he sailed with the *Alligator* back to Sydney on 3 June 1839, he was expecting to be able to promote the sale of land to settlers.

The journey south was reasonably quick, just 36 days, but the crew began to fall ill almost immediately. By the time the *Alligator* dropped anchor in Port Jackson, most of them were suffering from scurvy. It worried Governor Gipps and the government—if the *Alligator's* crew had scurvy, then surely it must also have been rife in the settlement.

Bremer was disappointed to be told that the land could not be sold freehold to investors after all, but he was allowed to advertise leases. He had already fielded about 50 enquiries from potential investors and was hopeful of securing the settlement's future though industry. He advertised the future lease of land in *The Sydney Gazette and NSW Advertiser* on 17 September 1839 to any 'persons of Respectability' wanting to set up businesses in the north, but not a single application came in, at any level of respectability:

> Sydney
>
> September 11th, 1839
>
> Notice is hereby given that persons of Respectability resorting to Port Essington for the purposes of Trade will be permitted to occupy for a period, not exceeding seven years, Town allotments containing each about half an acre of Land within one mile of the Pier at Victoria and Suburb allotments of five acres each within five miles of the same on the Conditions undermentioned.
>
> Parties desirous of availing themselves of this permission are requested to transmit written applications to that effect addressed to me at the office of the Harbour Master, in Her Majesty's Dockyard, Sydney, specifying the allotment they wish to obtain, and the time within which they will be

prepared bona fide to enter upon the land if approved.

The conditions are the following viz:-

The Lease to Continue for a period not exceeding seven years renewable or not at the discretion of the Commandant of Her Majesty's Government.

The Payment of an annual rent at the rate of five shillings per half acre.

The Lease to be determinable at any time by the Commandant on giving twelve months' notice.

All improvements to be effected at the expense and risk of the Lessee.

The Lessee not to destroy or injure timber etc. without previous permission.

J.J. Gordon Bremer

Commandant of Her Majesty's Settlement at Port Essington (*Gazette*, 17 September 1839).

In the very same paper, there were town allotments available in Williams Street, Woolloomooloo, and 20-acre farms in Wollongong, for freehold sale. If investors could *buy* freehold land in Sydney, why would they *lease* land on the north coast? Bremer's disappointment was bitter. He wrote to the Admiralty complaining, but—still optimistic that settlers and Malay traders would soon want to go to Victoria—he recommended increasing the garrison to 100 Royal Marines (Barrow, 30 October 1839). Undersecretary Sir James Stephen, in London, replied to the government in Sydney, with the first suggestion that Port Essington had not yet, and might never, prove itself, and the chance of abandonment was real:

> … I am directed to request that you will acquaint the Lords Commissioners that his Lordship has not at present anything to give on the subject; but that he proposes to instruct the Governor of New South Wales to continue to make any advances which may be necessary for the preservation of the Settlers at Port Essington and for preventing the entire abandonment of that place until some account can be received, from which Her Majesty's Government may be guided as to the ultimate retention or abandonment of it (Stephen, 21 June 1841).

Map 4: Labelled image of the Victoria Settlement site (Approximate positions) (Google Earth, 2020, 11°21'46.96"S, 132° 9'9.89"E).

Stephen remained a proponent of the settlement, however. In fact, he saw no way other than settling the north:

> ... The occupation of the northern shores of New Holland will ultimately be essential to the prosperity of our settlements to the southward, because, as population and wealth increase in the pastoral districts, it will be necessary to explore new sources for the profitable investment of capital accumulated there. To complete the greatness of the Australian nation, it will be necessary that they should have a greater variety than at present of climates, soils, products, and exports (Phelts, 2006).

Through all this, Bremer remained commandant of the settlement, and he was expecting to return to Port Essington. However, his career took a different route. The sudden death of Admiral Sir Frederick Lewis Maitland in India led to Bremer being promoted to Commander-in-Chief of the Indian Station. He was given command of Maitland's flagship, the 74-gun *Wellesley* in March 1840, and never returned to Port Essington. His 1849 biography says:

> ... To place on record here the various distinguished achievements that in design owed their birth, and in execution their success, to the presiding genius of Sir Gordon Bremer, from the organisation that left Singapoor [sic] in 1840 on its mission of triumph and glory to China, until the final chapter in Canton in 1841, would be to compile a history of the war itself ... His name ... will ever stand forth as connected with the brightest occurrences of that memorable epoch—that her Majesty testified her gracious approbation of his valour in conflict and his discretion as her Plenipotentiary in Council... (O'Byrne, 1849).[*]

---

[*] Sir Gordon Bremer died of diabetes, aged 63, at home in England in 1850 (Laughton & Lambert, 2009).

Chapter 2
Captain John McArthur, R.M. (1791–1862)

Up to the time of Sir Gordon Bremer's departure, John McArthur remained in Bremer's shadow. In 1838 he was 47 years old, five years younger than the 'white-haired' Bremer, and had been a lieutenant for 28 years. He served on seven ships before being promoted to captain in 1837.

In London, in early 1838, McArthur was appointed to the Port Essington post as the commander of the contingent of Royal Marines that sailed with Bremer to Australia in the *Alligator*, from Dublin. For the 12 years he was away—like military personnel everywhere—he remained an absent husband and father. He shared seven sons with his wife, Mary Elizabeth, the first two of whom, James and John, spent time in Victoria Settlement with him*.

McArthur had an older brother in New South Wales: Hannibal Hawkins McArthur (1788–1861) was a prominent businessman and pastoralist. The brothers shared a late uncle whose contribution to New South Wales is well known. John MacArthur (1767–1834) is

---

*   A coincidental connection with the north of Australia demonstrates how military families in Britain were entwined. HMS *Countess of Harcourt*, which was the convict transport and supply vessel used to settle Fort Dundas on Melville Island in 1824, was wrecked off the coast of Corfu in 1830. It was Mary McArthur's brother—Commander John Geary of HMS *Madagascar*—who rescued the distressed crew and soldiers of the 90th Regiment. Geary could trace naval officers in his family as far back as the time of Queen Elizabeth I (O'Byrne, 1849).

famous for his involvement in the wool industry and his part in the overthrow of Governor Bligh during the 'Rum Rebellion' of 1808.

Hannibal welcomed his brother to Australia and was able to furnish him with clothes and equipment for his new life in the north. Some of John's purchases from his brother, shipped to him in 1838, 1839 and 1840, are listed in McArthur's notebook. A note against three items says that they were sourced in Goulburn, New South Wales in 1840, where Hannibal farmed: a pair of 'trowsers' for 18/-, a waistcoat 12/6, and a pair of braces for 1/6. The mail-order system was slow in 1840, but it still worked, and it was handy to have family connections.

McArthur's appointment as the commander of the naval garrison of Royal Marines in Port Essington included the role of acting commandant of the settlement of Victoria whenever Bremer was absent. Despite some struggles for dominance with two other officers—both relatively short timers—he remained as commandant after Bremer's final departure, in June 1839. In the end, McArthur was to stay at Victoria for the settlement's entire existence. His devotion to duty, stoic resilience, and pragmatism, probably helped extend the life of the settlement for several years beyond its use-by date.

Because the British needed to examine their surroundings better, several exploratory trips were made in the first weeks after arrival around Cobourg Peninsula. Captain McArthur and his son, James, travelled west on foot on 7 November 1838, to find savannah grasslands, and a myriad of birds, including two 'native companions' (brolgas), which flew away. More importantly, they found several waterholes, and a narrow creek that was so deep in some places that 'with a pole eight feet long, I could but reach the bottom' (McArthur, 7 November 1838).

Lieutenant Peter Stewart, of the *Alligator*, also went to looking for water, and searched inland from Knocker Bay. He discovered a lake which was about knee deep, in which there were 'about 500 black swans' (probably magpie geese), and a small river with 'as good a water as ever I tasted' (Stewart, 16 November 1838). With some relief, the settlers knew the supply of fresh water was assured, so they could then concentrate on other things.

In May 1839, Stewart teamed up with the botanist, John Armstrong, and seven others from the *Alligator*, for a week's exploration of the peninsula, using two ponies to carry their supplies. They crossed many running streams, found good stands of timber ('cedars … 10 feet in circumference') and country damaged by hundreds of the descendants of the buffalo herd left by the Raffles Bay settlement in 1829.

They almost had a serious accident by lighting a fire at the base of an old tree. The fire took hold within its trunk, and the tree collapsed during the night. 'Had it fallen three feet more to the right, myself and two or three others must have been killed, and most likely more' (Stewart, May 1869).

John Armstrong, pleased at doing botanical work other than supervising the garden, discovered a large area of good land in the southern part of the peninsula. He thought it was the finest yet found for horticultural purposes (Spillett, 1972).

The party also found two 'large native huts', one of which contained a 'bundle of human bones, carefully bound round with a mat'. Stewart was careful not to interfere with them, 'for fear of giving offence'. This 'fear' was actually 'respect', such as Captain Collet Barker had successfully modelled in Raffles Bay, ten years before. The British seemed to want to learn about and understand the Iwaidja, so they tried to maintain good relationships with them. In this way, many of the Port Essington settlers contrasted markedly with the attitudes of some who came later and ruthlessly collected skulls, and other artefacts, to sell to European museums (Pugh, 2018a)*.

On 5 May, Stewart's little exploration party arrived at a broad creek they needed to cross, so they borrowed a canoe they found on the bank to help them:

---

* Lieutenant Lambrick did collect a skull in 1847 (Turnbull, 2017), which he gave to John Sweatman (Sweatman, 1847).

Figure 11: Artawirr, a bamboo didgeridoo, collected from Port Essington before 1844, now in The British-Museum (Oc1855, 1220.177) (Pastmasters, 2016).

Figure 12: A bark painting collected from Port Essington 'before 1868', now in The British-Museum (Oc1973-q-17.1) (Pastmasters, 2016).

… Here we found very convincing proofs that our black friends are not the most honest people in the world. In the canoe was a Canadian axe, with the Queen's mark, two bars of rod iron, and several pieces of iron hoop. On the other side of the river, in a hut, we found an iron dog (which I know had been made for the pier), another piece of rod iron, which they had contrived to point, and several handkerchiefs, old canvas, and pieces of red cloth (Stewart, May 1869).

The party of nine crossed the creek in the canoe two at a time, and all crossed safely except the last two, who capsized and had to swim. Stewart wrote that the stolen goods in the canoe sank to the bottom of the creek, and he was sorry, but it 'served them perfectly right'. No one was around, so they made reparation by leaving some bread, and then moved on further east. Earl was puzzled at the value of this pilfering by the Australians, stating that 'all the clothes, iron, axes &c ... goes into the interior' but he could not 'discover that they get anything in exchange but spears and perhaps food' (Earl, 13 July 1840).

Stewart, who refers to many Iwaidja as friends, was pleased to meet several men and women whom he knew from the settlement. 'None of them showed the least fear, but came forward with the greatest confidence', and led them to a campsite beside a river, and fed them with fish and crabs. Two of the 'friends', Alanget and Arradunga, agreed to guide them across the isthmus the next day, and then back to Middle Head and home. It was just as well they did because the land they needed to cross from there on was mostly bone-dry, and their guides were able to show them sources of fresh water. Stewart was amazed at their navigation skills:

> ... they hit Middle Head with a nicety, far better than we could have done with the best compasses ever made, and that in a track of upwards of 20 miles without, to our eye, a mark of any kind to guide them (Stewart, May 1869).

In the beginning of the settlement there was more to do than just build it. Whilst the *Alligator* was still in port, Charles Tyers[*], the *Alligator's* master and 'tide measurer', recorded the changes of the tides over seven months. He found a 'very irregular rise and fall, varying from two to thirteen feet'. More importantly, he prepared an excellent chart of Port Essington that was published by the Admiralty in 1840 and was still in use over a century later. Among the first ships to use it, on 17 July 1839, was a ship that was to become one of the most famous in history. Its sail was seen rounding Point Smith, and McArthur sent the yawl, with Crawford Pasco[†], the mate from the

---

[*] Tyers was discharged from the navy later that year, and 'took an appointment of Surveyor in the Colonial Office at a salary of £340 per annum, rising to £450. He deserves every shilling' (Bremer, 7 August 1839). He retired as Commissioner of Crown Lands for Gippsland, Victoria, in 1867.

[†] Pasco had a stellar career with the Royal Navy, retiring as a Commander in 1866. He was involved in Antarctic exploration and, in retirement, he helped start the Victorian Branch of the Royal Geographical Society (JSTOR, 1898).

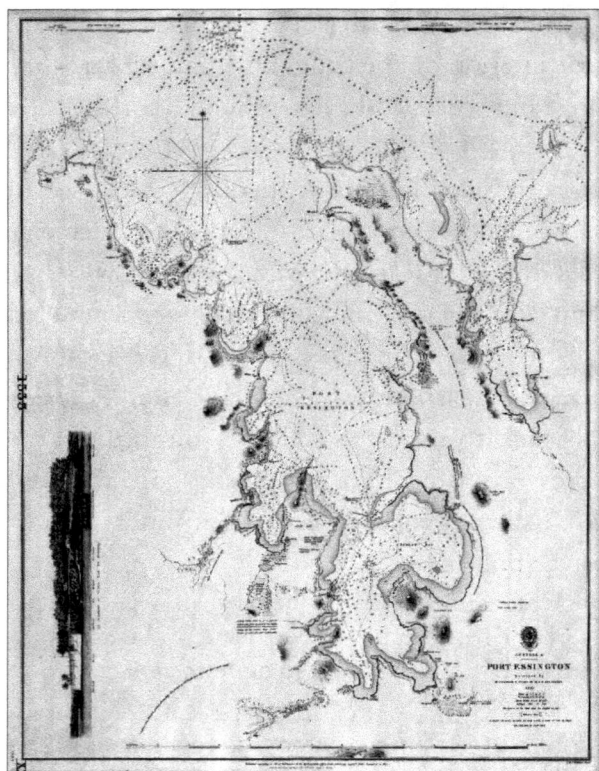

Map 5: Charles Tyers' chart of Port Essington 1839 (NTL, Rare Map 56).

Britomart, to pilot the ship into the harbour, using a brand-new copy of Tyers' chart. It was the sister-ship of the *Alligator*, HMS *Beagle*, under Captain Wickham, on her six-year survey voyage charting parts of the Australian coastline.

On board was the Royal Navy Surveyor, John Lort Stokes, and his journal is another that rings with optimism and praise for the 'vastly pretty' settlement. Stokes thought Port Essington to be a magnificent harbour, suitable for the future capital of northern Australia, and in his first visit of the new settlement, his strongest emotion was religious patriotism:

> ... We were of course extremely anxious to visit the settlement. Landing at the jetty, which we found a very creditable piece of workmanship erected under the direction of Lieutenant P.B. Stewart, we ascended the cliff, and on gaining the summit,

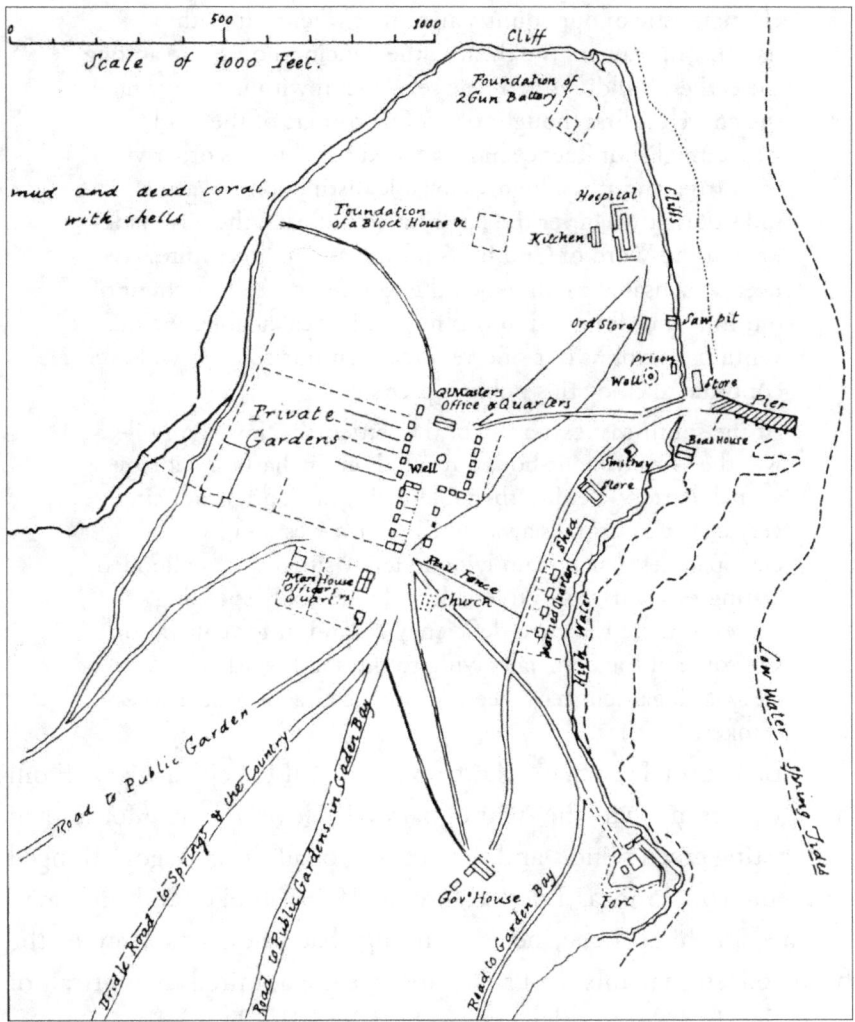

Map 6: The McArthur Map 1847 (HRA 1 XXV 1 373).

found ourselves on a small piece of tableland partially cleared. Seen through the trees, the dwellings of the settlers had an air of neatness, pleasing to the eye. Among the other buildings in progress was the church, which, planted as it was on the northern shores of the Australian continent, was expected to form a nucleus from which offshoots might by degrees draw within its influence the islands in the Arafura Sea, and thus widely spread the pure blessings of Christianity. It is highly characteristic of our countrymen, that where with other nations, the tavern, the theatre, the dancing-house, are among the earliest buildings in a new settlement, with us everywhere the church is first thought of. In few corners of the world, where English influence has extended itself, is this otherwise than true, and it is a highly enviable distinction. It seems, indeed, that wherever the flag of Britain floats, there is made known the Word of God in its purity; and as an empire has been vouchsafed us on which the sun never sets, the extent of our influence for good in this respect is incalculable. We may venture to express our sincere hope, that our country will ever continue to enjoy this noble supremacy.

At the south-east extremity of the settlement, raised on piles, was the Government-house, fronted on the harbour side by a small battery. Behind the table-plain, the land, producing very coarse grass, falls away to the south-west, and some clear patches which from lying in a low situation, are flooded during the rains, form tolerable soil. Generally speaking, however, there is a great deficiency of land fit for cultivation. On some of the best spots lying to the southward and westward, gardens have been commenced with some success (Stokes, 1846).

Benjamin Helpman, the ship's mate, also kept a diary. From him we learn that the white painted Government House had contrasting green blinds, and the prettiest of all the cottages belonged to Lieutenant Phineas Priest (Horden, 1989). Stokes and Helpman lunched in this cottage, never minding that Priest was away in the bush collecting plants. In Priest's absence, he admired the portrait of his wife, which was displayed prominently in the living room, hoping in vain that she was there in person.

The *Beagle* stayed a week in the port, with the crew undertaking maintenance and repairs, whilst Stokes measured the tides and did a little surveying, after which he declared Captain Owen Stanley incorrect in his placement of Government House on the charts. He had erred by 440 yards.

... The spot selected for our observations was Government House, where nearly a hundred observations with the sun and

Figure 13: Lt Phineas Priest's cottage (Stanley 1839, SLNSW).

Figure 14: Storehouse, Port Essington (Stanley 1839, SLNSW).

stars were made for latitude, the mean result being 11 degrees 22 minutes 21 seconds South, which strange to say, was nearly 15 seconds greater than Captain Stanley and Mr. Tyers' determination: this difference to me was quite unaccountable, as the instruments used in the *Beagle* were before and subsequently, satisfactorily tested at well determined places. The longitude being affected by the doubtful meridian distance between Sydney and Port Stephens, we can only give an approximate result; and therefore for the sake of the longitudes of those places referred to the meridian of Port Essington, we consider it 132 degrees 12 minutes East of Greenwich (Stokes, 1846).

Before the *Beagle* left, McArthur called a holiday, and invited the crew, and that of the *Britomart*, ashore for a sports day. There were games with the 'bat and ball', wrestling, and running races, all of which were won by the land-based garrison and 'nothing could exceed the good order and perfect harmony in which the day was merrily spent' (McArthur, 3 September 1841).

The *Beagle* was back in Port Essington on 18 August, with tales of major discoveries, including the Adelaide River and Port Darwin, and a story that amused them all: Lewis Fitzmaurice and Charles Keys, two stalwarts of the crew, were on shore taking measurements with a theodolite, when a dozen or more angry Wulna tribesmen appeared on the cliff above, stamping their feet, chomping their beards, and preparing to hurl their deadly spears at the intruders. Instead of running, the two unarmed mariners thought fast, and amazed their protagonists by making their defence a comedy. They broke into a lively sailor's dance and hallooed about in a crazy manner, whilst slowly easing out of range. The Wulna men lowered their spears and gawked in amazement, and the dancers made a dash to the boat, without any spears being thrown. On return to the *Beagle,* they told of their escape, and no doubt, calmed their nerves with a tot of rum. Wickham named the site 'Escape Cliffs', and Fitzmaurice and Keys had to endure months of teasing and mimicry by their shipmates:

Figure 15: Owen Stanley's depiction of the Theatre Royal, August 1839 (SLNSW).

… No one could recall to mind, without laughing, the ludicrous figure necessarily cut by our shipmates, when to amuse the natives, they figured on the light fantastic toe; and the readers, who look at the plate representing this really serious affair, will behold two men literally dancing for their lives (Stokes, 1846).

Such is how history is written: the name *Escape Cliffs* stuck, and in 1864, it was to become the site of settlement for the First Northern Territory Expedition from Adelaide in the first Australian attempt at settling the north (Pugh, 2018a).

Captain Owen Stanley felt idle during his long wait for the *Britomart* to be relieved. By August, the supplies were running low, and people were getting despondent and hungry. In Stanley's small library, which had travelled with him to places as distant as the Arctic, was a slim volume containing the script of a musical farce by Frederick Reynolds, named *Cheap Living*. In a small community, desperate for entertainment, it was easy for him to round up a group of amateur thespians willing to stage the play. He took over one of the prefabricated storehouses, empty for lack of victuals, constructed a stage at one end, and the Victoria Theatre was born*. The stage was curtained by a large ensign from the *Britomart*, the backdrops were painted with local ochres and clays, and the womenfolk lent their spare dresses to the female impersonators. Stanley was upbeat and tried to enthuse his players with as much energy as he could, but it was tough thing to do, as the food was running out. On 26 August, the sets were ready, the actors knew their lines, and tickets had been written and issued. Stokes kept his ticket as a treasured possession (Horden, 1989).

In the meantime, unknown to the settlers, an outbreak of scurvy had hit the *Alligator*, and '25 Patients, laboring under that disease, [were] sent ashore to the Military Hospital' in Sydney (Gipps, 1838). The Governor was so concerned that the settlement may have been similarly afflicted, that he hurried the preparation of two ships, HMS *Pelorus*†, under Captain Augustus Leopold Kuper‡, and a merchantman named *Maria*, with stores and refreshments for the community. A third ship was also readied; the *Gilmore*, under Lieutenant Drury, was hired in September, to take a load that included working oxen and cows. In the meantime, Bremer and the *Alligator* had been sidetracked to quell a disturbance on Norfolk Island, and, in fact, when the *Alligator* did finally return to Port Essington seven months later, it was with a new captain.

---

* *Cheap Living* was originally performed in Drury Lane in London. A second performance in Victoria Settlement occurred in 2010, in the ruins of the hospital kitchen, with the Honourable Tom Pauling, Administrator of the Northern Territory, acting as narrator in the play (see p. 255).

† HMS *Pelorus* was an 18-gun brig-sloop. Built in 1808, she saw action in the Napoleonic Wars, the War of 1812, and went on anti-slavery patrols off West Africa, where she captured four slavers and freed 1350 slaves. She was wrecked in 1844 while transporting opium to China.

‡ Kuper was the son of the chaplain to the Dowager Queen, but he was also Bremer's son-in-law, having married Emma Margaret Bremer in June 1837, when he had been Bremer's senior lieutenant on the *Alligator* (O'Byrne, 1849).

Figure 16: 'Victoria from the anchorage' (Stokes, 1846).

Figure 17: Port Essington, by Captain John McArthur
(National Library of Australia).

The garrison in Victoria, and the crews of the ships in the harbour, were fortunately not suffering from scurvy, but their food was running out nevertheless, and they were on short rations. Then, in the hours before the Victoria Theatre's first performance, the *Pelorus* and *Maria* arrived, with food, beer, and spirits enough to lift everyone's spirits. The play was delayed while the supplies were unloaded. They included 3,600 pounds of biscuits, cattle, mail, and newspapers. Once done, and the settlers had full bellies for the first time for weeks, the mood was brighter. The whole community, plus the crews of the *Britomart*, the *Pelorus*, the *Beagle* and the *Maria*, squeezed into the Victoria Theatre for the first play performance in northern Australia. It was a night to remember.

Captain Stanley especially celebrated, as the *Pelorus* was to relieve the *Britomart*, and he was to return to Sydney before the end of the year. On 26 August 1839, he hosted an early dinner party for 38 on the deck of the *Britomart* as a farewell to those staying behind,

The British in North Australia: Port Essington

Captain John McArthur, RM

Figure 18: New Victoria in 1839. Lithograph from *Voyage au Pôle Sud et en Océanie* by Jules Dumont d'Urville (Louis Breton 1840, PH1077-0001)

but as it happened, it took *Britomart* a few months longer to leave the port.

Once the settlement was resupplied, life settled down to a kind of normal. McArthur painted a memorable water-colour of Victoria that showed the hospital, church, and Government House, nestling among the trees (Figure 17). The Macassans returned home at the end of their season, and the Iwaidja, including women and children, built a semi-permanent camp down on the beach, and often visited the settlement. Life went on with little variation. The gardeners continued to clear land, planted vegetables and fruit trees, and prepared for the wet season. The stock had to be cared for—some of them had already run wild, so rather than set the others loose, the cattle had to be hand-fed with grass that was freshly cut each day and carried to them. Many of the chickens had also disappeared although a few could occasionally be seen scratching around the edge of camp, out of reach.

The first anniversary of the settlement passed quietly, as the humidity again began to rise, and thunderstorms rolled in from the east.

On November 25, Captain Stanley was readying the *Britomart* for her return to Sydney the next day. The *Pelorus* was moored nearby. Slowly, the weather started to change, and both Captain Stanley and Captain Kuper kept an eye on their ships' barometers during the day. Gradually, the wind picked up from the south east and menacing, low, grey clouds swept closer, with lightning flashing almost continuously within them. The barometer lost 8 points in a matter of minutes, and night fell just as fast:

> … Between seven and eight o'clock the wind drew round to the southward, and the barometer began to fall rapidly: at ten it blew furiously from the same quarter, and the barometer was as low as 29.10; many of the trees were blown down at this time. At midnight the wind drew round to the eastward, and blew a perfect hurricane, before which nearly everything gave way; the trees came down in every part of the settlement; the marines' houses were all blown down; the church, only

Figure 19: Éstablishment Anglaise a Port Essington 'Atlas Picturesque', plate 120, (Louis LeBreton 1840, SLSA B8964).

Figure 20: Government Gardens (Stanley 1839, SLNSW).

finished a week, shared the same fate: the barometer fell to 28.52 (Stanley, 1841).

Then the winds hit hard, building to cyclonic force, and whipping the seas into fury. The *Pelorus* rolled in the waves and shipped seas. A second anchor was dropped, but it was dragged inexorably towards the shore without gripping. *Britomart* somehow held fast, as her sheet anchors held, but *Pelorus* was pushed past her, towards the beach below Minto Head. Two distress rockets were fired, impotently, into the storm: there was nothing anyone could do.

> ... About two A.M. the wind shifted suddenly to the northward, from which point for about half-an-hour, its fury was tremendous; the government-house, built on stone piers, was blown away from them to a distance of nine feet; the sea rose ten feet and a half, by measurement afterwards, above the usual high-water mark. HMS *Pelorus*, having parted her cables, was driven on shore, and thrown over on her beam ends, on the north-east point of the settlement, where heeling over 82 degrees, her starboard side was buried nine feet in the mud, leaving the keel three feet clear of the ground (Stanley, 1841).

In fact, the *Pelorus* was driven into the mud with such force the men were thrown from their stations. Each and every wave crashed into her hard. The jolly boat and anything loose on deck was torn away. An hour later the winds changed direction, and the *Pelorus* was pushed over onto her side, until her mast was under water and her keel metres into the air. She stuck fast in metres of mud.

On shore, the winds brought a terror the like of which had never been experienced before by the young marines and their families. Storehouses were unroofed and seven of the marines' cottages blew down, whilst the remaining 14 lost their roofs, to become uninhabitable. All of the five officers' houses were damaged, and two of them were completely levelled. Government house was lifted off its piers and dumped at an angle. The church was almost completely destroyed—only its tower and basement remained. The prefabricated houses stood best, but the trees around them were blown 'naked of their foliage' (Spillett, 1972). The storm tide rose three metres above

Captain John McArthur, RM

Figure 21: Situation of the *Pelorus* the morning after the cyclone
(Stanley, 1839, SLNSW).

normal, and everything on the tide line was flooded and destroyed by the waves—all the stores kept under the victualling store were replaced with a 'great body of sand'. The boathouses and sheds, and five boats, were gone. Lieutenant Stewart's recently completed wooden jetty was also swept away, with many of the stones dislodged. The smithy's thatched roof disappeared into the darkness, and the highest waves damaged its walls. The hospital's doors and shutters were ripped from its walls, and the new panels, which had only been delivered a few weeks before by the *Gilmore* for its extension, were scattered widely. At least half were irreparably damaged. The gardens were stripped bare 'of almost every plant', and the well that serviced them—usually two metres above the tide mark—was filled with 'sea rubbish'. 'The whole country [was] covered with fallen trees and branches' (Kuper, 11 February 1840).

By dawn the weather had calmed enough to send a rescue boat to the *Pelorus*, whose crew remained clinging to the capsized deck. The roll call was depressing. Gunner John Kelly, Armourer John

Figure 22: Barrack Square (aka Victoria Square) after the cyclone
(Stanley 1839, SLNSW)

Bond, Able Seamen John Lyons and John Taylor, Ship's Boy David Bayliss and three Royal Marines—John Kennedy, Patrick Davis, and John Handcock—were missing. It was another 24 hours before the bodies of the first three—Kennedy, Taylor, and Bond—floated ashore, and another day for John Lyons' body to come in. Handcock's body turned up on the 29th, but John Kelly and David Bayliss took more than a week to find, because they were still on the lower deck, 'having been kept down by the weight of various articles that had fallen on them' (Kuper, 11 February 1840). Patrick Davis's body was never recovered.

Captain McArthur's report to Governor Gipps was sombre:
... the wreck which the forest trees still present—the effect produced on animals and animal nature in general, bear silent and solemn testimony to the desolation and terror accompanying this destructive visitation ... (McArthur, 12 May 1840).

The *Pelorus* was salvageable but saving her was to be a labour of several months and require the considerable engineering skills of

Figure 23: Ruins of church and the *Pelorus* people's tents
(Stanley, Jan 1840, SLNSW).

her commander, Augustus Kuper. She lay on her side in three metres of heavy marine mud, with more washed in during every high tide, twice a day, for 86 days.

McArthur did not mention an issue in his report that was building in the community during this time. Captain Kuper's rank was causing confusion in the small community. When Earl returned to Port Essington on the *Alligator*, he described the problem to his friend Captain Washington:

> ... We are sadly in want of a fixed government for since Sir Gordon's departure, his son-in-law, Kuper, has taken the reins out of McArthur's h[ands] on the plea of being senior officer, a[nd] I really do not know who is our chief. McArthur is in excellent health, and notwithstanding annoyances, is the same good-hearted old man as ever (Earl, 17 March 1840).

Captain McArthur considered that he was the senior officer in charge of Victoria Settlement, and that Kuper—despite being Bremer's son-in-law—was in charge of only his ship and the men attached to it. Tensions built up between them, but they were

The British in North Australia: Port Essington

Figure 24: HMS *Pelorus* at low water (Stanley, 1839, SLNSW).

minor compared with those that rose when Kuper's replacement arrived.

In the meantime, supplies were running short and there was much work to be done. The miserable job of clean-up and repair started over the next few days, and a stock-take of food and resources was taken. At least there was plenty of labour. Apart from a few minor injuries, there was no sickness in the settlement.

In heavy rain and continuing squalls, the settlers put up tents, cleared away rubbish, and gathered together many of the stores that were still usable. Perishable food that had been soaked by the rain or washed into the sea, was now mostly destroyed, and McArthur immediately ordered the settlers to go on half rations. The mental strain on the men was huge. Private Robert Male was caught stealing food and received 36 lashes in punishment.

Weeks were spent removing all the rigging from the *Pelorus* and building frames to right her. The main mast broke off at deck level under the strain.

Figure 25: HMS *Pelorus* at half tide (Stanley, 1839, SLNSW).

Figure 26: 'Situation of HMS *Pelorus* when pretty righted showing the purchases. Half tide. (Stanley, 1840, SLNSW).

On 10 January, a Dutch ship named *Ondenemer*, arrived with a cargo of 50 buffaloes, and more were brought by the English schooner *Lulworth* on 6 February. A week later, Captain Stanley felt he could at last obey his orders to quit Port Essington and return to Sydney. He would inform the government of the disaster, and organise a relief expedition, with more supplies and building materials. There was plenty of meat, but vegetables, fruit, rice, flour, and other foods were in short supply. McArthur therefore chartered the *Ondenemer* to sail to Kissa and Moa to seek victuals. When all three ships had gone, the settlement was without the comfort of marine support.

More effort was needed to right the *Pelorus*. She was stripped of anything heavy and portable, cables were tied to her, and a channel was dug under her keel. Empty barrels were placed on one side for buoyancy and every able-bodied man in the settlement manned the ropes on the day of the spring tide. Slowly, very slowly, as the tide came in, the men pulled, the water lifted, and the *Pelorus* inched out of the mud and rolled upright, quickly floating in four fathoms of water.

Work then started on cleaning out the mud, caulking the seams, replacing the masts and the rigging, and then refitting her as much as could be done with limited resources. Captain Kuper's knowledge of engineering and the forces required to lift her, and his enthusiastic command of his men, had saved the ship. It was ironic then, that just as the work was proceeding at a good pace, the *Alligator* unexpectedly arrived with orders from Bremer that Kuper was to take charge of her, and sail to the Opium War in China. Captain William Wylie Chambers R.N., of the *Alligator*, was then to transfer to the *Pelorus*.

William Chambers was the son of a Royal Navy Captain, and the grandson of the Attorney General of the Bahamas. He had joined the navy as a young boy in 1823 and was promoted to lieutenant six years later after passing his exams. He found a position on the 80-gun *Ocean* under his father, Captain Sam Chambers, based in Sheerness in Kent, England, and then served in North America and the West Indies on HMS *North*. In 1837, he transferred to the *Wellesley*, under

Sir Frederick Lewis Maitland as a first lieutenant, and was still in this role when Maitland died, and Captain Sir Gordon Bremer took over as commander. His brief duty as captain of the *Alligator* must have been a dream role, and history has no record of his feelings when he first saw the bedraggled *Pelorus* bedecked in mud, with broken masts and no rigging. Perhaps a clue arises in his subsequent behaviour in the settlement ...

Chambers' time in command of the *Pelorus* started easily enough. He needed accommodation in the settlement, so he moved into Government House, whilst his men set up tents among the ruins of the cottages. The *Pelorus* was still being renovated and, with Bremer gone, Government House was empty. The entire community had banded together and lifted the building and manoeuvred it back onto its piles after the cyclone. McArthur was living in his own cottage.

In February 1841, McArthur wrote to Governor Gipps about his problems with Captain Chambers. He outlined the orders he had received from Bremer and explained that he had shown Chambers 'Her Majesty's Commission' and the instructions he held. Chambers replied that they were irrelevant to him and that he would only follow Naval Regulations.

Perhaps Chambers had too little to do, but he objected to workers using oxen to drag timber across open ground in front of Government House. Instead, he told them to take a longer, more inconvenient route, around his land. Lieutenant Phineas Priest tried to intervene and negotiate access. Chambers refused and McArthur wrote him a letter telling him to stop interfering. Chambers was furious, and a war of letters began between them that lasted for the rest of the 12 months Chambers remained in the settlement. It was based on little more than their relative ranks—Chambers was technically the senior officer and wanted McArthur to remember that. He once addressed him as 'Captain of the Marines of the *Alligator*, lent to *Pelorus* for particular service' and refused to recognise his commission. In a later letter he reminded him that he was only the 'acting' commandant, and told

Lieutenant Priest that he believed neither McArthur nor Governor Gipps had any authority there at all (McArthur, 25 February 1841).

The bitter arguments McArthur had with Chambers must have caused him much anxiety, but his lack of formal commission also cost McArthur dearly in terms of income. Before 1844—when his commission finally came through—his salary was £191 per annum, but afterwards it rose to £600 per annum and later, £1000. McArthur's son, James, ran the commissariat store for nearly two years but was never paid, despite recommendations for a salary from Captain Bremer. Earl continued to be annoyed by the lack of clarity, although he supported McArthur: 'McArthur should have been the man' he wrote, but explained the problem was caused by the commissariat being placed on the books of the ship of war that happened to be in port (Earl, 13 July 1840).

Relationships between McArthur and Chambers deteriorated further after Chambers took it upon himself to order the whipping of several natives and producing in consequence a 'threat on the part of the natives to revenge themselves' (McArthur, 25 February 1841). In the end, neither man would cooperate with the other.

In this war of words, Chambers looks like the protagonist, but he believed he was correct, and was just following navy regulations. He no doubt also found the situation stressful and untenable and must have rued the fact that the commandant's civilian son, James McArthur, was the commissariat officer in charge of stores, and as a civilian was beyond his command. His father recorded the following exchange, perhaps with some unstated satisfaction:

> … on August 8th, Commander Chambers went to the storehouse and ordered the Acting Storekeeper to supply certain stores. Mr. McArthur replied that he could not comply with his demand until he received directions from Captain McArthur.
>
> Commandant Chambers exclaimed: 'Captain McArthur, Sir, is nothing to me. I am Commandant here.'
>
> Mr. McArthur: 'Indeed, Sir, I was not aware of that.'

Commander Chambers: 'Well, Sir, I am Senior Officer, which is the same thing.'

Mr. McArthur, still declining to act upon his order, he desired him to take care what he was doing and departed, apparently much excited … (McArthur, 25 February 1841).

McArthur appealed to the Governor to intervene in his dispatch of February 1841. Eventually he did, but by the time the orders arrived, Chambers had been gone from the settlement for 18 months, and his career continued unaffected. He was with Bremer on the *Wellesley* in the battle of Canton and showed such gallantry that he was promoted to the rank of commander in October 1841. He became 'second captain' of the *Albion* in 1843, and worked on 'various Particular services' for the rest of the 1840s (O'Byrne, 1849). What the 'particular services' were, I was unable to uncover. One tidbit that does appear in the records: while at Port Essington, Chambers collected a number of birds and presented them to the British Museum. These included the golden green pigeon, Smith's ground pigeon, and a male southern sandpiper (Anon., 1844). Thus, Chambers joined an increasingly long list of wildlife collectors in northern Australia.

It took 18 months for the *Pelorus* to be replaced. On 2 September 1842, HMS *Chameleon*, a 10-gun brig-sloop under Lieutenant Hunter, arrived to be based in the port. McArthur lamented that she was not instructed to take the 'Victualling Department', but nevertheless, within weeks, she was sent to Sourabaya (Surabaya, Java) for supplies and to take George Earl on a study tour of the islands, particularly Macassar.

HMS *Pelorus* was in service for only another 14 months. Chambers left Port Essington on 17 March 1841 and took her to Singapore. It was intended that she would take part in the Opium Wars, but instead she was laid-up and sold, only to become an opium trader, under a Captain Triggs. On Christmas Day, in 1844, she hit a reef off Borneo, and was wrecked. The crew of 20 were rescued, and—according to the *Singapore Free Press*—so were 70 chests of opium (SFP, 25 January 1845).

Apart from quarrels among the officers, daily life continued mostly uneventfully. Captain Stanley said that everyone was 'pretty well', but that their lives were 'monotonous' and 'very trying' (Stanley, 10 June 1841). Occasionally it was enlivened: on 30 June 1840, for example, there was a 'considerable shock of an earthquake; it lasted about one minute and a half' wrote McArthur. Earth tremors in the north are regular events: Earl asked the Iwaidja about them and wrote to his friend in England that 'the natives state they are not uncommon. They say it is caused by the Malays dancing. What on earth can they mean?' (Earl, 13 July 1840).

Captain McArthur was not a hard disciplinarian—like Chambers appears to have been—but he had a job to do, and the discipline of the British military forces in the nineteenth century was harsh. The 36 lashes he ordered for Private Robert Male after he was caught stealing food was necessary and understandable by all the men. McArthur well understood his role: boys and men who broke the ships' laws could be caned (usually boys), flogged, or, as a capital punishment, hanged from the yard arm. In most cases in the navy, flogging was done with a 'cat-o-nine-tails' whip, after a public hearing and in front of the entire crew or company, so it would be a deterrent to others. Sometimes, particularly after a theft among the crew, the miscreant would be made to walk slowly between two lines of his colleagues, and they would each flog him with small multi-tailed whips as he passed. This was known as 'running the gauntlet'. The worst floggings were done in port, and they were called 'around the fleet'. The convicted sailor or marine would be taken around every Royal Navy ship present in the port and flogged on each in turn. This was sometimes fatal, and, luckily, no one at Victoria transgressed to such an extent that such punishments were needed.

All ships and colonies in Australia were required to provide an annual 'Return on the number of cases in which flogging was inflicted' (HRA Series 1, Vol 19, 1839). Flogging appears rarely in the Port Essington records—it was most often carried out as a punishment for drunkenness. The *Alligator's* log of 10 December 1838 records the first punishment in the port:

> ... Parties on shore erecting Public Buildings, making a pier, and digging wells. Punished David Stewart (AB) with 18 lashes for theft and drunkenness (Bremer, 1838).

Theft was a problem during the heavy wet season rains in early 1840, after McArthur had put the men on half rations because food was running out. About the same time that Robert Male was punished, Private William Handy (the brick-maker) was given 24 lashes, under Captain Chambers' orders, for being drunk and insolent. Chambers also disrated the bosun's mate, John Hendry, to 'able seaman', for a similar offence. Alcohol was a particularly difficult problem in settlements where endemic diseases preyed on those with reduced ability to defend themselves. Binging on alcohol, as many sailors still do when they reach ports, creates a susceptibility to disease because there is a paralysing effect from high blood-alcohol levels on the immune system (Currie, 2020), which means diseases become easier to catch.

The volume of alcohol delivered to Victoria was huge. Casks or cases of brandy, gin, Madeira, porter, beer, claret, Maraschino, muscatel, champagne and more, arrived regularly.*

Captain Watson, on the civilian ship *Essington*, had continual trouble with the crew drinking and must have envied the ability of naval captains to use harsh discipline measures. He recorded problems with them a number of times:

> Nov'r 7th The only purchases made today were a few Pigs. Several Canoes came off in the course of the day, from which the men bought some kind of liquor which intoxicated them and made them very insolent and abusive.
>
> Nov'r 13th Experienced a great deal of trouble with the

---

* McArthur recorded the prices of the alcohol in his notebook: 1 cask of brandy £8.8.0, gin £2.10.0, a case of claret 20 sh, 52 dozen bottles of beer £33.16.0. The officers topped it all off with a little smoking: 2000 cigars arrived in June 1845 at '40#' each, total £6.13.4. (and this was only a month after 1000 cigars were purchased for £3.6.0!) (McArthur & McArthur, 1849).

men since they were constantly drunk with an obnoxious liquor, which the Natives distil from the Cocoa Nut Tree. This morning the Cook went on Shore in a Canoe without permission, and the Blacksmith whom I had taken to assist me in my trades ashore, also thought proper to leave without consent.

Nov'r 14th Those of the people who are sober, are employed ballasting and Watering. The Cook and the Blacksmith returned on board both in a state of intoxication; They were very quarrelsome and put the Ship into a state of complete confusion. The Blacksmith was detected in the act of selling Iron hoop, the property of the Owners of the Schooner and when spoken to upon the subject, he gave a great deal of abuse. I am not surprised that Ships should be cut off among the Islands, whilst the Sailors are so much addicted to drunkenness, for it will be found that where a Ship has been cut off, the Sailors have been generally under the influence of liquor, and that the Natives have taken advantage of this circumstance… No trade of much consequence today.

Nov'r 16th I was obliged to witness the old scene of drunkenness among our men; the Blacksmith positively refused his duty when ordered to do some little job. I was compelled to employ a Native Canoe in consequence of both my boats being away (Watson, 1838).

The possibility of trade with the East Indies, either directly—as Watson successfully showed, despite the issues of a drunken crew—or via the annual movements of Macassan fishermen, was one of the driving forces of the settlement.

Macassans first came to Port Essington around 1780 (MacKnight, 1976). Matthew Flinders met six praus from Macassar in the English Company Islands, during his circumnavigation of Australia in 1803. When they were first spotted, the Englishmen thought they were 'piratical Ladrones who secreted themselves' among the islands to avoid pursuers. They had already seen stone fire pits, broken pottery and the 'remains of blue cotton trowsers, of the fashion called moormans' (Flinders, 1803) at several places along the coast.

Figure 27:
Trepang boilers
(Masson, 1915).

The English approached the praus fully armed and carefully. But a Malay cook on the *Investigator* was able to act as an interpreter, and Flinders was delighted to meet Pobasso, the *nakhoba, or* leader, of the praus. He was a short, elderly man and his prau, Flinders was astonished to learn, was one of 60, strung out along the coast of Arnhem Land, crewed by about 1000 men. He told the Englishman that he had travelled to the English Company Islands on at least six previous occasions out of the past 26 years and had been among the first Macassans to do so (Austin, 1964).

Trepanging had been a small industry on the Kimberley coast from about 1720. Perhaps some praus had been blown east by the monsoon one year. Their crews would then have found trepang all along the Arnhem Land coast, and greatly expanded their opportunities.

The praus returned every year. When Fort Wellington was established, Macassan-British relationships developed well while Captain Collet Barker was in charge. However, the short time of the fort's existence meant that little was actually achieved, although the Macassans did enjoy the protection the garrison offered them:

> ... In 1829, which was the last year of the existence of the former station at Raffles Bay in the vicinity of Port Essington, the Commandant mentioned, in a letter to Sir Edward Owen, that between the 23rd of March and the 11th of May, 1829,

Figure 28: 'Prow off Port Essington February 13, 1840' (Stanley, 1840).

thirty-four proas, manned by 1,056 persons, visited the settlement, and that all of their captains said that a great many more would arrive in the next season, and further expressed the utmost satisfaction at the prospect of a permanent British establishment, and gratitude for the reception, they met with. The new settlement formed by Sir Gordon Bremer has already been visited by some of these people… It appears that the natives entertain an inveterate hostility to them, and often molest them to a formidable extent. They cannot land and cure their fish in security. This gives the Malays a further motive for desiring the protection of a civilized community, independently of any commerce which they may be disposed to enter into on the spot (Arden, 1 October 1843).

It was an industry as yet untapped by the British, but maybe there could be mutually beneficial arrangements made.

It was known that on many parts of the coast there were 'feelings of hostility' between the Aborigines and the Macassans, which often led to bloodshed. The British garrison's presence as a protector of the fishermen on the north coast would put a stop to that, and that would encourage more to come, thought Bremer, who heard of regular battles with the visitors:

Figure 29: Painting at Malarrak in Arnhem Land, possibly of a Macassan trepang drying shed (Taçon & May, 2020).

… at Goulburn Island they were attacked about three weeks since and five of their number killed. They afterwards revenged themselves by the slaughter of seven of the islanders (Bremer, 4 April 1839).

Captain McArthur felt that the Australians held a 'rooted hatred to the Malays'. In May he reported that some Macassan turtle shell collectors had killed one man and a boy who were well known to the British (McArthur, 12 May 1840).

Some tribes along the north coast were friendlier than others. The Macassans were not welcome at all, for instance, on Melville Island. The Tiwi continued to repel any outsiders, it is thought, because of a history of raids by slavers in the seventeenth century (Pugh, 2016).

But, in other parts of the coast the Macassans were welcomed and expected each year. The coastal tribes would spend the off-season gathering turtle shells to trade with the travellers. They would also offer their labour for tobacco or other items. In the rock shelters of Arnhem Land several artists recorded their contacts with the Macassans over the years, painting *keris* knives, praus and even a trepang drying shed (Taçon & May, 2020).

East of Port Essington there were known to be 'good natives' who particularly welcomed the Macassans and the trade they offered. So, the 'rooted hatred' noted by McArthur was not everywhere and might have been an overstatement for anywhere. The idea that Aboriginal people had an 'inveterate hostility' towards foreigners is also not supported by the fact that many Aborigines jumped on board praus, worked their passage to Macassar, stayed a season, then returned home the next year. Searcy called this 'the grand tour' and it was quite

The British in North Australia: Port Essington

Figure 30: Macassan Camp, Port Essington, April 1839. Le Breton, *Atlas Pittoresque*, (pl. 116. NLA).

Figure 31: Macassan Trading Prahu (McArthur, NTRS 3601_p112).

commonly done (Searcy, 1909). In 1828–29, Barker estimated that there were around 100 Aboriginal men gone to Makassar from Raffles Bay area (Mulvaney & Green, 1992). Earl noted that:

> ... many natives visit Macassar annually, chiefly from Carpentaria where the people are described as being far milder than our neighbours of the Cobourg Peninsula (Earl, 13 July 1840).

Most travelling Australians appear to have come and gone from Macassar with impunity, though they might not have been always safe: in 1875 four men from Port Essington were returning home when they were sold by the prau's captain to some islanders, for a quantity of tortoise shell. The islanders then apparently 'made a feast of them'. Such an end is possible, but unlikely.

The Aborigines, including many from Port Essington, were usually looked after by one or other of the leaders of the trepang industry—Daeng Remba, or Daeng Tompo, when in Macassar. In the 1960s, C.C. MacKnight interviewed old trepangers in Macassar and identified several houses where the Aborigines boarded. One of the houses was still standing and being used as a school. MacKnight heard that there were 17 Port Essington Aborigines living there in 1876 (MacKnight, 1976). Earl wrote that:

> ... nearly every prahu [prau] on leaving the coast takes two or three natives to Macassar and brings them back next season.

The consequence is that many of the natives all along the coast speak the Macassar dialect of the Malayan language. A few have been converted to Mohammadanism; one of these, Caraday, a chief of one of Goulburn's Islands, visited us soon after our arrival in Port Essington. He had been circumcised and refused to eat pork (Earl, 1846).

Macassarese became so well-known along the north coast, it operated as a lingua franca among the tribes. Earl found it very frustrating:

> ... You ask for vocabularies. I am in the most ridiculous perplexity about them. After having collected many words, I found that I was making vocabulary of a horrid patois of the Makassar dialect: in fact, nearly all the words the natives use when speaking with us are Macassarese' (Earl, 13 July 1840).

Some of the Macassans journeyed to the same parts of the Australian coast for so many years that they developed strong relationships with the locals. For instance, Bapak Padu, a grey-haired captain of the *Bonda Tamalaba*, and leader of four other praus that arrived in Port Essington in April 1839, had been visiting the coast for more than 30 years and employing the same Iwaidja men and women year after year. Padu and his men camped on the beach next to Victoria Settlement for three weeks. Every day they would spread out across Port Essington in canoes. Each canoe would return laden with trepang collected on the mudbanks of the harbour at low tide. The slimy animals would be simmered in large cauldrons for several hours, and then smoked to dry in racks in the drying houses, before being packed ready for transport. On 3 April, in just one day, 'upwards of 700 lbs weight of trepang' was brought to their camp for boiling. Bremer wrote that would amount to £15 income. He also estimated the praus would be taking at least £500 worth of tortoise-shell back to Singapore.

Padu, in a spirit of cooperation, left Timbo, one of his men, with the British for several months to act as an interpreter. George Windsor Earl, who was just beginning his exploration of the local languages, must have been very happy with the arrangement, but

Timbo wasn't around long—he went bush with several Aboriginal mates and disappeared into 'the interior' for a month or more. When he returned he had 'glowing accounts of the interior, its inhabitants and his reception there'. This type of interaction may have been the exception, rather than the rule, but 'it was almost normal for Aborigines to visit Macassar' (MacKnight, 1976).

Bapak Padu was a genial old man, much respected by both his crew and the British, but this was to be his last trip to Australia. Two years later, Earl heard from Menangbari, the youngest of the crew, how Padu and the crews of three praus had been taken by Philippine pirates in the waters off Flores, whilst on their journey home. They were, as far as he knew, then kept as slaves on the island of Mindanao (Earl, 1846).

During the 1839 and 1840 seasons the British traded well with the visiting Macassans. From notes on the trades we can cast off the image of British Royal Marines constantly suffering by having to wear stiff English uniforms in the tropical heat. Instead—especially as the uniforms wore out or were kept for special occasions—many would wear Macassan cotton clothing they bought or traded from the praus. This was particularly necessary when the 'slops' from the store were used up (Earl, 9 June 1841).

In June 1841, the Macassans brought more goods to sell than the Europeans had money to buy them, but then—unfortunately for the British—the Macassans' desire to trade with them faded. When asked why, they said it was because anything they received from the British would likely be charged heavy duties or seized by the Dutch authorities in Macassar.

In Port Essington there was the occasional arrival of other interesting people to break the monotony of settlement life. When the *Gilmore* arrived on 12 July 1840, with timber and supplies to replace those lost in the cyclone, John Gilbert—a passenger on board—requested permission to research and collect plants and wildlife on Cobourg Peninsula. Gilbert (1810–46) came from South London and trained as a taxidermist for the Zoological Society of London. He is most well known as a naturalist and collector of zoological and plant specimens for the great British ornithologist, John Gould. As a 28-year-old, he was the 'chief collector' on Gould's 1838 expedition to Tasmania, on £100 per annum. In 1839, he had also gone to the Swan River settlement in Western Australia to collect birds and mammals. Returning to Sydney late in 1839, he arrived about three weeks after Gould had returned to London. As a result, he shipped his specimens to Gould and then needed to look around for another project.

Now 30 years old, Gilbert considered travelling to New Zealand with Captain Stanley in the *Britomart*, but instead joined the *Gilmore*. Arriving in Port Essington with letters of introduction from both Governor Gipps and Captain Stanley, he was warmly welcomed by McArthur (Chilsolm, 1966). He stayed eight months, until 17 March 1841, existing on stores he had brought with him. In that time, he collected and recorded more than 200 species of plants and animals from the Port Essington area alone, with a particular emphasis on birds and their eggs. McArthur was so supportive of Gilbert's work he had special quarters built for him at Government House and lent him a 'decked boat' for collecting expeditions.

Gilbert developed a good working relationship with several Iwaidja men. In particular, with one man—never identified in Gilbert's journal—who guided him through the bush to some huge nests of the orange footed scrub fowl, *Megapodius reinwardt*. These are rainforest birds, nowadays commonly seen in suburban parks and gardens of Top End settlements. They are megapodes, large footed birds who lay their eggs in huge mounds that they construct from leaves and earth. The composting of the leaves provides the heat for the developing chicks, who are immediately independent when they hatch. The largest mound Gilbert found was in Knocker Bay—it was 4.6 metres high and over 18 metres in circumference (Powell, 2016).

Figure 32: The Orange Footed Scrub Fowl (MacGillivray, Zoological Society of London, 1876).

John Lort Stokes was also charmed by this bird:

… One discovery which was made through the medium of the natives, was that the large tumuli noticed by Captain King and others, and supposed to be raised by the inhabitants, are the works of a bird; some of them are thirty feet long and about five feet high; they are always built near thick bushes in which they can take shelter at the least alarm. The edifice is erected with the feet, which are remarkable both for size and strength, and a peculiar power of grasping; they are yellow while the body is brown. Nothing can be more curious than to see them hopping towards these piles on one foot, the other being filled with materials for building. Though much smaller in shape, in manner they much resemble moorfowl. The use made of the mound is to contain eggs, which are deposited in layers, and are then hatched by the heat generated in part from decomposition. The instant that the shell bursts, the young bird comes forth strong and large, and runs without the slightest care being taken of it by the parent. Of the number of eggs laid by each bird, seldom more than two are hatched… It seems difficult to credit that a bird so small could raise a structure so large (Stokes, 1846).

Gilbert sent more than 60 new species of birds to Gould*, and collected thousands of other specimens from all over Australia. One of them was a special, brightly coloured little finch that he found in the Northern Territory. He personally carried it from Port Essington to England and delivered it to John Gould. Sadly, Gould's wife, Elizabeth developed an infection giving birth to her eighth child, Sarah, and died of puerperal fever about the time of Gilbert's visit. John was left with six children. Elizabeth was an artist who illustrated many of the plates in her husband's publications, including 84 in *The Birds of Australia*. Gould was devastated by her death. In 1844 he named the finch *Amadina gouldiae*† in her honour (Alvis, 2019). We know it as the Gouldian Finch.

Many of Gilbert's specimens ended up in museums across Europe and the United States. Approximately 8% of the Australian 'type' specimens, (from which a species is first described), were collected by him. Alan Powell suggested that 'John Gilbert's sojourn at Port Essington left probably the most lasting legacy of those eleven years' of settlement (Powell, 2016).

John Gilbert found a kindred spirit in one of the other civilians in Port Essington. The botanist John Armstrong (?–1847) joined the settlement after having experience in the tropics collecting for Kew Gardens in London, and growing food in British Honduras (Belize). He was employed as the Government Gardener, but Armstrong's main interest was discovering and collecting the plants that surrounded them. He therefore continued to collect for the Royal Gardens at

---

* Gould's collection of birds was valuable. In 1847, he offered it to the British Museum. The price was £1000 including the eggs, or £800 without them (Schauensee, 1957). The equivalent purchasing power of £1000 from 1847 is now approximately $A235,000.

† An analysis of mitochondrial DNA in 2009 changed its placement from the genus *Amadina* to *Erythrura*.

Figure 33: Gouldian Finches are named after Mrs Elizabeth Gould (John Gould, 'The Birds of Australia', 1841).

Kew—which still holds his collections*.

Armstrong found his duties as the settlement's gardener unsatisfying and frustrating, particularly when he could see how active John Gilbert was in his collecting. On arrival, he had led a party of Royal Marines and put in a considerable effort to clear the garden plots and plant the seeds and cuttings they had brought with them. The gardens initially did well, but much of the fruit fell off the plants before ripening, and rats ate many of the pumpkins before they were harvested. Armstrong reported that the soil was horticulturally poor, and only about one acre out of twenty any good at all, and the difficulties of getting enough water to the plants during the dry season were almost insurmountable. Armstrong's frustration grew. He found too little time to collect plants, and wrote to a friend at Kew, saying that he would not stay as gardener/collector for £500, but would stay as collector for £50.

Figure 34: Sugar gliders (Gould: 'Mammals of Australia' 1841).

On 20 July 1840 Armstrong went to see McArthur and told him that he refused to work in the garden any more. He felt he would never be able to provide the vegetables and fruit the colony

---

* The naturalists were not the only collectors in the settlement, and we may never know how many private collections were made. For example, hidden deep within the almost illegible writing of Doctor Richard Tilston's will, he bequeathed his collection of birds to someone named Elizabeth. Surgeon Sibbald collected plants and sent them to Edinburgh (although the online Edinburgh Herbarium currently only lists plants collected by him in Tahiti, perhaps because only 30% of their collection is digitised to date). Several plants are named after Sibbald (plants.jstor.org).

needed with a workforce of just two marines, and he wasn't able to do the botanical collecting he so desired, (even though he had already shipped 597 specimens to London on the *Britomart)* (Spillett, 1972). McArthur was conciliatory and gave him an opportunity to learn more about how to grow plants in the tropics by sending him to Timor on a short trip. McArthur hoped that Armstrong would be inspired by new knowledge. John Gilbert joined him, and together they sailed to Timor on the *Lulworth* in October 1840.

In Timor, Armstrong met the Governor of Coepang (Koepang) and was seduced by the Timorese vegetation and the collecting possibilities he saw. He returned to Port Essington only to resign and pack up his collection and his personal gear. As far as his new farming knowledge went, Armstrong declared that:

> … the islanders were ignorant of all science, and that he had gained 'no information whatever, the people being centuries behind us' (McArthur, 20 September 1842).

Captains McArthur and Chambers agreed that Armstrong should resign because there was no 'beneficial result to the public service from his remaining at Port Essington' (4 November 1840). Two years later, McArthur was no doubt thinking of Armstrong when he wrote:

> … no man ignorant of the treatment of soil in tropical regions can succeed without considerable experience and possessing the good sense to abandon preconceived notions and prejudices … (McArthur, 20 September 1842).

Armstrong sent more specimens of plants from Port Essington to the Royal Gardens at Kew in London. The herbarium lists 103 specimens collected by him, 35 of which are type specimens (Wallis, 2020).

Armstrong then moved to Timor and received 'every assistance in collecting botanical specimens for shipment to England'. He never returned to Victoria, although he did call into Raffles Bay in 1846 on a brief collecting expedition and named a yellow-flowering *Goodenia* there after himself.

Armstrong's Australian collection held at Kew dates from 1838 until August 1846, and his Timor collection between 1840 and 184.

There are six plant species from the Top End named after him*. John Armstrong died in Timor on 21 January 1847†.

Of course, the plants and animals that surrounded the British were almost all novel to them. Everyone who kept a journal mentioned them, and they often demonstrated a good knowledge of natural history. For example, John Lort Stokes—who had previously spent five years travelling with Charles Darwin—described many in detail:

> ... Great numbers of kangaroos were also found here, which at the period of our arrival the settlers were just getting into the way of killing. There are three varieties, of which the largest weighs about 160 pounds.
>
> I must further allude to a most beautiful little opossum which inhabits these parts. It is about half the size of a full-grown rat and designated as *Belideus ariel* [sugar glider]. Its colour and fur greatly resemble the chinchilla, and I have little doubt that the skin is valuable and might be made an article of trade. This animal has a membrane between the fore and hind paws, which aids it to some extent when leaping from bough to bough. It is a great enemy to the wild bee, devouring them and their nests; the bees the natives discover by tapping the tree and listening for a buzzing from within. Those we saw, amounting to nearly a hundred, were about the size of a fly, of a dusky black colour, and strange to say, were hovering round an empty tar-barrel. They have been unsuccessfully tried in hives at Sydney.
>
> Extensive hauls of fish were made on Point Record, amongst which one species, there called salmon, was most excellent eating ... (Stokes, 1846).

---

* *Cycas armstrongii, Euphorbia armstrongiana, Goodenia armstrongiana, Isotoma armstrongii, Phyllanthus armstrongii, Syzygium armstrongii.*

† Armstrong is incorrectly listed on the cemetery sign in Victoria as having died there.

Chapter 3
Health and happenings

Victoria Cemetery was in a pretty park surrounded by shady trees on the western edge of the settlement. It was needed almost immediately after settlement: Henry Dance, a young cook from the *Britomart,* died of consumption (tuberculosis) on 10 November 1838. Bremer wrote that Dance 'thus became the first tenant of the calm and peaceful spot I have selected as the Cemetery'.

Henry Dance did not have to wait long for company, as Susan Seagar's baby died at birth a few weeks later. Several months then passed peacefully, but when the cyclone hit the community, and particularly the *Pelorus,* in November 1839, the cemetery was a busy place for several weeks. All except one of the cyclone's victims were buried there—Patrick Davis's body was never found.

After that, for the next three years, there were almost no deaths in the Victoria—only James Meldrum of the *Pelorus,* who died on 10 June 1840. McArthur and others commented regularly in their journals and letters about the good health of the people: 'Happily,' wrote McArthur in February 1841, 'we have had very little sickness and none of a character to excite the least anxiety' (McArthur, 25 February 1841).

In the next few months there were only three cases of 'febrile symptoms', but they cleared up with medical treatment, and McArthur congratulated himself for keeping the community healthy by providing an 'occasional change of fresh meat by purchasing pork' (McArthur, 15 May 1841).

In September 1841, McArthur reported a number of cases of mild fever, scurvy, and diarrhoea. He said he sent five 'convalescents' across the harbour to Observation Cliff and Coral Bay, where medicine, the sea breeze and better climate benefited everyone except the patient with scurvy. About that time John McArthur junior arrived. He was the captain's second oldest son (after James) and would stay with his father until the end of the settlement. Leichhardt was impressed by him, in 1845:

> '...Mr John McArthur was a very amiable openhearted upright young man, whom I liked very much' (Webster, 1986).

In April 1843, Captain Sir John Everard Home—commander of HMS *North Star*—arrived in Port Essington to prepare a report on its progress. The war in China had come to an end, and Hong Kong was now ceded to Britain, so the Admiralty could expand its horizons and focus on other parts of the empire. They wanted to know how well Victoria Settlement was succeeding in agriculture, both in the cultivation of land, and the production of livestock. They also wanted to know about the volume of shipping using the port and what Sir Everard would conclude about the future potential of the area. McArthur must have enjoyed the report—Sir Everard was pleased to be upbeat about his belief in the settlement's future, saying it offered 'great hopes of success to a permanent settler':

> ... Although the present state of Port Essington is by no means inviting to a casual visitor, it holds out in my opinion great hopes of success to a permanent settler. Its geographic position is admirable ... The natives ... appear to be of a mild and obliging disposition ... there are five never failing wells of excellent water ... The sea produces fish in great quantity... Pearl fishing might be carried out with great success ...
> (Home, 19 April 1843)*.

Sir Everard visited the hospital, but at that time it was only occasionally used, so he paid little attention to the building. However,

---

* A section of the report is attached as Appendix 5, where it can be read in conjunction with McArthur's 1847 report and map of the settlement.

just as he was completing his report some of the men began falling ill. One of the Royal Marines, Private John Durwood, collapsed with 'congestive fever' and died within days, despite having the most 'healthy and general robust constitution amongst us' (McArthur, 27 February 1843). His was the first death since James Meldrum, and it was a harbinger of the difficulties to come.

Then George Earl—whom Sir Everard interviewed about the prospects of the settlement—fell sick. McArthur was concerned enough to send him (with his steward, Shadrack Phillipus) to Sydney when Captain Home sailed. Six marines were also invalided out on the *North Star* when she left on 22 April 1843.

McArthur was sorry to see Earl depart, but he sent a note to the Governor stating that Earl was a 'Gentleman eligible to the appointment of Magistrate and a Commissioner of Crown Lands; should it meet His Excellency's approbation' (McArthur, 22 April 1843). Earl was duly promoted.

About this time a group of London-based merchants enthusiastically put together a proposal for starting businesses at Victoria, on the condition that they had sole rights for a number of years. The proposal may have been a good idea, but 19 months later—after enquiries were made as to its progress—Lord Dalhousie (the man responsible for the growth of the railways in India) had to rummage through 'one of his boxes' to find the paperwork. It was untouched and forgotten. The proposal never arrived in Australia. It was a huge embarrassment better left undiscussed. By the time it was found, the merchants had lost interest (Cameron, 1989).

In April 1843, the *Alligator* also left the port, heading to Hong Kong. On board her were Privates Fawkes and Fish, who were discharged, and Lieutenant Phineas Priest, McArthur's second in charge. The latter must have failed in his duty somewhere along the way, because on 22 April 1843, McArthur wrote to the Colonial Secretary that he had been 'under the necessity of suspending Lieut. Priest from duties for some time; he is now superseded'. Unfortunately, McArthur gives no

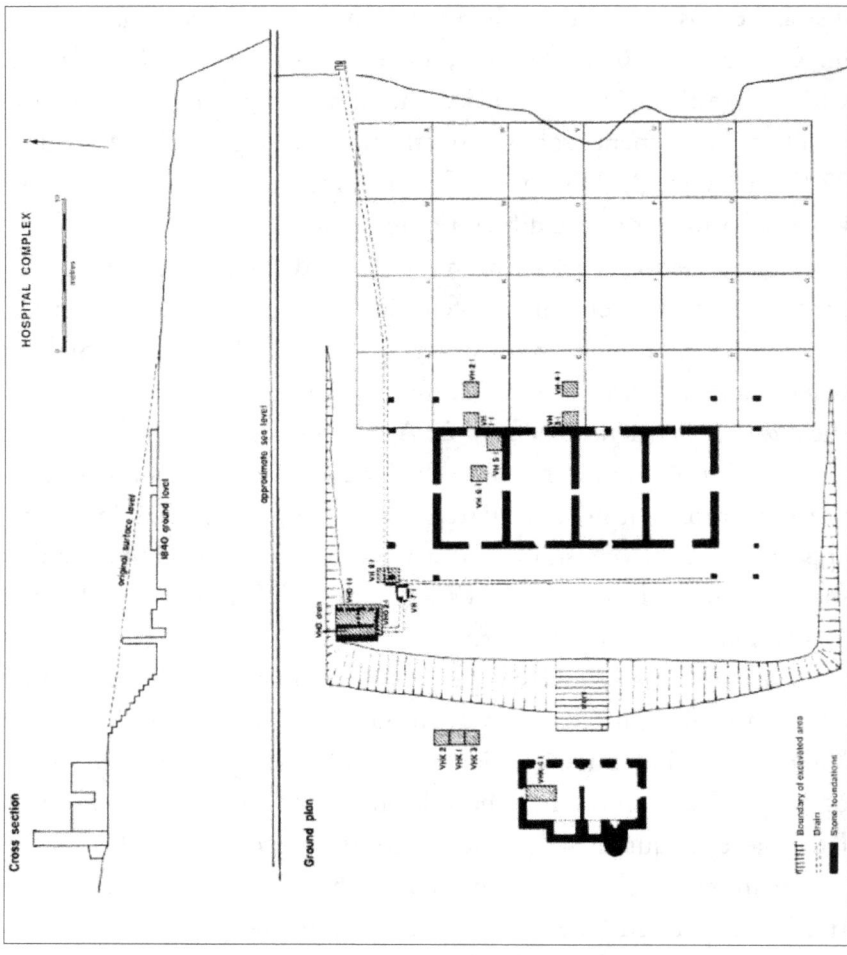

Figure 35: Victoria Hospital consisted of four wards. The hospital kitchen was the stone building on the left of this plan. It was built by borrowed Prisoners of the Crown (Allen, 1973).

further explanation, but it cannot have been too serious—Priest was promoted to captain on 18 December 1846 *(Navy List 1846).

Phineas Priest was replaced by Lieutenant Henry Timpson, who had arrived on the *North Star* with Captain Home. As one of his duties, Timpson joined McArthur on the 'bench of magistrates' at

---

* Phineas Priest (Paymaster) died during 1847. He is listed in 'Colburn's United Service Magazine and Naval and Military Journal', Part 3. There are no details.

Victoria, but he too was relieved by November, leaving McArthur 'alone in the Magistracy'.

Sir Everard Home left behind a huge supply of aging stores, transferred from the commissariats supporting the war in China, and McArthur expressed the wish that he could stop some of the requisitions he had sent to Sydney months earlier. However, he was pleased to have an excess of stores when the distressed crew of the *Manlius*—a large ship carrying a cargo of cotton—called in for shelter against the monsoon. Eleven of her crew of 36 were admitted to hospital with scurvy, and if it had not been for the extra supplies, the settlement would have run short for themselves. They also had plenty in reserve for the survey ships *Fly* and *Bramble*, both of which McArthur expected to be in Port Essington before long.

With Earl and six Royal Marines sent to Sydney to convalesce, several deaths were avoided, but a month after Durwood died on 10 March 1843, Private John Lewis succumbed to a fever, and a week after him, Private Richard Curtis and then a boy named James Green*. McArthur's report stated that he had 'lost three of the most robust of our men by congestive fever' (McArthur, 22 April 1843). Then Private John Bray died on 26 May, 'he had long suffered from an obstinate disease in the ears … during the severe changes we have experienced this season, he caught cold, and finally it terminated in fever, and seems to have attacked the liver chiefly' (McArthur 24 May 1843).

Suddenly many people were sick—even the Aborigines in the neighbouring camp. The hospital filled up, and soon five marines lay dying of the 'remittent' fever: malaria. Another was suffering the 'ague', and five others 'under the disease'. Everybody in the community and on the ships—except for one man—caught fevers to varying levels. Unfortunately, someone who arrived in the port in early 1843 must have been carrying a malignant form of malaria. The *Anopheles* mosquitoes, which unwittingly carry the malaria parasites from one

---

* The information sign in the cemetery incorrectly states these men died in 1840.

victim to another, were already in the settlement, so the disease spread quickly. Despite having three years of healthy existence, MacGillivray blamed the location of the settlement:

> ... There can, I think, be little doubt that much of the unhealthiness of the garrison depended on local influences. The situation of Victoria, at the distance of sixteen miles from the open sea on the shores of an almost landlocked harbour, was unfavourably for salubrity, although in other respects judiciously chosen. Occasionally for days together the sea breeze has not reached as far up as the settlement, and the heat has been almost stifling; usually however the sea breeze set in during the forenoon, and after blowing for some hours was succeeded by a calm, often interrupted by a gentle land-wind. Within 400 yards of the hospital a great extent of mud overgrown with mangroves, dry at low water, must have exercised a prejudicial influence; at times when crossing this swamp, the putrid exhalations have induced a feeling almost amounting to nausea. And if anything more than another shows the comparative unhealthiness of the settlement, it is the fact, that invalids sent to Point Smith (at the entrance of the harbour) or Coral Bay—both of which places are within the full influence of the sea breeze—speedily recovered, although relapses on their return to Victoria were not infrequent (MacGillivray, 1852).

Many of McArthur's workforce were out of action. Fourteen of the 33 privates were too ill to work, and Dr Whipple, the assistant surgeon, joined them in June. By the time he recovered enough to return to work, there were three sergeants and 21 privates on the sick list, suffering from a mix of 'intermittent fever and ague'. Only a few were diagnosed with malaria. Work still needed to be done, however, so McArthur borrowed some sailors from the *Chameleon* to build a beacon on Point Smith, which became a small round tower about 10 metres high*. Whilst building it, the men were joined by convalescents from Victoria, with excellent results for their health.

On 19 July 1943, the brig *Royalist* of 18 guns—under Lieutenant Phillip Chetwode—arrived to relieve the *Chameleon*, which sailed

---
* The tower is still there, albeit renovated.

immediately for England. An odd character was working on board, who stood out because he made several 'direct contradictions' in his story. Richard Cooper (or Cooke)* turned out to be an escaped convict, who had been shipwrecked in Torres Strait, made his way to Singapore, and had volunteered as crew on the *Royalist*. He had apparently absconded from Yass. McArthur was very suspicious of him and had him locked up in the little prison built near the port road for a few days, with a plan to send him to Sydney on the next available man-of-war.

Fever hit the *Royalist's* crew almost as soon as they had arrived. Within three weeks, Privates Mick Reardon, Leon Marcutt and James Deveraux were all dead.

Captain McArthur fell ill too, and though not as severely as others, it still took him weeks to recover[†].

HM Survey Vessel *Fly*, under Captain Francis Blackwood, R.N.[‡], arrived on 19 August 1843. McArthur had not been expecting supplies to arrive, so suddenly, Victoria was in a state of surplus. Even better, Blackwood brought a supply of quinine and he sent it to the hospital. There was immediate improvement in the nineteen patients currently there. The *Fly* stayed a week, and exchanged the Assistant Surgeon, Frederick Whipple, with Surgeon Archibald Sibbald[§], who stayed at

---

* A Richard Cooke arrived in Van Diemen's Land on the *Pyramis* as a Prisoner of the Crown on 24 March 1839, on a 7-year sentence, but no others of that name arrived in the time period. By the time this man was shipped back to Sydney, in the *Bramble* in October 1844, he was calling himself Robert Squires and claiming he had stowed away on the *Flora Kerr*, which had been wrecked. He made it to Singapore and found work as a blacksmith before volunteering to work on the *Royalist*. In the end, Squires claimed he had actually finished his sentence and was free. There are two 'Robert Squires' in the convict lists, neither of whom belong in this time period: 1829, 7 years, ship *Georgiana I*, and 1831, 14 years, ship *Strathfieldsay*, so he remains a mystery.

† Entomologist Peter Whelan suggested several species of malaria could have been in circulation concurrently, perhaps *Plasmodia falciparum*, and *P. vivax* (Whelan 2020).

‡ Blackwood was later a strong advocate for steam ships travelling to Australia (Bogue, 1848).

§ Sibbald later did some excellent research in Sierra Leone, Africa, into the effects of 'quinine wine' in malaria prevention (Buren, 1865).

Victoria for the next 15 months. A naturalist, John MacGillivray, also disembarked and stationed himself at Victoria in order to undertake natural history explorations across the Cobourg Peninsula.

The *Fly*, and HMS *Bramble*, had been surveying Torres Straits to see if there were any clear passages for shipping to pass through them. In 1844, the newspapers were already reporting that they had 'discovered a channel, clear of all dangers, and three miles broad, nearly in a direct line through Torres' Straits' (TSR, 16 March 1844). It was, alas, fake news and not so; ships continued to hit unknown reefs in the Straits.

Whilst convalescing in Sydney, George Windsor Earl accepted the appointment of Magistrate and Commissioner of Crown Lands, and he had returned to Victoria in May 1843 on the *Bintang*, with a cargo of sheep and 10 hogsheads of porter. He was saddened to find the garrison 'suffering very much from ague', and blamed the tropical climate, the undernourishment of the men and the position of the town; repeating that it was 'surprising' to see how quickly the sick recuperated after a few days at Point Smith.

Earl's own health deteriorated again, and he was finally invalided to England on the *Royalist** in October 1843 with three sick marines—albeit without the ship's commander—because on 15 September, Lieutenant Phillip Chetwode and Private Henry Brown, both died of fever.

The *Royalist* left on 5 October 1843 about three weeks after the *Fly* arrived. For those three weeks it can be imagined how MacGillivray

---

* Earl was back in England by 1845, but he returned to the far east, promoting cotton and trade among the islands. He spent several years in administrative positions, including his last one in Penang. He died, aged about 52, in 1865, on a ship en route to England, and is buried in Penang. He was a recognised expert on tropical settlements and was an important consultant for South Australia's First Northern Territory Expedition at Escape Cliffs, 1864–6. His hydrography work inspired Alfred Russell Wallace to describe the bio-geographical boundary, which became known as 'The Wallace Line'. Earl described the inhabitants of the East Indies archipelago as 'Indu-nesians', which is said to be origin of the name 'Indonesia'.

and Earl—who had an extensive knowledge of the surroundings—talked late into the night and compared notes.

On the *Fly* was also a group of 12 Prisoners of the Crown. They did not escape McArthur's notice. His workforce of marines was next to useless with 'debility', so he asked Captain Blackwood if he could borrow them for a few weeks and use them to repair some of the buildings in the settlement. The *Fly* was expected to return in the new year, and Blackwood would be able to collect them then. It was quickly arranged, and Lieutenant Ince from the *Fly*, remained in charge of the convicts whilst in the settlement. The *Bramble* arrived soon after, and Captain Yule left the seven convicts he had on board under a similar arrangement. Some of the prisoners were masons and 'mechanics', but not all—William Weston, for instance, was a 'gentleman's servant' who had been transported in 1840 for stealing a pair of opera glasses.

The convicts were healthy and able to do work the marines could not. 'Mechanics' had been essential at Fort Wellington 15 years before, as they had the skills the settlement needed. The Royal Marines and soldiers were usually otherwise unskilled young men, and there were grumblers among the marines at Victoria—they had expected to be guards of convict workers, rather than have to do the work themselves. They were thus relieved for a while.

The convicts were very useful, and the more urgent repairs to the buildings were quickly done. As the wet season approached, the general health of the settlement improved, and spirits rose. Everyone was expecting that relief would arrive soon. The earliest arrivals had survived six years on the north coast, just a year shorter than many of the convicts' sentences.

Over the wet season of 1843–4, an average of sixteen people reported sick every day. Often it was the same men who had just recovered, having relapses.

Private Joseph Sheppard died on 26 January 1844. Then McArthur's second son, John McArthur, was admitted to hospital. He was gravely ill for several weeks, but slowly recovered (Spillett, 1972). McArthur's two sons had the unpaid role of writing out and copying the commandant's correspondence. This was particularly important because McArthur—now in his mid-fifties—was suffering failing eyesight and there were no spectacles available to him. When young John was sick, McArthur laboured hard to write his own dispatches. When he was sick himself during July 1843, he apologised that his health would not 'avail' him to communicate.

Some of the ill suffered from a 'febrile illness', which may not have been malaria. Professor Bart Currie—from the Menzies School of Health Research in Darwin—analysed soil samples he collected in the Victoria Cemetery. He found the melioid bacterium, *Burkholderia pseudomallei*, which is spread widely across the Top End of the Northern Territory, with many cases of melioidosis occurring each wet season. Melioid most easily attacks people who are already debilitated, such as diabetics, alcoholics and the malnourished. Currie suspected the bacterium may have been guilty of several mis-diagnosed deaths in Port Essington, although on balance, he agrees with the diagnoses of malaria. Further evidence for the presence of melioid during the 1840s, Currie says, comes from the fact that sheep—who McArthur discovered were very difficult to keep alive in the port—are 'melioid magnets', whereas cattle are resistant to infection (Currie, 2020)*.

Sergeant John Edgecombe died on 5 March, and the hospital ran dangerously low on medicines until the *Bintang* arrived with some quinine and hogsheads of porter. After Assistant Surgeon Whipple had noticed that beer improved the men's health, it replaced the issue of spirits. McArthur believed 'that beer is very efficacious in preserving the stamina of men subjected to considerable labour and exposure'† whereas spirits could be 'a more bitter scourge than malaria'‡ (McArthur, 25 April 1845). The

---

* See the foreword by Professor Currie in this book.
† This is a belief which is still strong among the workers of the Northern Territory.
‡ This is a belief which is still strong among the spouses of the workers of the Northern Territory.

Royalist had gone to the islands to obtain medical supplies, and news came back to Port Essington by a merchant vessel named *Hebe*, that she had suffered damage to her masts, and would be delayed for at least a month. The hospital desperately needed quinine, castor oil, calomel and salts, and other drugs. McArthur sent the decked boat, *Lady Jane*, out of the port to Cape Croker to flag down any passing ship and attempt to buy medical supplies, to no avail.

Illness continued to plague a number of the men, even after they had survived Port Essington. For example, Robert Wasson went on to join the HMS *President* at the Cape of Good Hope Station, but quickly joined the sick list there:

> ... Robert Wasson, aged 29, Private Marine, taken ill at sea; sick or hurt, febris interm, says that he was one of the marines who were employed [farming?] a Colony in South Australasia called Port Essington, where he contracted intermittent fever, he now complained of languor, headache and sense of chilliness; put on sick list 15 December 1845, discharged 6 January 1846 to duty (Jones, 15 December 1845).

McArthur summed up the situation in Victoria in August 1843:

> ... Our numbers are thus reduced to forty-six, which includes two women and three children*. Of these only the storekeeper and one private soldier have escaped the endemic up to this time, and as relapses are of frequent occurrence, so it may be suspected the causes of this sickness are still existing, and I believe will exist until the change of the Monsoons.
>
> We had last month a subaltern, medical officer (dangerously), three serjeants, and twenty-one privates actually on the sick list: the virulent fever has attacked but few comparatively, and the majority of cases were speedily mitigated by medicine.
>
> The intermittent we do not regard with such seriousness but a few of the men, perhaps constitutionally hypochondriacal have wasted in flesh and seem to be somewhat desponding in mind ... (McArthur, 24 August 1843).

---

* Mrs Margaret Mew and her three daughters, Mary Ann, Eliza, and Margaret (born 7 January 1841, at Victoria), and Susan Seagar. (Kaziah Davis, and her son Josiah, left with Pte Joseph Davis on the *Pelorus*).

In Sydney, Governor Sir George Gipps read McArthur's reports on the fever with alarm, and asked Lord Stanley of the Admiralty to relieve the garrison without delay.

Another marine died on 3 June 1844 from a 'debilitated constitution'. Other men were clearly weakening, and the death toll was mounting. Luckily, by the middle of 1844, 1 concluded that the malaria epidemic that so devastated everyone was 'if not totally suspended, so abated this season as to remove anxiety'. However, the men's weakness continued, and the lack of a labour force allowed the gardens to fail and the termites to run riot in every building in the settlement. And five buffalo mysteriously died.

Gipps was also under pressure from London to keep in contact with the settlement, at least *monthly* during the wet season. He needed to patiently explain to them that ships were rarely available, and that Sydney was 2000 miles from Port Essington! The bureaucrats in London clearly had no concept of the difficulties and distances involved*.

The British government also needed to decide what to do regarding land sales in Victoria. As early as 1841 they were dithering:

> On June 27, 1841. Sir George Gipps, the Governor of N.S.W. received a dispatch from Lord John Russell in which he was informed "You will perceive it to be the wish of Her Majesty's government that you should continue to make any advances which may be necessary for the preservation of the settlers at Port Essington, and for preventing the entire abandonment of the place until some account can be received by which her Majesty's government may be guided as to the ultimate retention or abandonment of it..." (Campbell, 1916).

In early 1843, there was a merchant ready to set up business in the settlement and he requested five blocks of land. Antonio d'Almeida was the owner of the merchant vessel *Heroine*. He came from Singapore, and was a junior partner in his family's firm,

---

* The problems of transport were not insurmountable, given enough time. For instance young John McArthur was able to send money to his mother, as recorded in the notebook: 'July 8th—gave a five pound note No 65965 to my mother on James' account (McArthur & McArthur, 1849).

d'Almeida of Singapore, headed by the Portuguese Consul-General, Commandador d'Almeida. The company was excited to be able to expand their business to the north of Australia. The Commandador had already encouraged the establishment of plantations of fruit trees at Port Essington and had sent a supply of young trees on the *Heroine*. Antonio d'Almeida wanted to base himself at Victoria, and have his ship ply its trade among the islands to the north. He applied for permission to build a house; and it was granted. However, ` was careful to make sure he understood the prohibiting conditions as they stood, following Bremer's recommendations (see Appendix 5.3).

Antonio's plan was to arrive the next December with a house and a team of mechanics to build it on his 'five town allotments'*. In the meantime, he was contracted to import 49 buffaloes, a number of pigs and 'some other necessities'. He arrived with them on the *Heroine* during February 1843.

McArthur had fielded several enquiries by other prospective settlers; but found they quickly withdrew when learning the terms of settlement. He remained hopeful, however, of welcoming the arrival of many other merchants who were willing to set up in Victoria. He therefore encouraged the Colonial Secretary to quickly sort out the legal matters relating to the sale of land to foreigners. McArthur recommended that land needed to be cheaper in Victoria than elsewhere, because of the lack of facilities available—why would anyone 'pay the same price for land which [they could] obtain in a temperate climate when all the pursuits, objects, and agents are alike familiar to them'? (McArthur, 20 September 1842). McArthur also came to realise that the Macassans were unlikely to ever be in a position to buy land there. They were all hired 'by the Chinese established at Macassar'. The Chinese were therefore the target market:

---

* The use of this terminology is curious—there were no pegs in the ground, or survey maps of Victoria marking where allotments were placed, nor, apart from the mapping by ship's navigators, does there appear to have been any surveying of blocks of land or building sites done, as at Escape Cliffs, 20 years later.

> ... but, if this port be opened under liberal regulations, it is not easy to foretell the consequences on these densely populated places, now impatient of Dutch rule—or of Dutch interference. Doubtless a great revolution would soon take place throughout the whole archipelago, and British influence would universally prevail throughout ... (McArthur, 20 September 1842).

McArthur was a Royal Marine through and through. He could not picture a world where people would not prefer British rule over other European powers.

Chapter 4
Relief and reinforcements

In 1844, relief was on its way. On board the convict transport ship, *Cadet*—sailing directly from Dublin with a cargo of 160 Irish convicts—was Lieutenant George Lambrick, Lieutenant William Wright, Assistant Surgeon Richard Tilston, three sergeants (Copp, Masland and Isaacs), 3 corporals (Conway, Quinn and Brooks), a drummer, 45 privates, 6 wives and 3 children (Cameron, 2016)*.

The Royal Marines were the guard for 160 convicts, whom the *Cadet* was required to deliver to Hobart. After that, they would travel to Port Essington and become the relief garrison. The journey to Hobart was marred by several incidents. Firstly, diarrhoea spread among the passengers and crew, and Private James Lee died of 'inflammation of the bowels' somewhere in the South Atlantic. He was buried at sea with full honours and—as the journey continued—the diarrhoea epidemic ended. There was also a short delay when the *Cadet* caught fire in the middle of the Southern Ocean. Luckily, it was quickly extinguished.

The *Cadet* arrived in Hobart on 25 August 1844 and remained there for a month while Lieutenant Lambrick supervised a refit of the men's accommodation. Lambrick also collected a good supply of medicines for the garrison, because he had heard of the illness in Port Essington.

The British Government finally announced its decisions about the future of the settlement. Victoria was to remain a military outpost

---

* Mrs Esther Norman and her baby daughter both died en route, leaving Private William Norman to raise his son, John, alone.

but would no longer have a man-of-war attached to it or be established or supported as a colony. The *Royalist* had departed Victoria in October the previous year, and she would now not be replaced. It meant the protection of the settlement by the navy had ended, and no extra money would be spent. One exception was McArthur's salary, which rose to £600 per annum.

On 3 June 1844, a small sail on the horizon announced the arrival of a boat. It turned out to be a pinnace belonging to HMS *Fly*, skippered by the mate, Mr. Harvey. He, and the 14 men with him, had endured a torrid time getting to Port Essington after they had been separated from their ship off the south coast of New Guinea, in heavy weather. The crew had also repelled an attack by New Guineans in canoes. None of the British were hurt, 'but the natives suffered a loss of their most dauntless men, and after a few rounds of musquetry, retired'. Harvey had the presence of mind to sail direct to Booby Island and the Torres Strait 'post office', leave a message there and collect some provisions for the 1100-kilometre journey across to Port Essington.

It was a busy time at Booby Island. The *Hyderabad*—under Captain Robertson—with a cargo of horses bound for India, had been wrecked near Murray Island on 25 May 1845. As horses drowned around them, 31 of the crew and passengers managed to get to the Island. Then the long boat was sailed to Port Essington with 28 people on board. McArthur had no ship, so there was nothing he could do for those stuck on the island, but he knew the *Fly* would probably call there. There were several other ships likely to pass as well—so he expected that they would be saved.

He was right: the stranded did not have to wait long. The *Midge*, an assistant ship to the *Fly*, and a schooner named *Shamrock* found them chewing through the provisions left on the islands for just such occasions. There were other survivors there too: the captain and crew of the *Coringa Packet*, a brig from Sydney, had also been wrecked nearby. Captain Chilcott had brought 15 of his crew and passengers to the island but had left 25 Lascar crewmen near the reef that sunk his ship. The *Shamrock* cheerfully gathered them all up, and took them all to Port Essington, and dropped them off at Victoria. Eleven of the survivors elected to stay with the *Shamrock* till her next port, but this still left 76 extra people in Victoria who needed feeding and accommodation. At least five of them were children.

One of the primary reasons for the settlement at Port Essington was as a refuge for shipwrecked sailors and their passengers. The settlement seemed to be achieving this goal, but only in a limited way: the distance from Torres Strait was one major problem—1100 kilometres. The difficulty of finding the opening to the port from a small boat was another; despite the 10-metre tower being built on Smith Point. It replaced a temporary 16 metre wooden beacon (McArthur, 1 December 1846).

After he had returned to Sydney on the *Fly*, Captain Blackwood, voiced his criticisms of the distance any shipwreck survivors were expected to travel to get to Victoria. He began pressing for a new settlement—this time on Cape York—which would better assist those who were wrecked in the straits (Blackwood, 16 September 1845). At least twelve ships were wrecked in Torres Strait between 1838 and 1845, but only three of the crews made it to the settlement (*Montreal*, *Hyderabad*, and *Coringa Packet*) (Powell, 2016).

And when they had arrived, the survivors must have wondered what hell they had arrived in. The thin, pallid faces of the marines were a warning. The cemetery told them everything else they needed to know. As John MacGillivray reported:

> … The climate of Port Essington is decidedly unhealthy,- the burying ground of the settlement tells this tale in language not to be misunderstood … (MacGillivray, 15 October 1845).

They needed to get out of there before they became victims of the fever themselves. Luckily for them, the *Fly* and the *Prince George* arrived in the port on 12 June. They were able to take all the shipwreck survivors, either to Singapore on the *Fly*, or to Sydney on the *Prince*

George, and they all left on 18 June. Just in time too, because, as it turned out, fever reappeared in the garrison just two days later. Private Charles Swan died of it on 20 June 1845. McArthur described Swan as 'a person very unfit for this climate, being liable to determination of blood to his head. In fact, he was decidedly apoplectic' and his death throes were terrible to watch. Soon after, fever had also claimed the lives of Privates Mark Curthoys and George Larner.

McArthur was told he could sell land at £1 per acre if he could find Malays or Chinese willing to invest. In the end, however, he advertised land for lease only via a public notice he sent to Singapore on the *Fly* on 18 June. There would be 'Town Allotments' and 'Country Allotments'. The former would cost from 20 to 30 shillings an acre, depending on access to the harbour. Country allotments would cost just one or two shillings per acre, with land-locked allotments free for the first year. A Mr Bissex from Singapore was interested. He was the Master of the *Sri Singapura*, and he applied for some land to establish a trepang harvesting business, and then headed to China to hire some workers. He was never seen again, though word came back that he was ill, and on his death bed, in Hong Kong. He had left several workers at Victoria in a camp on Middle Head. Some of them were employed at building a small boat called the *Gipsy* for John McArthur Junior. Captain McArthur had to eventually repatriate them to Singapore, which he did via the *Angelina*.

The conditions of lease were so onerous that most people interested in setting up a business or a farm at Port Essington soon withdrew. The land regulations 'served to hinder rather than encourage enterprise' (Donovan, 1981). Any lease holders had to be independent for at least six months, and they could expect no support or provisions from the garrison. Applicants also had to be Chinese or Malays who could farm. Only 50 men, women, and children in total would be allowed, until the system proved itself. McArthur suggested there might be employment for wives or older children who could work as cooks or servants, but work was not guaranteed.

Professional farmers would have been a boon to the settlement. The marines had a great deal of trouble keeping their plants and animals alive. The sheep appeared easily poisoned by shrubs that 'contain matter of deleterious quality' and their bodies would swell to an 'enormous size and the animal dies, apparently in great agony'*. Post mortem examinations showed diseased kidneys and livers and the flesh appeared 'unwholesome, and in many instances disgusting' (McArthur, 3 September 1841).

But by 1845, McArthur had learned much from early mistakes and had built up significant experience in animal husbandry. He reported to Sir George Gipps that he 'decidedly abandon(ed) the buffaloes as bad stock on every consideration' (McArthur, 25 April 1845). Buffaloes were too large to consume when slaughtered, and too much of their 'indifferent' meat was wasted. About a third of them were lost anyway, through disease, eating poisonous plants, or by running away soon after arrival. Sydney sheep were also unsuccessful, but pigs were excellent imports. So, McArthur decided not to import any more buffaloes or sheep—just pigs, and *Bali Sapi*, or banteng cattle (*Bos javanicus*), from Bali. The economics of the trade needed to be tested, as there was a concern that d'Almeida, on the *Heroine*, would not come unless he was bringing buffalo, because the profit margin would be too small with other stock.

McArthur was still having difficulty keeping his garrison alive, and the death toll was climbing. Not all the deaths were attributed to diseases caught in the port, of course. There were those who were already consumptive, and those who drowned during the cyclone. Nonetheless, the number of victims of the settlement was rising, and McArthur was about to find out that it was not necessarily anything to do with the length of time people spent there, because 'young fresh faces' were about to arrive.

---

* The sheep were mostly killed by the poison in ironwood leaves (*Erythrophleum chlorostachys*) (Dr Lorna Melville, personal communication 2020).

The *Cadet* finally appeared on 19 November 1844, after a slow trip from Hobart via the west coast. In November, the heat and humidity of the Top End wraps up people like a blanket, and much of the journey was spent on deck to avoid the stifling heat below. After months on board, the passengers on the *Cadet* were looking forward to their destination as much as the residents of the settlement were looking forward to being taken away.

The ship slowly approached the pier, and crowds gathered to welcome her. Peter Spillett imagined their arrival:

> … their faces were alight with excitement at the realisation that the long-awaited relief had arrived, but a closer look revealed the drawn, yellow faces of ones who had been long deprived of a proper diet and medical care and the aftermath of long illness. They returned the stares and found young, fresh faces, men and women alike, dressed unsuitably for the torrid climate, eager for service and a chance to settle ashore after the long voyage from England (Spillett, 1972).

It took three weeks for the *Cadet* to refit and fill her water tanks, and for the worn-out relieved marines to pack up their belongings. Many had souvenirs from the Iwaidja and the Macassans—which were worth good money to collectors back home. Everything needed careful packing and storage in the *Cadet's* holds.

The married couples moved into the married quarters, which were a line of tiny cottages not far from Government House, with round chimneys above cooking hearths that were more suited to cold climates than the torrid tropics. The 'Cornish chimneys' are now famous and star among the souvenir photos taken by modern visitors to the site.

Single men swapped their berths on board for the thin mattresses of the huts gathered around Victoria Square. In the small gardens behind each hut, they took over the tending of the previous tenants' banana and pineapple plants. The Victoria Hospital was emptied of its patients, as their care was transferred to the naval surgeon, Dr Bower, on board the *Cadet*. For a brief moment, no one in the settlement was on the sick list.

Captain McArthur—in what might be the only emotion he displayed in his dispatches—admitted to a profound sense of loss as he watched the first detachment sail away on the *Cadet* on 9 December. He, and his son John, were the only ones remaining behind.

The new detachment had hardly settled in to their termite-ridden huts when illness appeared among them. As the wet season progressed, McArthur watched as the newcomers suffered from the climate. Two years later, he concluded that:

> ... the present detachment, generally speaking, does not endure the climate of this region so well as the last did. We have a long sick list—nine patients in hospital, and three convalescents capable of no active work (McArthur, 1 December 1846).

February 1845 passed with an average of four patients a day in the hospital, suffering from 'dyspepsia (indigestion) and debility (physical weakness)', but in March, fever reappeared again, and twice that number joined the sick list each day. On 19 March, there were 11 men on the list, with five of them suffering from the 'remittent fever'. On the last day of March, four of the ten patients in the hospital were 'febris' (with fever). One of them, Private Joseph Thorpe, died the next day, and there were two more in danger of joining him in the cemetery.

In Sydney, rumours about the settlement were rife, but not all were about illness and death. In 1845, a journalist wrote that the settlement was about to be converted into a penal colony under the superintendence of Captain Alexander Maconochie[*]. He even reported that the captain was about to arrive on HMS *Anson*, which had already been fitted out for the role. However, the journalist was alone with such knowledge and its origin is obscure (Anon, 15 November 1845).

---

[*] Captain Maconochie was Governor of Norfolk Island (1840–4) and was a penal reformer ahead of his time. By November 1845, he was already back in England campaigning for reform, and he became the 'father of parole'. He never planned to take convicts to Port Essington, and in fact, was instrumental in the decline of transportation as a punishment.

Lieutenant George Lambrick, R.N. was Captain McArthur's second-in-command. He earned an extra 4 shillings a day as the acting paymaster and quartermaster and took over all the accounts and victualling responsibilities from young John McArthur. It was a thankless task: an annual letter from the 'paymaster' in London reprimanded him for not providing an annual report by January 1, to show that the settlement was 'alive and solvent'. The London clerk—for whom 'Brighton represented remoteness'—was a bureaucrat

Figure 36: Victoria Square, by H.S. Melville. Four marines lived in each thatched hut, and they grew food plants in small gardens behind them. George Earl and James McArthur, and then Lieutenant Lambrick and his family, lived above the spirit store on the right (SLSA B-8409).

unable to understand the difficulties in getting mail to the settlement. His letters took up to a year to arrive! (Masson, 1915).

Lambrick had little experience with accounts and needed a local clerk, but McArthur was sure he was 'intelligent enough' to work through them. Lieutenant William Wright was left with the day-to-day management of the 45 newly arrived privates, helped by three sergeants and three corporals. Almost immediately there was some grumbling. The men had been told their duty in Victoria would

Figure 37: Monument over Mrs Emma Lambrick's grave at Port Essington Victoria in 1915 (SLSA B-10134).

amount to guarding convicts. Both Fort Dundas and Fort Wellington had been built and worked by convicts, and many in England assumed that the same was happening in Victoria. It came as a shock to the Royal Marines that the farm labouring and menial tasks of running the settlement fell to them. There were no convicts.

George and Emma Lambrick and their two children moved into the 'very comfortable wooden house over the spirit store' on the north side of the square, that had previously housed George Earl and James McArthur*.

Emma Lambrick, who was just 21 years old, left England with an 8-month old baby girl, also named Emma. She was pregnant with her second child, George, and he was born on the *Cadet* during the passage up the Western Australian coast. He was a sickly child who

---

* James McArthur is thought to have left Victoria and returned to London on the *Brittomart* in August 1841. He was there in December 1845, however. Leichhardt wrote that McArthur's 'two sons were living with him' and compared the 'proud' James, whom he didn't like and avoided, to the 'amiable' brother, John. (Webster, 1986). It is possible that James had returned for a visit, but I can find no other reference about him.

never thrived, and he died at the end of March 1845. Mrs Lambrick had a third child in October 1845; but he too was sickly and weak.

John Sweatman, who was clerk and accountant on board HMS *Bramble**, came to know Lambrick and his family quite well. Sweatman described the lieutenant as 'rather a nervous man' because he was not 'accustomed to accounts' and was 'fidgety, lest his (accounts) should be informally got up' (Sweatman, 1847). He need not have worried; Sweatman said Lambrick's accounts were admirable, and he helped him prepare a set to forward on to the Admiralty Paymaster in London.

Whilst he was in Victoria, Sweatman slept at the hospital, sharing a ward with Dr Tilston, Father Confalonieri and others. He took all his meals with the Lambricks and wrote that Mrs Lambrick was a 'quiet, agreeable woman', in poor health. Sweatman felt sorry for her because she was a 'lady' and, whilst there were three other English women in Victoria, they were wives of the men. McArthur wrote that Emma was 'a truly amiable and sensible woman. How she endures the privations she is exposed to, I cannot comprehend'. Neither could Sweatman:

> ... she said she was very happy, but I could not fancy it, with no society, no amusement, no one but her husband to speak to, and he constantly occupied with his duties. She however, had an unfortunate baby who was always sick and who perhaps served to keep her employed, particularly as she had but one female servant, a Malay girl, whom she could not put much trust in ... (Sweatman, 1847).

No other mention of the Malay girl can be found, but the Lambricks certainly had a young Iwaidja girl, named Memorimbo living with them for more than a year. She was about 10 years old, 'clean and decent', and she would wait on their table and undertake other chores, wearing a petticoat given to her by Emma. Lieutenant

---

* Sweatman was on board the *Bramble* in the years 1842–7, under Lieutenant Yule, on a surveying voyage to the north-east coast of Australia, Torres Strait and the south coast of New Guinea. (Sweatman, 1847).

Lambrick spoilt the relationship by trying to stop the young girl from cruising 'about, all hours of the night' and she eventually 'bolted to her tribe' where such restraints were unheard of (Sweatman, 1847)*.

Both Emma Lambrick and her baby boy remained sickly during 1846, and by October, Emma was severely ill. Her young son was cared for by the other women in the settlement, which released George Lambrick to care for his wife. However, there was little he could do, and she succumbed to the fever that had already taken so many. She died quietly in late October, aged just 24 years. Distraught, the anguish continued for George Lambrick, and increased when the baby also died a month later. Lambrick built a permanent monument to them, which still stands above their graves in the lonely Victoria Cemetery.

---

* Memorimbo grew up to be called 'Flash Poll' and she appears later in this story.

Chapter 5
The *Lizard* and the *Gipsy*

Occasional regattas were held between two small boats that were based in the port: *Lizard* and *Gipsy*. Where the *Lizard* came from is uncertain, though she was anchored with the *Alligator* on arrival in 1838 and could be the boat referred to as the 'decked boat' towed behind her.

The *Gipsy* was a small cutter built 'across the water' in a camp on Middle Head in 1846, by a carpenter called Stuckey. He was aided by Mr Edward Selby and some 'Manila men' who had been left by Mr Bissex—the master of the *Sri Singapura*—from Singapore[*].

Next to their camp, using a single mattock the 'Manila Men' had dug a '29 feet deep' well in just three weeks. McArthur was very impressed—until it filled with salt water:

> ... there was thirteen feet water in the well but all salt. The fact is they have gone too deep with it and the only chance of doing anything with it now is to empty the water out and fill it up again to above high water mark level (McArthur & McArthur, 1849).

McArthur probably contracted the boat-builders from Mr Bissex, to build the cutter. Howsoever it was arranged, Stuckey and Selby did not get on well together:

> ... Aug 2 Sunday, Stuckey did not send the boat over this morning as directed by Mr Selby. He took over the carpenter

---

[*] Evidence for this comes from McArthur's notebook, where he refers to them as being Mr Bissex's problem, and the fact that their names do not appear on any British lists.

Figure 38: Two paintings of Middle Head, Port Essington, where *Gipsy* was built (Stanley 1839, SLNSW).

of the *Bramble* with him last evening and when he came over this evening Stuckey was not sober. I found fault with him but seeing the state he was in refused to say anything more

Figure 39: *Lizard* and *Gipsy*, sketch probably by John McArthur junior (1847, NTRS 3601_p 107).

Figure 40: Sketch by McArthur in his notebook (NTRS 3601_p 129 (McArthur & McArthur, 1849).

to him tonight. Immediately after leaving me he went on the pier and meeting Mr Selby began abusing him and struck him three times. Mr Selby returned to give him in charge in the meantime. Stuckey took the boat and went away. Tomorrow Mr Selby intends taking out a warrant for him (McArthur & McArthur, 1849).

The *Gipsy* was close to the heart of young John McArthur. He records a number of events involving her, with sketches, in the McArthurs' notebook (see Appendix 5.4).

In November 1846, *Gipsy* was already suffering from the effects of termites, which can only have been attracted when the boat was on the beach:

Figure 41: Regatta at Victoria with HMS *Britomart* (Stanley 1839, SLNSW).

Nov 2nd Had the carpenter to look at the *Gipsy*'s bottom and found it necessary to take out the greater part of the main keel which with some of the butt end has become perfectly rotten. Her keel appears to have been much damaged by white ants being nearly hollow throughout the centre (McArthur & McArthur, 1849).

Gipsy was leaking badly, but further damage to her keel was caused by Selby dragging her across rocks without removing the heavy ballast first. This resulted in an argument between young McArthur and Selby, that ended in the latter's dismissal from having anything to do with the boat. McArthur recorded their argument, verbatim:

Monday Evening Nov. 30th, 1846.

Sent for Mr Selby at ½ past 8 o'clock when the following conversation took place

Well Mr Selby I suppose you have hauled the *Gipsy* up to stop the leak.

Yes Sir.

Well I am surprised knowing the state the boat is in you hauled her up without taking the ballast out.

Well then, all I know is you must be surprised.

I don't understand your talking to me in that way Sir—

And I don't understand your talking to me in that way Sir (folding his arms)

Don't you indeed. Well then for the future you will do nothing to the boat without consulting me—

I shall do nothing of the sort—

Well then, recollect you will have nothing more to do with the boat or anything else—

Well then you will settle with me.

I shall do nothing of the kind—

But I will see whether I can't make you—

And I will see if I can't bring you to your senses Sir—

Pooh! You bring me to my senses? Pooh! Do you think you can treat me like a child?

And do you think I will be treated as a child Sir? Or let you be master?

Noted at ¼ past nine. (signed) J. McArthur (McArthur & McArthur, 1849).

The next day young McArthur wrote a note to Selby threatening future trouble. It was copied—or perhaps drafted—in the McArthurs' notebook:

I have received your note and must inform you that your contract is not fulfilled.

I hereby order you to return to the discharge of your duties a refusal of which you will abide the consequences. Mr Selby Dec 1, 1846.

(initialled) JMcA.

A final comment a few pages later in the notebook suggests they came to a parting of their ways on the same day:

Dec 1st Edwd Selby refused further work after being very insolent.

By the next year, most of the *Gipsy*'s problems had been fixed, and she was taken on a week-long expedition out of Port Essington to Croker Island. John McArthur kept a log of the journey in the notebook, which is reproduced in Appendix 5.4.

On 1 October 1847, the brig *Freak* arrived with several more reinforcements for the settlement: Surgeon John Irwin Crawford, who took over the medical supervision of the settlement. On board were Lieutenant George Sheddan Dunbar; a corporal[*]. An additional six Royal Marines were also on board. They included Private James Tossell, who was married with a child, so work was immediately commenced on new married quarters for his family. The *Freak* also brought six months provisions for the settlement and £200 of coins for Lieutenant Lambrick to pay the men. When she left two weeks later there were four invalids on board, heading home to a healthier life England.

The next excitement at the settlement had its origins in events that occurred in Sydney four years earlier.

---

[*] The corporal has never been identified, and it is thought that he died at the settlement during the epidemic of the next year.

Chapter 6
Overlanders

In 1843, the Legislative Council of New South Wales created *The Select Committee on the Proposed Overland Route to Port Essington* for the 'purpose of inquiring into the practicability' of a route to Port Essington from New South Wales. The committee consisted of Mr Elwin, Mr Wentworth, Dr Lang, Mr MacArthur, Mr Suttor and the chairman, Dr Charles Nicholson. They examined how such an overland route would:

> ... be attended with important additions to our geographical knowledge of the interior of Australia, and is an object the accomplishment of which is also likely to be attended with great advantages to the commercial and other interests of this Colony, by opening a direct line of communication with the Islands of the Eastern Archipelago—with India, and other parts of Asia Resolved ... (Lang, 1847).

The committee also needed to consider what support the government should provide to any proposed expeditions to the north. From as early as 1841, Edward John Eyre, fresh from his extensive explorations in South Australia, wrote to Governor Sir George Gipps. He offered to lead an expedition from Moreton Bay to Port Essington, but nothing had come of it. Even Captain Charles Sturt had been tempted by the north, as he followed the Darling River to its source; but the distances and difficulties were too vast for his expedition.

Nobody then knew what was in the far interior of the continent, and there were varying degrees of support from government members, both for the expedition and in the commercial development of Port Essington. At the time, they had yet to decide whether to develop the settlement at all, or whether to abandon it like the two previous attempts in the north. Land had still not been released for sale, and there would be no immigrants willing to invest the time and money in the settlement until there was more security of tenure.

The Select Committee interviewed everyone they could find who had experience in the north of Australia and the tropics. This included Dr Braidwood Wilson, who had spent two months at Fort Wellington before it was abandoned in 1829 (Wilson, 1835). Also, on the committee was John Mackay, a long-term resident of the islands north of Australia, and George Earl, who had recovered from the illness that had caused his retreat from the north. Earl was quizzed about what was happening in Port Essington, and the likelihood of the settlement's success as a port of trade and agriculture, and the possible sources of cheap labour and other immigrants. They also wanted to know his opinion of the existence of an inland sea and the undiscovered rivers that may drain them. Earl thought the Gulf of Carpentaria would be the most likely place for these rivers, as even Matthew Flinders had not been close enough to the shore to see (SMH, 31 October 1843). Other titbits of information Earl had gathered were of interest. For instance, he said the bark of *Morinda citrifolia* was collected by the Macassans for export to sell as a source of red dye for cloth (Earl, 1846). This plant is well known in the Top End and around Asia, where it is often called 'rotten cheese fruit' or 'vomit fruit', for the pungent odour of its ripe fruit. Earl also mentioned that the hard timber from the ironwood tree (*Erythrophleum chlorostachys*) was harvested and exported and used by the Macassans to repair their praus. There was much interest in Sydney and London about the Macassans and their annual voyages to Australia, harvesting huge amounts of trepang and other resources from Australian shores. The questions and Earl's answers were published verbatim in the *Sydney Morning Herald*. Earl spoke of an industry as yet untapped by the British and a potential market for

British goods, and—as far as the Select Committee was concerned—a reason for Victoria's existence, and any future government support for an overland route to Port Essington:

> ... 17. *By the Chairman: Is the coast of the Peninsula visited by prahus from the islands?* Yes.
>
> 18. *Do they frequent the coast in great numbers?* The number of prahus varies every year according to the state of the market in China; if the price of trepang is high a greater number come than when the contrary is the case; last year there were upwards of forty prahus, which is the largest number I have known to visit the Coburg Peninsula during one season.
>
> 19. *What crew do these prahus generally carry?* They vary from twenty-five to fifty men.
>
> 20. *Where do they come from?* From Macassar on the Island of Celebes.
>
> 21. *Do they return to Macassar?* They return to Macassar, touching at Timor or the Serwatty Islands on their way.
>
> 22. *What do they take besides trepang?* Trepang forms the bulk of their cargoes; they also obtain tortoise shell in considerable quantities from the natives, together with the bark of the Morinda citrifolia [Cheesefruit], which is used in the Indian Archipelago to dye cloth a red colour.
>
> 23. *What do the natives take in exchange?* Macassar sarongs, an article of clothing worn by the Indian Islanders, resembling a large petticoat, is more sought for by the natives than anything else.
>
> 24. *Do the natives wear these petticoats?* They do; they suffer, perhaps, more from the cold than the natives do here, and find these very comfortable; the natives save up their tortoise shell, and exchange it also for rice, sugar, and for a preparation of rice and sugar, of which they are very fond; but the principal things which they receive in exchange are these sarongs and axes.
>
> 25. *Have you any idea of the value of the exports from Port Essington and the neighbouring coast?* I have made a rough calculation, but owing to the nature of the trade, it is difficult to make a correct estimate of the value of the produce exported.

26. By Mr. Elwin: *What is the tonnage of these prahus?* They vary in size from twenty to seventy tons; the average is between fifty and sixty tons.

27. By the Chairman: *Do you think the people are disposed to take English manufactured goods?* They have already taken a considerable portion and are glad to get them when they can (*SMH*, 31 October 1843).

Shadrack Phillipus, Earl's Kissa-born servant, was brought before the committee and asked if his countrymen were likely to migrate to Port Essington if there was paid work for them. 'Yes,' he said, 'they would all want to go' and would work for wages of six or seven rupees a month. As if to prove this, Phillipus returned to Port Essington in 1847, and was immediately employed as McArthur's linguist.

Everyone interviewed by the committee agreed: Port Essington had a bright future. People from Kissa, Timor Laut, Timor and Singapore would flock there for paid work; and some were prepared to come immediately. The horticultural potential of the land was as yet untried, but looked very promising: timber, buffaloes and other resources were there for the taking. If only they knew where the inland sea was, and where the great rivers that flowed from it came to the sea. Developing an overland route to Port Essington might solve these questions, they thought. Expeditions overland to the north would 'doubtless contribute more or less to promote that great movement of commerce, wealth, and enlightenment towards the east, already in rapid progress' (Chronicle, 27 Jul 1844).

The Committee handed down its report in October 1843, and it was published in full by *The Australian* on 26 October. They were unanimous in their support of an overland expedition; but wanted to do it cheaply, using equipment already owned by the Surveyor General's Department, and using a cheap source of labour:

> … The greater portion of the men to be engaged, might consist of selected prisoners of the Crown, who might be induced to volunteer their services upon the promise of Conditional Pardons, or other indulgences, by the Executive

Government; and the supplies of provisions might be furnished at the present period, at a rate, which, in consequence of their cheapness, would render the outlay comparatively small (Nicholson, 26 October 1843).

Dr John Dunmore Lang, a member of the committee, was in full support of the exploration for his own reasons. He was a promotor of growing cotton in Australia, and thought that Port Essington's future lay in agriculture...

Figure 42: Dr Ludwig Leichhardt, 1813–48 (anon, NLA)

In fact:

> England could soon make itself independent from America in opening a settlement at Port Essington, though Malay labour would be required in a climate like that of the north coast of Australia; the cotton obtained in Port Essington, has been sent home, and the first judges have pronounced it to be of the first quality (Lang, 1847).

The exploration was also supported by all the biggest names in Australian exploration at the time. Sir Thomas Mitchell was very keen on it. He told the committee that:

> ... Tropical Australia is wholly unknown within the coast lines; the proposed undertaking would be creditable to the Colony; and, both as to the immediate results to be expected and the objects to be ultimately accomplished thereby, this seems to me the most important expedition that ever could be undertaken in Australia ... (Lang, 1847).

With Edward Eyre distracted by other projects, and Sir Thomas Mitchell unavailable, a 31-year-old Prussian explorer, Dr Ludwig Leichhardt was chosen by the Government to be the leader of an expedition that would travel overland, from one of two starting points suggested by the Committee: either Moreton Bay in Queensland, or from Fort Burke, in western New South Wales.

The government was going to pay £1000 to fund the expedition, until the plans fell through because Governor Gipps withdrew his support. Viewing the current economic circumstances of the colony, he was not willing to take the risk. He said, 'I fear I should be hardly justified in undertaking ... an expedition of so hazardous and expensive a nature' (Lang, 1847).

Undaunted, Leichhardt raised private funds for his expedition, and he built a team of volunteers around him. In June and July 1844, the team was busy planning the trip and finding the needed support. His objective was 'to investigate the interior of this great country in the direction of Port Essington, to reach which place will be the great endeavour of the party'. To do this he needed help:

> ... the assistance of every well-wisher to an undertaking so generally interesting, and which may possibly be conducive to the further advancement of this great colony, is earnestly requested (Aldis, 24 Jul 1844).

A tobacconist in George Street, Sydney—Mr Aldis—ran a media campaign for Leichhardt, and collected items and cash donations to help him on his way. Leichhardt needed everything from horses and saddles, to 'six red woollen shirts' and a frypan. The public were forthcoming; some of the 'well-wishers' would end up getting geographical features named after them.

Against considerable odds, Leichhardt's party was ready to go by 1 October 1844. They left from Jimbour Homestead on the edge of the known lands on Queensland's Darling Downs. They and bore not just the interest of the scientific community, but also the knowledge that their findings might affect decisions made about the future of the settlement in Port Essington. Accompanying Leichhardt was a group of men of varying bush experience: John Gilbert (the naturalist who had already spent nine months collecting at Port Essington in

1840–1), John Roper, James Calvert, John Murphy, William Phillips, and two Aboriginal guides, Harry Brown and Charlie Fisher (Blyton, 2015).

The journey took so long that the explorers were given up for dead. They nearly were dead. They were weak and emaciated—and becoming more so—when Leichhardt met two Aborigines who asked him for food. In English! But Leichhardt had none, and the men were not impressed. What sort of white man had no food?

> ... You no bread, no flour, no rice, no backi,—you no good! Balanda plenty bread, plenty flour, plenty rice, plenty backi! Balanda very good ... (Leichhardt, 1847).

The two men 'Backi-backi' and 'Rambo'—who was a 'short sturdy fellow with remarkably large testicles'—showed Leichhardt how to take palm hearts out of the small palms that grew everywhere. They then set them on the right path towards Port Essington. Leichhardt knew then that Victoria was within reach, but it still took another three weeks of struggling to reach it. They met more Aborigines who knew some English:

> It is difficult to express our joy, when English words were heard again, and when every sign which the black-fellows made, proved that we were near the end of our journey — particularly as December advanced, and the setting in of the rainy season was to be expected every moment (Leichhardt, 1847).

On 17 December 1845, after fifteen months and 4,800 kilometres, the exhausted explorers arrived in Port Essington, and they:

> ... were most kindly received by Captain McArthur, the Commandant of Port Essington, and by the other officers, who, with the greatest kindness and attention, supplied us with everything we wanted. I was deeply affected in finding myself again in civilized society, and could scarcely speak, the words growing big with tears and emotion; and, even now, when considering with what small means the Almighty had enabled me to perform such a long journey, my heart thrills in grateful acknowledgement of his infinite kindness (Leichhardt, 1847).

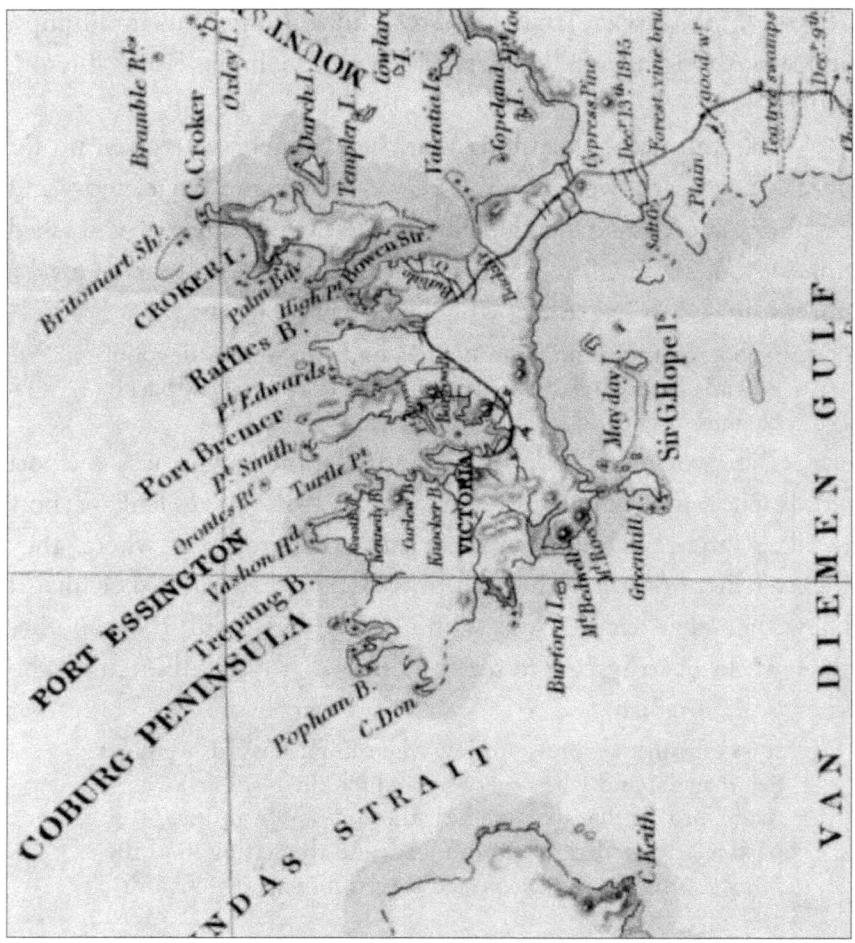

Map 7: The final leg of Leichhardt's 3000-mile journey from Moreton Bay (Leichhardt, 1847).

But the most experienced member of the expedition, John Gilbert, was not with them. In 1840, when he had been collecting in Port Essington, Gilbert had been friendly with John McArthur, who had special accommodation constructed for him within Government House. He may therefore have been looking forward to returning to the settlement and catching up with an old friend. However, on 28 June 1845, somewhere near the Mitchell River in the Gulf of

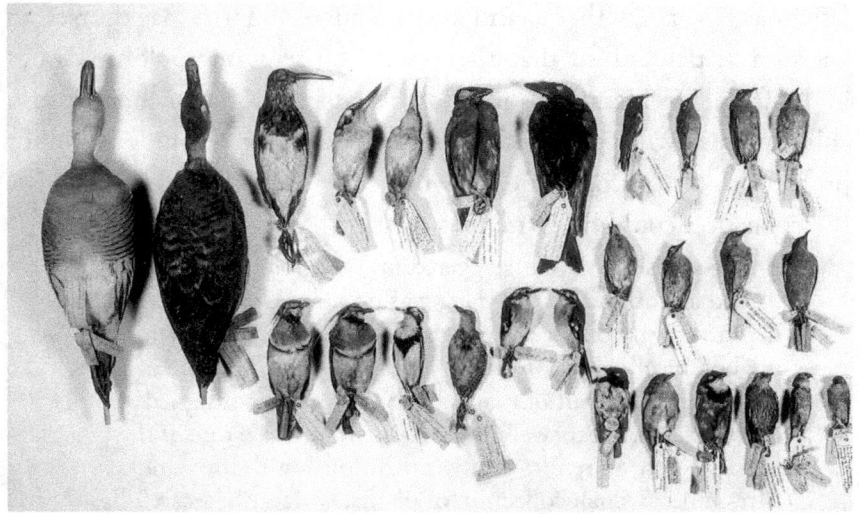

Figure 43: Ornithological specimens from the Port Essington Expedition, collected by John Gilbert and carried to Victoria Settlement by Leichhardt after Gilbert's death. Liverpool Museum (www.environmentand society.org accessed April 2020).

Carpentaria, Gilbert was killed by a spear in the lungs. His last words, 'Charlie, take my gun: they have killed me', were said as he pulled the spear out by himself (Roper, 1846). Perhaps the attack came because the travellers had transgressed important laws by camping on sacred ground. In his last diary entry, Gilbert described a strange ring of stones the Aborigines had left near where they were camping:

> … what the ring is for would be very interesting to know, perhaps in some way connected with their superstitions…
> (Gilbert, 28 June 1845).

Another reason often stated for the attack is an alleged abuse of local women by two of the team. Either of these reasons gave the local tribe justification for the punishment of the intruders. Gilbert was buried under a tree near the camp, and his grave was disguised by a fire. It has never been found.

Gilbert collected zoological specimens right up to his death—a *Climacteris* treecreeper and a finch were skinned just before dinner.

Leichhardt carried them, and many others, on the packhorses to Victoria settlement so that they could be sent on to John Gould in London for identification and/or classification. Leichhardt also collected his own specimens. He sealed them in green-hide boxes for protection, but unfortunately—when four of his horses drowned—the collection could be carried no further:

> ...This disastrous event staggered me, and for a moment I turned almost giddy; but there was no help. Unable to increase the load of my bullocks, I was obliged to leave that part of my botanical collection which had been carried by one of the horses. The fruit of many a day's work was consigned to the fire; and tears were in my eyes when I saw one of the most interesting results of my expedition vanish into smoke. Mr. Gilbert's small collection of plants, which I had carefully retained hitherto, shared the same fate. But they were of less value, as they were mostly in a bad state of preservation, from being too much crowded. My collection had the great advantage of being almost complete in blossoms, fruit, and seed, ... (Fensham, et al., 2006).

Another of Leichhardt's party, John Roper, was hit by six spears in the attack. He lost an eye, but his injuries were not fatal. Roper was a 'limited young man', thought Leichhardt, and 'foolhardy' and no bushman, according to Gilbert. He had found it hard to build the respect of his companions—but he survived the ordeal of the trek[*].

The explorers spent a month in Victoria, recuperating. Leichhardt spent the time preparing his maps and preliminary report. He also added to his plant collection, adding a *Tephrosia* just before Christmas (see www.eflora.nt.gov.au). He continued his journal through most of this time:

> ... There are two gardens, one with a rich black soil, mixed however with sand, which makes it mild. Here [are] Coconut palm, the Banana, the breadfruit, and the sowersob [sic]... the

---

[*] John Roper returned to New South Wales and eventually became the mayor of Albury, in 1862 (Orlovich, 1976). The Roper River, in the Northern Territory, is named after him.

other garden, nearer to the sea side, is on a shallow crust of the decomposed rock of the place. It produces good pumbkins [sic], melons, cucumbers, vegetable marrow, but nothing else (Webster, 1986).

In early January Corporal John Conway—who had spent eight months in the hospital—died of consumption, but the health of the community seemed to be improving, with only three others on the sick list. McArthur reported on 1 December 'more favourably than hitherto' on their state of health when there were just nine patients in hospital. A party of convalescents had spent time at Point Smith which improved their health enough for them to help finish the construction of the 10-metre stone beacon. From then on the beacon defined the opening to the harbour, and marked an approach from the west that aided ships' masters to avoid the Orontes Shoal (McArthur, 1 December 1846)[*].

On 9 January 1846, the *Heroine* arrived with a cargo of beer from Bali, and everyone was issued a bottle a day—which greatly improved morale.

On 17 January, Leichhardt's party left Port Essington to return to Sydney on the *Heroine*. He left a forwarding address in McArthur's notebook:

To the care of -Lynd Expi_ [sic]
Barrack Martin General
Sydney

It was good riddance for McArthur, who disliked Leichhardt on sight, and he called him 'bitter, virulent, malicious, dishonest, shifting and mean ... the very lowest stamp' (Spillett, 1972). Oddly, E. M. Webster, Leichhardt's biographer, found the opposite, quoting McArthur as saying; 'I shall really feel his loss, never having met with a more intelligent and amiable man'. Perhaps McArthur would have softened his views if he could have read what Leichhardt wrote about him:

---

[*] Several ships have been wrecked on the Orontes Shoal and other reefs off Vashon Head since then. For instance: The *Red Gauntlet* in September 1887, the *Calcutta* in 1894, with a cargo of 500 tons of rice from Saigon heading to Noumea (*NTTG* 24 August 1894), and the steamer Australian in 1906 (*NTTG*, 23 November 1906). Also, several pearling luggers were lost in the area during the 1920s and '30s.

> ... I shall never forget Capt. MacArthur [sic]. I am proud that I have been able to make him my friend. A man of so various knowledge and of so sound information is rare anywhere, but uniting it with such an amiable disposition, such willingness of communication and, if I could use the term, of conversational bartering (ready to give and take, he becomes a rara avis, there most where knowledges and sciences abound (Webster, 1986)

When the explorers arrived in Sydney, it was to a tumultuous and triumphant welcome:

> ... At length, on the 25th of March, 1846, the city of Sydney was electrified at the sudden apparition of Dr. Leichhardt and his party ... direct from Port Essington; having accomplished the grand object of their expedition, and thereby achieved, with the scantiest means and with consummate ability, an exploit scarcely paralleled in the annals of Geographical Discovery. To traverse with so small a party and so inadequate an equipment a country hitherto untrodden by civilized man — to traverse that country during fifteen months successively, for a distance of nearly 3000 miles — a country, moreover, inhabited by fierce barbarians, and subject alternately to distressing droughts and terrific inundations—the heroism of the enterprise can only be equalled by its brilliant success. Dr. Leichhardt has virtually added a vast and valuable province to the British Empire and has greatly extended the domain of civilized man. The real benefits and advantages of his discoveries can scarcely as yet be either felt or appreciated; but inasmuch as they have opened up a boundless extent of pastoral country to the northward and westward, they will be felt and appreciated in the first instance by the colonists of Cooksland ... (Lang, 1847).

The government was pleased that the self-funded cross-country exploration had been so successful; and a public subscription of £1400 was raised and paid to the surviving members. The colonial secretary, Earl Grey, passed on the congratulations of the British government:

> ... you will express to Dr. Leichhardt the high sense which Her M.'s Government entertain of his Services, and their acknowledgment of the great personal Sacrifices, which

he appears to have made in pursuing the enterprise (Grey, 18 August 1846).

It was not only politicians who lauded Leichhardt's efforts, but poets too:

Thy footsteps have return'd again, thou wanderer of the wild,
Where Nature, from her lonely throne, in giant beauty smiled.
Pilgrim of mighty wastes, untrod by human foot before,
Triumphant o'er the wilderness, thy weary journey's o'er!
...
Proud man! In after ages, the story shall be told,
Of that advent'rous traveller—the generous—the bold,
Who scorning hope of selfish gain, disdaining soft repose,
Taught the dark and howling wilderness to blossom like the rose
... by E.K.S. (Lang, 1847) p337.

The British in North Australia: Port Essington

Chapter 7
Iwaidja

Sir Gordon Bremer, Captain McArthur, George Earl, and others built up good relationships with many of the Iwaidja. 'We get on famously with the natives' said Earl (13 July 1840).

Some of the Iwaidjas' early willingness to spend time with the British may have come from their memory of—or spoken reputation of—Captain Collet Barker at Raffles Bay a decade earlier. When Langari delivered his 'long address, shedding many tears' to Bremer in 1838, he was mistaking the new commandant for the old (Earl, 1846).

Like Barker, both Bremer and McArthur 'strenuously opposed all violence towards them' and—although misdemeanours from Iwaidja were punished—they were punished in the same way as British miscreants; and the Iwaidja respected that. They also must have been grateful the British did not copy the Macassans:

> … McArthur manages them well. They pilfer occasionally, for which they are punished with a caning, or a confinement for a week in irons. The latter they consider the greatest punishment… The Macassans I find sometimes put them to death for having been engaged in attacks on them … (Earl, 13 July 1840).

McArthur learned that solitary confinement affected them 'in the same manner that it does children when shut up in dark closets' (20 September 1842). Stanley wrote that 'two days confinement [had] more effect than any corporal punishment however severe' (Stanley, 1 November 1841).

George Windsor Earl questioned the Iwaidja as he gained more knowledge of their languages. He was curious about their history and what was happening across northern Australia. He concluded that the British had arrived after a period of great change:

> ... Indeed, it would seem that at no very distant period, the pressure of a powerful people in the interior of the continent had driven one tribe in upon another, until several distinct communities have been crowded up within the Cobourg Peninsula, where, until very recently, they have been making war upon each other, to such an extent that two of these have, within the memory of natives now living, been reduced from numerous bodies to mere scattered remnants ... (Earl, 1846).

Aboriginal groups along the coast were also decimated by events other than war. With the annual visits of Macassans—then the Europeans—came malaria, leprosy, smallpox, influenza, eye diseases (ophthalmia) and venereal disease such as syphilis: all of which the Aborigines had no inherited defence against.

Earl described four different tribes on the peninsula, which this book refers to under the umbrella term of Iwaidja.

Yaako, inhabiting Crocker Island and the country around Raffles Bay.

Yarlo, the Port Essington tribe.

Iyi, who inhabited lands west of Port Essington.

Oitbi, occupying the southern shore of the peninsula, the islands of Van Diemen Gulf and the extreme upper limits of Port Essington (Powell, 2016).

The difficulty in collecting anthropological information with limited communications is highlighted by MacGillivray's conclusions about the same people in the same area:

> ... The natives of the Cobourg Peninsula are divided into four tribes, named respectively the Bijenelumbo, Limbakarajia, Limbapyu, and Terrutong. The first of these occupies the head of the harbour (including the ground on which the settlement is built) and the country as far back as the isthmus, the second, both sides of the port lower down, the third, the north-west portion of the peninsula and the last have

Iwaidja

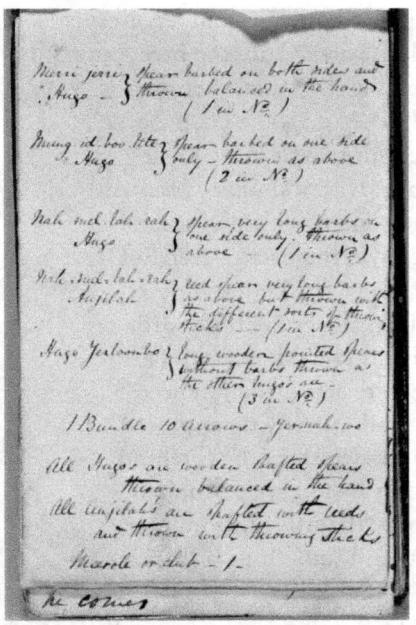

Figure 44: The McArthurs' notebook, recording Iwaidja spears (McArthur, NTRS 3601_page 35).

possession of Croker's Island, and the adjacent coasts of the mainland. From the constant intercourse which takes place between these tribes, their affinity of language, and similarity in physical character, manners, and customs, they may be spoken of as one (MacGillivray, 1852).

Several curious characteristics of the Iwaidja continued to confuse the settlers. For example, in the time of Fort Wellington, the settlers had never met any Iwaidja women. Now, however, 'the females come into the settlement without reserve' (McArthur, 2 November 1840). There appeared to have been a major change in attitudes among them during the preceding decade that no one could explain.

Also, whenever the white men gave any of the Iwaidja clothing, for instance—as it was much coveted and keenly collected—it would disappear immediately:

> ... It was generally remarked that the old clothes given to these savages disappeared in a most mysterious manner. They were understood to be sold to the natives inhabiting the loftier parts of the interior, but of this I entertain very considerable doubt (Stokes, 1846).

Major John Campbell—the second commandant at Fort Dundas from 1826—later addressed the Royal Geographical Society in London*. During his time in the north he travelled to the Cobourg Peninsula and spent some time with the Iwaidja he met:

> ... In personal appearance they bear some resemblance to the natives about Port Jackson: they are, however, better made and

---

* Campbell's paper is reproduced in part in *Fort Wellington* (Pugh, 2020).

have more intelligent, and perhaps more savage countenances as they go entirely naked; their skin, particularly the breast and thighs, is ornamented, or disfigured with gashes; their hair is long, and generally straight, yet I observed some crisp. Some of them have a fillet of network about two or three inches wide bound tightly round the waist, with a similar ornament round the head and the arms, and sometimes a necklace of network depending some length down the back. Several of them have the front tooth in the upper jaw knocked out ... They paint their face, and sometimes the entire body with red earth: and those who are inclined to be dandies draw one or two longitudinal lines of white across the forehead and three similar on each cheek, while a few who appeared to be 'exquisites' had another line drawn from the forehead to the tip of the nose. The septum is invariably perforated; but it is on particular occasions only that they introduce a bone or piece of wood through it, and sometimes a feather ... (Campbell, 1834).

MacGillivray described the Aborigines as 'scarcely differ(ent) physically' from others he knew in New South Wales. He claimed that there were never any feelings of hostility from them towards Europeans, unlike that which was experienced both at Fort Dundas and Fort Wellington (MacGillivray, 15 October 1845).

Captain McArthur—or his son—was intrigued with the variety of Iwaidja spears and probably made a collection of them. In their notebook, there is a description of the spears, their Iwaidja names, how they were made, and how they were used (See Figure 44).

Lort Stokes was also impressed by the Iwaidja:

... These aborigines were certainly a fine race, differing in some matters from the other natives of Australia; their hair was neither curly nor straight, but crisp. The custom of extracting a front tooth prevails among them, while the nasal cartilage here as elsewhere was perforated ...

... I noticed in particular that they did not make use of the boomerang, or kiley, but of the throwing stick or womera, of a larger kind, however, than any I have observed elsewhere; the head of their spears was made of stone. They have a smaller kind, chiefly used to kill birds and other animals at a considerable distance. They have also large heavy clubs, while the natives on the South coast carry only the short throwing stick. They go wholly naked, except when entering the settlements, on which occasions they wear a few leaves. Their canoes were chiefly obtained from the Malays…

… I here saw the only musical instrument I ever remarked among the natives of Australia. It is a piece of bamboo thinned from the inside, through which they blow with their noses. It is from two to three feet long, is called ebroo, and produces a kind of droning noise. It is generally made use of at corrobories or dances, some of which express feats of hunting and war, while others are very indecent, and reminded us of similar exhibitions in the East (Stokes, 1846).

George Earl agreed with Stokes. He found the people to be superior to others he had met:

The natives of the N. coast differ little from those of the southern parts of Australia, except in being superior in personal appearance. Their intercourse with the Bughis has given them some idea of commerce, and the former obtain large quantities of tortoiseshell from them in exchange for iron, rice, and old clothes. We have been on excellent terms with them throughout our stay at Port Essington (Earl, 1841).

The 19-year-old Sweatman's observations of the Iwaidja seem almost envious:

… they are a merry light hearted people and although an European would think their mode of living the very extreme of wretchedness, they are far happier than many who enjoy every comfort (Sweatman, 1847).

John Sweatman's comments would have been decidedly different if he had written them several months later. The general health of the Iwaidja was indeed mostly good during the early years of the settlement. In 1841 several had suffered from 'catarrh, inflammation of the chest, and ophthalmia', but McArthur's biggest worry for them was that they were being 'ensnared into habits of smoking tobacco as I conceive this seduces to the love of ardent spirits… by the time this evil is open to them, I fear they will fall an easy prey' (McArthur,

3 September 1841). Several contracted malaria, or other fevers in 1843, but they never suffered an epidemic of disease. That is, until 1847!

During an early and uncharacteristically cold dry season, a bronchial influenza arrived on the north coast. In October, McArthur described how most of the Iwaidja on Cobourg Peninsula fell into 'such a state of destitution and wretchedness that it aroused the pity of all who came in contact with them' (Spillett, 1972). The disease quickly spread, many died, and many others were too weak to help themselves. The Europeans mostly went unaffected by the disease, but the Iwaidja had no defence against it.

McArthur fed those near the settlement with rice and sago and provided tea and sugar. Doctor Tilston also did as much as he could to help them. They heard that as many as 60 Iwaidja had died beyond the peninsula, in Mountnorris Bay. Father Confalonieri also nursed many out at Black Rock, but many more may have died without ever being noticed by the Europeans. How the influenza arrived is unknown, but just prior to its appearance, several ships had called into Port Essington: the *Angelina* under Captain W. Morgan, and the *Juno*, under Captain Henry Bray. With the sudden cooler weather of the dry season, the virus took hold and McArthur felt that—if the English hadn't been there to help the Iwaidja—the tribe may have died out completely (Spillett, 1972).

McArthur's actions towards the Iwaidja were consistent throughout his 11 years in Victoria. He genuinely cared about their welfare and was respected by them. There was one incident, however, that marred their relationship.

Corporal William Masland arrived on the *Cadet* with the relief garrison in April 1844. At one point he was promoted to Sergeant and selected by Captain McArthur to be a Constable of Police in the settlement. His main role then, was to try and curb anti-social behaviour caused by 'intemperance'. Arguably, he was the first military police officer in the north.

In August 1846, Masland, four armed marines and an interpreter chased two Iwaidja men across the harbour and arrested them for theft. They warned them, through the interpreter, that if they attempted to escape, they would be shot.

Unfortunately, both prisoners managed to slip out of their manacles and dive overboard as they passed South Head. Masland ordered them back, but it was just after dark, and the men dived underwater and avoided recapture, until the constable drew his revolver and fired. One of the men was hit and was either killed by the shot or drowned with his injury. His body washed up on a beach the next day.

Captain McArthur was horrified. This was the first death of an Aborigine by violence in the eight years since settlement; and McArthur was proud of his unblemished record. Masland was arrested and placed on bail. All the reports and evidence were forwarded to the Supreme Court in Sydney. McArthur added a note suggesting that Masland was not motivated by malice. He had always been very humane towards the Iwaidja in the past. His defence, that he was carrying out his duty as an officer to prevent the prisoner from escaping, was held up by the Attorney-General in Sydney. Masland was, he said, justified in the shooting, so he was never prosecuted in a court. He also kept his role of constable in Port Essington, until the settlement was abandoned.

That, however, was not the end of the matter for the Iwaidja. The dead man's relatives wanted revenge. Killing an Englishman was too dangerous, so they took it out on another Aborigine, a man named Neinmal, of the Binanolombo people.

Neinmal had led an extraordinary life since the coming of the British. Now recognised as one of the most important Indigenous naturalists of the nineteenth century, he was John MacGillivray's advisor, consultant and assistant for two years (Olsen & Russell, 2019). As MacGillivray recorded:

> Many of the Port Essington natives have shown a remarkable degree of intelligence, far above the average Europeans,

Figure 45: Neinmal by H.S. Melville (Greenwood, 1863).

uneducated, and living in remote districts among others I may mention the name of Neinmal of whose character I had good opportunities of judging, for he lived with me for ten months. During my stay at Port Essington, he became much attached to me, and latterly accompanied me in all my wanderings in the bush, while investigating the natural history of the district, following up the researches of my late and much-lamented friend Gilbert. One day, while detained by rainy weather at my camp, I was busy in skinning a fish. Neinmal watched me attentively for some time and then withdrew, but returned in half an hour afterwards, with the skin of another fish in his hand prepared by himself, and so well done too, that it was added to the collection …

He accompanied me in the *Fly* to Torres Strait and New Guinea, and on our return to Port Essington begged so hard to continue with me that I could not refuse him. He went with us to Singapore, Java, and Sydney, and from his great good humour became a favourite with all on board, picking up the English language with facility, and readily conforming himself to our habits, and the discipline of the ship. He was very cleanly in his personal habits, and paid much attention to his dress, which was always kept neat and tidy. I was often much amused and surprised by the oddity and justness of his remarks upon the many strange sights which a voyage of this kind brought before him. The *Nemesis* steamer under weigh puzzled him at first, he then thought it was "all same big cart, only got him shingles on wheels!" … The poor fellow suffered much from cold during the passage round Cape Leeuwin and was ill when landed at Sydney, but soon recovered. Although his thoughts were always centred in his native home, and a girl to whom he was much attached, he yet volunteered to accompany me to England, when the *Fly* was about to sail, but as I had then no immediate prospect of returning to Australia, I could not undertake the responsibility of having to provide for him for the future. I was glad then when Lieutenant Yule, who was about to revisit Port Essington, generously offered to take him there. While in the *Bramble* he made himself useful in assisting the steward, and, under the tuition of Dr. MacClatchie, made some proficiency in acquiring the rudiments of reading and writing.

At Port Essington, the older members of his family evinced much jealousy on account of the attention shown him, and his determination to remain with Mr. Tilston, the assistant-surgeon, then in charge, and endeavoured to dissuade him from his purpose. While upon a visit to his tribe he met his death ... His natural courage and presence of mind did not desert him even at the last extremity, when he was roused from sleep to find himself surrounded by a host of savages thirsting for his blood. They told him to rise, but he merely raised himself upon his elbow, and said: "If you want to kill me do so where I am, I won't get up, give me a spear and club, and I'll fight you all one by one!"

He had scarcely spoken when a man named Alerk speared him from behind, spear after spear followed, and as he lay writhing on the ground his savage murderers literally dashed him to pieces with their clubs. The account of the manner in which Neinmal met his death was given me by a very intelligent native who had it from an eyewitness, and I have every reason to believe it true, corroborated as it was by the testimony of others (MacGillivray, 1852).

Hardon Sidney Melville—a draftsman and an artist on the *Fly*—sketched Neinmal and provided a description for James Greenwood, which was published in Greenwood's 1863 book, *Curiosities of a Savage Life*:

> ... The aboriginals of Australia have a custom of 'adorning' the body by slitting the fleshy parts loopwise and underlaying the semi-detached piece with clay, producing a sort of 'ridge and furrow' pattern more curious than pleasing. Mr H.S. Melville, while attached to Captain Blackwood's exploring expedition, made the acquaintance of one of these cicatrised gentry.
>
> 'Neinmal was a native of Port Essington and was taken on board the *Fly* on an experimental tour. He adopted 'Jack's' costume and much of 'Jack's' manners, for it was 'Jack' which had most to do with Neinmal's civilisation. A great element in Neinmal's personal makeup were his cicatrices being scored according to native custom horizontally across the body, much as a cook would serve a loin of pork—the operation, I am told, was performed by some sharp instrument; but an oyster shell may supply the want of a better—the wound is then

Figure 46: Aborigines in front of the hospital. According to Olsen, Neinmal is the man third from the left (Herman Melville, HMS *Fly*, NLA-148363905-1)

filled up with clay, and the skin healing over forms raised ropy ridges, giving to the body much the resemblance of an old tree which has suffered from the mutilations of a schoolboy's knife at different stages of its growth. Neinmal's trunk had much this aspect, and he was very proud of the adornment, although it must have reminded him of the torture he had undergone (many die under it). When he was exhibited to some of the Torres Strait natives, they regarded him with veneration, their admiration being expressed by the most emphatic 'Whi-warg!' ... (Greenwood, 1863).

Neinmal's journeys may have made the other men in the tribe angry for what they saw as desertion or disloyalty, or perhaps—as Sweatman thought—they were jealous. Sweatman noted that the girls 'used to get hold of [Neinmal] and tell him what a disgraceful thing it was for him to wear clothes etc'. Jealousy creates strong motives and the innocent Neinmal may have been chosen as a target for revenge, solely because he had developed strong relationships with the British.

MacGillivray used Neinmal's death as an exemplar of Aboriginal laws of punishment and revenge:

> A Monobar native (inhabitant of the country to the westward of the isthmus) was shot by a marine in the execution of his duty, for attempting to escape while in custody, charged with robbery. When his tribe heard of it, as they could not lay their hands upon a white man, they enticed into their territory a Bijenelumbo man, called Neinmal, who was a friend of the whites, having lived with them for years, and on that account he was selected as a victim and killed. When the news of Neinmal's death reached the settlement, some other Bijenelumbo people took revenge by killing a Monobar native within a few hundred yards of the houses. Thus, the matter rests at present, but more deaths will probably follow before the feud is ended. Both these murders were committed under circumstances of the utmost atrocity, the victims being surprised asleep, unconscious of danger, and perfectly defenceless, then aroused to find themselves treacherously attacked by numbers, who, after spearing them in many places, fearfully mangled the bodies with clubs. (MacGillivray, 1852).

One mistake from the constable—no matter how 'justifiable' under British law—cost the Iwaidja three, or more, of their own. If further payback killings occurred, they were not recorded, as the British left soon after these events.

The longer the British stayed in Port Essington, the more interested they were in the local Aborigines. Surgeon Archibald Sibbald, for instance, watched in astonishment as an Iwaidja man closed his own spear wound using a nail and a thread of bark. The Iwaidja man had previously watched the doctor suture another man's wounds, caused by a bite from a crocodile.

Sibbald was also interested in the cicatrised scars the Iwaidja decorated their bodies with. In an eccentric Victorian-era scientific exploration of them, he asked the Iwaidja to give him a cicatrice on his own shoulder:

> … The manner of doing it is as follows; they take a lancet; sharp shell in their native state & cut two perpendicular lines,

the length (it) is to be, they cut with a scraping motion as is done in etching … then they take different coloured earths or chalks … mixed on a leaf for a palette, & getting a small stick, bite the end to make it hold like a paint brush, this they paint over the scars alternately of different colours & ascending to the number of markings to be raised this operation of painting goes on every day, till [the scar] is large enough; but whatever may [please them] would not similarly a European, so I put a stop to it on the 4th day (Sibbald, 1844).

Sibbald appears to have understood more about the enormous cultural divide between the British and the Iwaidja than many other diarists; but only in that he was aware that he would never grasp the complexities of Aboriginal life. Most Aborigines kept their distance from the British. Only a few, like Neinmal and Jack Davis, truly allowed their lives to be examined, but even then, only to a certain extent. As Sibbald (1844) noted 'they have a language they speak to us in & another we do not understand'. Even Captain McArthur recognised that there was a reticence among the Aborigines: 'they prefer the adoption of some of our language rather than we should acquire theirs' he wrote. McArthur was no linguist, but his notebook does show a small collection of Iwaidja vocabulary on the names of birds in the area: *māngār*—partridge, *inmoolar*—epaulette dove, *morcoitch*—Torres Strait pigeon … (McArthur & McArthur, 1849).

There is no in-depth information about Iwaidja beliefs discovered during this time. The British were never told, for example, that Cobourg Peninsula is believed to be the place where the creation ancestor, Warramurrungunji, first came ashore from the Arafura Sea, long ago in the Dreamtime. Linguists Nick Evans and Murray Garde collected the story from Croker Island elder, Tim Mamitba, in 2004:

… Warramurrungunji … came ashore on the northern part of Croker island, having crossed the ocean. Once she was here, she gave birth to many children. And she healed herself by sitting on a combination of sand and hot ashes where there are now many sand dunes. She first came ashore at Malay Bay … In each place she left some of her children. She kept on like that, leaving children in many places. She used to carry them on her shoulder in a dilly bag. She would assign each group a country, telling them, 'You're going to speak this language'. She also went to Eastern Arnhem Land, and she travelled inland, placing all the groups of children in different places and giving them different languages. We don't [know] where she lay to rest. Maybe much further inland, where the kangaroos and wallabies live. The escarpment country. We don't really know where she's buried, where she is now, but we know she started here on Croker Island … (in (McKenna, 2016).

During the decades immediately after the British left, the Iwaidja suffered terrible epidemics of disease. Foelsche thought Malay trepangers introduced smallpox, known locally as 'mea-mea' or 'oie-boie', when visiting Cobourg Peninsula (Foelsche, 1886). Smallpox, Foelsche was told by Jack Davis—who remembered many pock-marked elders when he was a child—had killed 'plenty blackfellows'. Judy Campbell, after extensive research into this disease, concluded that it had first appeared among Aborigines around 1780, just at the beginning of the trepang fisheries (Campbell, 2002).

By 1886 the Iwaidja population was reduced to just 30 members, consisting of seven men, twelve women, nine boys and two girls. Today, many Iwaidja descendants of these survivors still live on their own country. Some work as rangers and land managers in the Garig Gunak Barlu National Park. About 150 other Iwaidja make their home in the community of Minjilang*, on Croker Island, where they retain their cultural links to the land and sea.

---

* According to the West Arnhem Regional Council, about half the population of 300 in Minjilang speak the Iwaidja language (the other language groups are mostly Mawng and Kunwinjku) (www.westarnhem.nt.gov.au).

Chapter 8
The *Heroine* and the priest

Fresh from taking the triumphant Dr Ludwig Leichhardt and his party to Sydney, the schooner *Heroine** was returning to the north. The *Heroine* was the ex-convict transporter owned by Mr d'Almeida which had been so useful in the early 1840s—bringing pigs and buffaloes to Port Essington. She was in company with two other supply ships: *Sapphire* and *Enchantress*.

On board the *Heroine*, Captain Martin Mackenzie was the most experienced commander of the three, so he led the way through the Great Barrier Reef. Unfortunately, his navigation was not good enough. On 4 April 1846†, the three ships were near the Cumberland Islands‡, some 20 miles west of where Mackenzie thought they were and travelling at 8 or 9 knots. Then, without warning—just before 1 A.M.—the *Heroine* hit rocks with 'such violence that the foretopmast went over the side' (Sweatman, 1847).

Eight of her people were killed. Reverend Nicholas Hogan and Reverend James Fagan were asleep in a cabin below and they drowned in their beds. Mr Earl, the brother of George Earl planning to visit

---
* The *Heroine* first arrived in Port Jackson transporting convicts, on 19th September 1833, after 128 days at sea, plus two months 'in quarantine' because of a smallpox outbreak.
† The date is disputed, but 4 April 1846 is the date stated by Captain Richard Essenhigh of the *Enchantress*, who witnessed the wreck and picked up survivors (*Sydney Morning Herald*, 18 November 1846).
‡ The Cumberland Islands, which includes the Whitsunday group and others, are near Mackay in Queensland's Great Barrier Reef. The Northumberland Islands, mentioned by Sweatman, are nearby.

him, and his wife managed to get out on deck. Earl tied himself to his wife, but the rope he chose was a part of the rigging. As a result, they were dragged to the bottom as the ship went down. Also drowned were an unnamed Chinese man and three of the Javanese crew.

On board the ship were '5 natives of Port Essington'*, one of whom was 'Jack White'. With other passengers and the seamen, they swam to the rocks, or to the small boat that was under tow. They were later rescued by the boats of the *Sapphire* and the *Enchantress*.

Another priest, and three women, managed to cling to the maintopmast as the ship sank. They were rescued by Nelson, the chief mate's Newfoundland dog . The dog swam them, one by one, to safety on the reef†.

Captain Mackenzie swam the wrong way—in the dark and confusion, he headed out to sea. Tragically, he tied his infant daughter to his back, but the little girl died from exposure before morning and Mackenzie reluctantly let her drift away. When dawn broke, 5 hours later, he could see the *Sapphire* in the distance. Luckily, he was spotted by the mate, just as the ship was bearing up, and rescued.

Mackenzie lost his child and his life savings. Also gone were 300 sovereigns the ship was transporting to Port Essington to pay the garrison. George Lambrick, the paymaster, was eagerly awaiting them because the men were paid in cash‡, but the sovereigns were now lying on the sea floor. The Government usually only sent cash on warships, but since the *Royalist* had left the port, Victoria had been without one. In fact, there was no warship anywhere in Australia at that time (Spillett, 1972), and the men had not been paid for months.

There were 40 survivors from the wreck, and they were

---

* Except for 'Jack White', these men are not named. It shows there was a growing number of Iwaidja who travelled with the British (see Neinmal for instance).

† Nelson was later killed by a crocodile in Port Essington (Sweatman, 1847).

‡ Paying the marines in cash had started after the arrival of the *Cadet* at Port Essington. McArthur worried that his control of his men was then weakened, as they could now buy illicit spirits and tobacco from ships and gamble their wages away (Spillett, 1972). The cash also needed to be transferred by ship, which created its own set of problems, as the loss of the *Heroine* shows.

The *Herione* and the priest

Figure 47: Father Angelo Confalonieri

transferred to the *Enchantress* and delivered to Port Essington on 13 April 1846.

The priest who owed his life to Nelson the Newfoundland dog, was Father Angelo Confalonieri, a Catholic missionary from Lake Garda in Northern Italy. He had been sent from Rome by Pope Gregory XVI with 20 other Irish, French, and Italian missionaries to evangelise Australia (McKenna, 2016). He was appointed the 'Vicar-General of Port Essington' in Perth but now was destitute. He had lost everything in the wreck, including his two assistants—the Reverends Hogan and Fagan. Despite this, Sweatman was impressed by Confalonieri. He described him as 'very gentlemanly and well educated … liberal minded and tolerant on all points of religion'.

On arrival in the port, the destitute priest threw himself on Captain McArthur's mercy, asking him for any help he could give. He promised that his superior in Perth, Bishop John Brady, would repay McArthur for any receipts he produced. Confalonieri owned nothing. McArthur took pity on him and provided him with food and clothing, paper, pencils, and accommodation. Confalonieri was not a British subject, so McArthur was unsure of how much help he could officially give, so he took the responsibility on himself. He paid for a month's rations and generously offered to continue providing them until Confalonieri could provide for himself.

Confalonieri was a clever linguist and the only European of the time to study the Iwaidja language in depth (Harris, 1985). He was extremely short-sighted and had lost his glasses in the shipwreck, but he could charm and communicate well with people. However, there were still great difficulties, such as mischievous intents among his informants: when he was collecting vocabulary, the larrikins among the Iwaidja would sometimes teach him obscenities instead of the words he wanted:

> 'When the poor padre came to address the natives, he wondered how it was that they laughed so at his sermons' (Sweatman, 1847).

Confalonieri's mission was to live with the Aborigines and convert them to Christianity. Originally unaware of the tribes' semi-nomadic life, he had planned to set himself up in a 'village' near the Alligator Rivers. However, his plans changed when he learned there were no permanent villages anywhere in the Top End and McArthur convinced him to remain closer to Victoria for safety. A hut was built for him on the opposite side of the harbour near Black Point, about 20 km from Victoria. He lived there with a young Iwaidja man, known as Jim Crow*, who worked as his language assistant and translator, and probably as a general servant.

Confalonieri made a short victualling journey to the Ki Islands on the *Bramble* when Lieutenant Yule, accompanied by the *Castlereagh,* sailed there to buy pigs and other food items.

Confalonieri had money loaned to him by McArthur, and he bought a small boat called a sampan to use for his mission. Unfortunately, he didn't have it long—it was soon stolen by two English sailors who deserted from the *Castlereagh* whilst they were still in the Islands. Lieutenant Yule refused to wait whilst the sailors were located because he had 98 wild pigs breaking out of their bamboo holding pens and fighting 'like cocks jumping up at each other', on the deck of his ship. He therefore needed to return to Port Essington as quickly as possible. Even so, two pigs managed to jump overboard and drown before the crew had even weighed anchor. Six more were lost on the way.

---

* In the 1830s a popular American entertainer, Thomas Rice (1808–60), blackened his face and performed a racist song-and-dance act supposedly modelled after a slave. He named the character 'Jim Crow' and over the years the character became the basis of the 'Black and White Minstrels'. There was a 'Jump Jim Crow' dance craze in Sydney in 1835. Confalonieri's assistant was probably named after this character.

Confalonieri's troubles were not over. According to Sweatman, he was helpless in the most ordinary domestic matters. For example, he didn't know how to mix and cook flour. He also had to beg the garrison for everything, including a spoon. They hardly had one to spare—but it was 'miserable to eat pease [sic] soup with a fork', he said (Sweatman, 1847).

Once the shipment of pigs was unloaded and the paperwork done to transfer them to Lambrick's domain, Confalonieri was left to settle into his hut, and the *Bramble* was taken to anchor near Point Record.

The ship was suffering from a plague of cockroaches, which were an 'intolerable nuisance'. Sweatman said it was impossible:

> … to sleep below for them, for apart from the nuisance of having such disgusting animals crawling over one they used actually to eat away the skin from our extremities while we slept… they flew about like birds, I have even seen the lights put out by them… (Sweatman, 1847).

Sweatman had done a study on the effects of the cockroaches on the ship's bread supply. He had taken a 112-pound bag from the stores at Victoria, had the officers sign and seal it in the ship's bread room, and left it alone for 20 days while they sailed to the Ki Islands and back. When it was again weighed, it totalled 65 pounds, and 'the bag was eaten to rags and the biscuits like honeycomb'. Sweatman worked out that he had lost 3000 pounds of bread since they had left Sydney.

The ship's crew had tried smoking the cockroaches out, and this had worked for a while, but by June 1846 they were back in force. Lieutenant Yule paid the ship's boys to collect them, by the pint, between dark and 8 P.M. each night. They would catch at least two or three pints for their efforts, every day. This started to become too expensive for the lieutenant, so a new plan was needed.

At the beginning of August, the *Bramble* was moored off Point Record. The crew then unloaded all the stores and equipment onto the beach and erected a sail as a tent. They then lived under it for the next three months.

Clearing out the ship was a big job, and it took until 14 August before the *Bramble* was completely emptied. Then, at high tide, she was taken around to some sand flats and a 'scuttle' was cut in her side at low tide. She then filled with water from the incoming tide:

> ... At high water, she was completely covered above the tops of the roundhouses abaft; and the cockroaches came up by millions to take refuge on the rigging, and the crew stood by with buckets: ... to wash them down and a regular water frolic took place: the sea was covered with the dead who were washed ashore in heaps where the natives gathered them up in handfuls to eat them*! (Sweatman, 1847).

The ship was drained with the tide, the scuttle closed, and the ship was pumped dry. A few worm-eaten planks were then replaced, while stoves burned below to dry the lower decks. Then she was completely cleaned and repainted, and the stores examined minutely to ensure not a single cockroach was allowed back on board. More than 500 gallons of cockroaches were shovelled out; and about the same amount were washed away by the sea!

All this was done in the dry air of August, and a pleasant camp was had by all, despite the annoyance of clouds of little black flies during the day, and mosquitoes at night. Sweatman tells of regularly swimming off Point Record, and although no 'alligators' ever appeared, to be sure they were safe the Englishmen regularly:

> ... collected a dozen or twenty women and children and made them bathe with us, as well for the fun we used to have with them, swimming, diving, playing leapfrog &c as to make a good noise and hubbub in the water & so frighten the sharks away. Moreover, people say, though I do not know if it's true,

---

* This might be 19th century hyperbole, designed to horrify Sweatman's readers. Cockroaches can be eaten but need cooking first. Their secretions can be highly acidic, and they regurgitate an odorous brown substance, which smells disgusting. It is doubtful that anybody would ever eat them raw or 'by the handful'. By their description Whelan feels that they were American cockroaches (*Periplaneta americana*) (Whelan, 2020).

that a shark always prefers a blackfellow to a white if he has a choice... (Sweatman, 1847).

The process of emptying and drowning the *Bramble*, then drying her out and repacking her, took a little under three months. She was finally ready to return to Sydney cockroach free. But the drowning process had not killed the eggs. Soon the insects were swarming once again through the holds and cabins. The whole process had to be repeated the next summer, in Sydney.

On board the *Bramble* as she left on 12 September 1846, was Lieutenant William Wright, invalided out because of worsening epilepsy.

Meanwhile, at Black Point*, Father Angelo Confalonieri became more adept at speaking Iwaidja†. He was more and more accepted by the people. They respected him for his kind manner and willingness to join them in their 'wandering and desultory' way of life. He happily travelled unarmed, but remained 'childlike', because he needed to be cared for every step of the way.

The priest found that the Iwaidja adults were hard to pin down for religious education. Nevertheless, he:

> ... continued to teach the blackfellows to say a few prayers, of whose meanings they had not the remotest notion: indeed I was told that they were occasionally to be heard repeating them in the square of the settlement with many gestures as rather a good joke than otherwise ... (Huxley, 1848).
>
> He collected together as many of the children of the Limbakarajia tribe as he could induce to remain in the neighbourhood. He endeavoured to instruct them in the elements of his religion, and taught them to repeat prayers in Latin, and follow him in some of the ceremonious observances of the Roman Catholic Church. Like other children this amused them, and so long as they were well fed and

---

* Also called 'Black Rock Point'.
† Throughout this text, the term *Iwaidja* is used for both the language and the people. Confalonieri identified seven tribes using a similar language, but modern linguists may despair, and complain that the Iwaidja dialect used by people living in the area today is unlike the Iwaidja collected by Earl, Confalonieri, and others. See Harris, 1985, for a discussion of this point.

supplied with tobacco, everything went on as he could desire (MacGillivray, 15 October 1845).

There were several drugs brought to Australia from Macassar on the annual voyages: alcohol, tobacco, betel nut and possibly opium. It was probably for the use of the captains and crew at first (though religious Muslim would not have been drinkers). But, when the Macassans observed how welcome alcohol and tobacco were to the tribes along the coast, more were brought for trade or payment for labour (Brady, 2020)*.

Many Aboriginal men would have seen opium smoking in Makassar first hand—hundreds of men undertook 'the grand tour' to Makassar with the praus, stayed there for the off-season, then returned the following year. Some may even have married there and stayed for years. In 1845, MacGillivray wrote that Aborigines 'frequently' accompanied the Macassans (MacGillivray, 1852). Thus, not only could they have observed and participated in opium smoking, they also would have had the opportunity to obtain the pipes and could return to Australia with them. Then, because opium was mostly unavailable on the north coast in the 1840s, the pipes became a preferred way of smoking tobacco. Sweatman was bemused by this:

> … they smoke to excess, every child that can walk has a pipe in his gills and I have seen men get absolutely intoxicated on smoke alone … (Sweatman, 1847).

As part of his mission of converting Aborigines to Christianity, Confalonieri taught Iwaidja children to pray in English. Decades later, 'Flash Poll' could still recite the Lord's Prayer. However, Sweatman says Confalonieri eventually despaired of his mission:

> … had they any idolatry of their own, he said, they might have rooted it out and taught them Christianity instead, but

---

* MacGillivray's comment regarding tobacco is interesting. Tobacco very quickly became a mode of payment by the British, in a practice that continued in the Northern Territory for over a century. Numerous researchers have studied its use as a currency and questioned how it all started. Initially, tobacco was one of the most popular items that Aboriginal people could obtain from the Macassans (MacKnight, 1976).

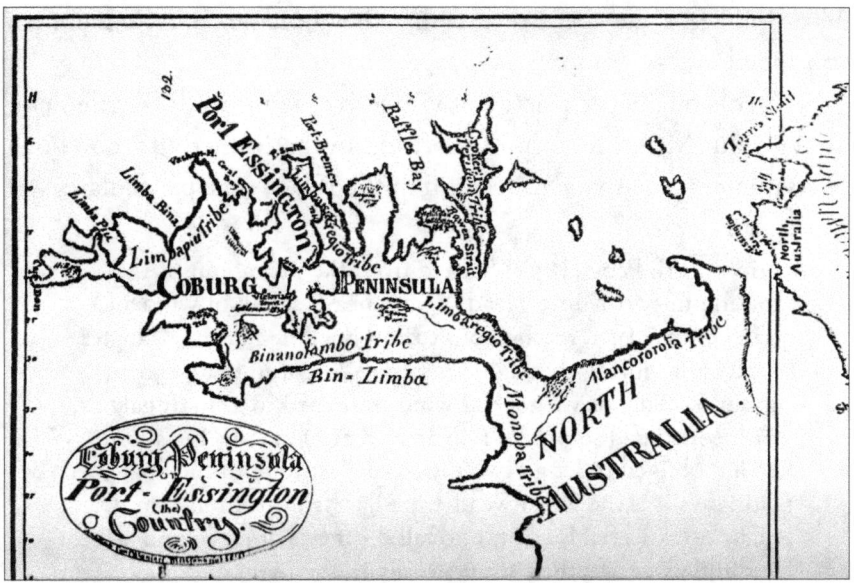

Map 8: Confalonieri's map of the tribes of Cobourg Peninsula (Spillett, 1972).

having no idea of religion whatever, he feared it would be impossible to make them understand anything about it … (Sweatman, 1847).

Confalonieri's plan, after he had fully mastered the language, was spread 'The Word', among the tribes as far west as the Alligator Rivers and east to Van Dieman's Gulf. He worked out that the Iwaidja people were actually divided into seven tribes, and he drew a map of their tribal areas, and collected dialect variances in the Iwaidja language.

Unfortunately, Confalonieri did not impress all the Iwaidja. One day, several elders from the Black Point area tricked him into checking his boat one day. While he was away, they ransacked his hut and stole from him. When Confalonieri reported the men to the commandant, McArthur identified them as men who had already been expelled from the settlement for bad behaviour. Then the elders took offence. They asked what right did a man who lived alone have to talk about them in that way? They then declared themselves to be enemies, although they never fulfilled the evident threats that they became, and Confalonieri continued to travel among the people unarmed.

Occasionally the priest was visited by men from the settlement. Young John McArthur kept a short log in the McArthurs' notebook of a sailing trip he made to see him in the *Gipsy*, on a particularly wet weekend in 1847[*]:

> Friday 26th Feby [1847] Started from the pier about 8 AM towed out past Minto Head. A very heavy squall of wind and rain about 9 P.M. reached out to and anchored at the triangles, much rain during the night. Saturday 27 got under weigh about 5.30 am as we got out wind freshened to a smart gale with continued squalls of rain arrived at Don Angelo's about 11 am obliged to let go two pigs of ballast to hold the boat the Don says it is the worst weather he has had this monsoon. Last night he expected his house to fall. I dined with him and as he said the worst weather was generally in the night and the boat had already driven considerably, I determined to get out of his place before dark and get anchorage on the weather shore.

Perhaps foreshadowing the disastrous government policies of the next century, Confalonieri came to believe that the only way the natives were to become civilised was to remove the children from their families and raise them as British citizens. McArthur agreed, but he was having troubles of his own at the time. Like Lambrick and others in the settlement, he had employed an Iwaidja boy to work around his house and run errands for him. But through his role as a civil magistrate he had 'interfered' in the affairs of several Iwaidja men who were involved with a tribal killing of men from Goulburn Island. The Iwaidja told him it was none of his business, and he should refrain from anything other than issues to do with whites. They said they expected to be executed if they killed a white man, but they had the right to deal with their own people as their law allowed. As tensions rose, the boys who worked in the settlement left and either refused to return or were not permitted to by their families.

When the wet season arrived at the end of 1846, Confalonieri

---

[*] This is reproduced in full in Appendix 5.4.

stayed near his hut, endured the rains and the insects, while he prepared his word lists. He also translated the *Lord's Prayer*, the *Hail Mary*, the *Creed*, and the *Catechism of Christian Doctrine* (which contains the Ten Commandments), into the local Iwaidja dialect. When the dry season followed in 1847, he was sufficiently well known to attract a large number of Aborigines seeking help from him for an influenza epidemic that hit them hard (Pryor, 1990). Doctor Tilston regularly crossed the harbour from the Coral Bay convalescents' resort to help him, and they saved more than a few lives.

Confalonieri attended his mission for just over two years, living most of it in his little Black Point hut, or travelling across Cobourg Peninsula with the Iwaidja. But, in June 1848, a boat happened to pass the point and a marine dropped in to see him, only to find him sick in bed, with a fever that had already burned for a week. He was rushed to the hospital and the care of Dr Crawford. He never recovered and he died on 9 June 1848. His bones still lie in a lonely grave on Cobourg Peninsula. All his bones, that is, except one. His scapula was removed and dried according to his dying wish (Pryor, 1990). It was then sent with a small cross to his sister, near Lake Garda in Italy, and was placed in their church's ossuary.

Confalonieri remained a topic of conversation for the remainder of the settlement's existence. Thomas Huxley never met him, but was curious:

> ... Thinking about the desolate life of the man, I said to Crawford ... 'I suppose this man was a thorough enthusiast, for it is difficult to imagine what else could have supported him through such trials'. Crawford told me that I quite deceived myself, that he had had much conversation with the priest, and that he seemed wholly without religious feeling, well acquainted with theology and a strong stickler for the doctrine of his church, but more like an advocate than a believer ... he was in an especial sense a soldier of his church, i.e. like most soldiers he did his duty religiously but cared not two straws for the quarrel in which he fought (Huxley, 1848).

MacGillivray saw the priest's diary and discovered that much of

Confalonieri's time was spent waiting. He had written a letter asking for help. It was published in the *Catholic Press* on 6 March 1847, and the result was enough donations to fully kit him out in his mission for years to come. He then waited in hope for everything to arrive. Hope faded to despair when they did not:

> ... While leading this lonely life he seems gradually to have given way to gloomy despondency. I recollect one passage in his diary (which I once saw for an hour) where he expresses himself thus: "Another year has gone by, and with it all signs of the promised vessel. Oh! God, even hope seems to have deserted me".
>
> At length, a vessel from Sydney arrived, bringing a large supply of stores of every kind for the mission, but it was too late, for Father Anjello [sic] and his sorrows were alike resting in the tomb. One day news came that he was ill; a boat was sent immediately for him and found him dying. He was removed to the settlement and next day he breathed his last—another, but not the last victim to the climate. His deathbed was described to me as having been a fearful scene. He exhibited the greatest horror of death, and in his last extremity blasphemously denied that there was a God! (MacGillivray, 1852).

By the time the donated equipment arrived in Port Essington on the *John and Charlotte*, poor Confalonieri had been dead and buried for nearly six months. Among the cargo was a large packing case marked 'piano'. Everyone thought it was a 'veritable piano forte, sent to console Don Angelo's solitary hours and perhaps help his performance of the mass' (Huxley, 1848), and they were curious to see it. Some of the sailors swore they heard jarred strings from within, as the crate was shifted from the ship.

The most curious was Captain Owen Stanley who had an 'especial vocation for prying into all concerns'. He ordered the crate opened, but no 'rosewood grand' was to be seen. Instead it was a box crammed full of 'priest's vestments and other baubles'. The inscription on the box, when examined more closely, said 'Posa Piano' ... *Handle Carefully*. Unfortunately, the vestments were of no use to anybody.

Confalonieri is remembered in Darwin in the name of Angelo Street, and a plaque on the wall of St Mary's Cathedral commemorates him as the Territory's first Catholic missionary. Also, in Palmerston there is a Confalonieri Park.

The British in North Australia: Port Essington

Chapter 9
Decline and departure

McArthur was well aware of the settlement's decline, and he tried to arrest it during the 1847 dry season. However, on 20 November 1847—just as the wet season was starting—there was a long, undulating earthquake that shook the settlement and cracked the buildings, making them immeasurably worse. Water cascading from heavy dark clouds found every crack, and barely a single building remained waterproof. The shingled roof of Government House was so rotten, it rained inside nearly as much as outside. McArthur knew that if nothing were done, there would not be a usable house in Victoria. To compound matters, *Mastotermes darwiniensis*, the giant northern termite, was happily chewing through anything made of wood or leather. The buildings on stone piers fared better, but any timber touching them would be attacked ferociously. Constant vigilance was needed: the hospital was the best of the lot because 'Lt. Lambrick has always succeeded in extirpating them,' McArthur wrote, 'but they first effect much mischief; the framing and roof have been undergoing frequent repairs' (McArthur, 16 October 1847).

At the same time, in Sydney, everyone but the Government seemed to be talking about how Victoria would soon be abandoned:

Notwithstanding all that has been said in favour of the station by Mr Earl, Sir Gordon Bremer, Captain Stokes, and others, there is but one opinion, and that is that Port Essington is not the best part of the north coast of New Holland for a British Colony, and I am not wrong when I surmise that the

Government themselves are well aware of this fact, from the decided discouragement given to the sale of lands, and to the settlement of capitalists, and other permanent residents (Bogue, 1848).

In Victoria, even the solidly constructed blockhouse would soon be turned to paper and dust by the termites. McArthur experimented with different types of timber, even building a house using ti-trees and bark. Most buildings were thatched, and this needed regular changing. McArthur discovered that roofs with a steeper pitch lasted longer, as the water ran off faster. Weatherboards rotted fast in the climate and needed continual painting to save them, and as they were imported from Sydney, they were very expensive.

Eventually, as the wet season came to its humid close in April 1848, work started on repairs and maintenance. During the dry season, the shingles on Government House were replaced, and the pier was strengthened. Since the *Heroine* had been wrecked, the settlement's regular resupply was less assured, but the privately owned *Tam O'Shanter* arrived with stores from Sydney on 10 June. Consequently, with fresher food and better weather, the health of the garrison started to improve. Fruit and vegetables were harvested from the gardens in greater quantities than ever before, and new cultivations were made (McArthur, 18 August 1848). In September and October, four private vessels arrived with stores. The *Cacique* had medical supplies and livestock and took two of the invalided Royal Marines to Singapore; the *Sir John Byng* landed a healthy bull, and more stores; the *Pelacca* and the *Suwa* brought barrels of preserved food. Lieutenant Lambrick complained that most of the barrels were already over a year old, and some were as many as 20 months old. As the supplies might be stored in the settlement for 12 months before being needed, their age was a severe problem.

The schooner *John and Charlotte* arrived in November with a huge amount of supplies from Sydney (Huxley, 1848). There were 264 gallons of rum, and medicines for Dr Crawford, and 900 yards of duck cotton to make clothing. Also. at last, a pile of boots and shoes.

On 9 November 1848, the survey ship *Rattlesnake*, under Captain Owen Stanley, visited Port Essington on its four-year cruise, surveying New Guinea and the Great Barrier Reef. Stanley had not been in the port since he had left with the *Britomart* in 1841. He was now surveying through the Torres Strait to the Gulf of Carpentaria. Before leaving Sydney, he had written a letter to several newspapers, saying where the *Alligator* would be and:

Figure 48: Captain Owen Stanley

… in the event of any ships being unfortunately wrecked in attempting the outer passage this season, it would be better for the crew to join this vessel than to attempt to cross the Gulf of Carpentaria to Port Essington (Stanley, 12 May 1848).

The wisdom of choosing to search for a moving survey ship, in a small boat, in a huge expanse of water—versus an 1100-kilometre journey to a fixed point—was questionable. However, Stanley's letter added support to the argument that Port Essington was too far from the straits to be of easy access to wrecked seamen.

Corporal Richard Mew (later Colour Sergeant) was on board the *Rattlesnake* at this time. Mew had been attached to Victoria settlement for five years. He had lived in one of the 'Cornish' cottages with his wife, Margaret, and their three daughters, Mary, Eliza, and Margaret; the last of whom was born there. It must have been an interesting experience for him to return.

Apart from Owen Stanley, three other diarists of note were on board the *Rattlesnake*: Thomas Henry Huxley, the artist Oswald Brierly, and the naturalist and notable linguist, John MacGillivray. MacGillivray was returning to the port after a three-year absence. None of them was impressed by the Port Essington settlement …

The British in North Australia: Port Essington

Thomas Huxley, then aged twenty-one, was travelling as an assistant to Surgeon John Thomson. He had many interests, and during the journey wrote several scientific papers. When they were published, they were of such high quality that Huxley was voted onto the Royal Geographical Society*.

The young man was, of course, excited to be visiting Victoria Settlement after weeks at sea, so he hurried to the rail for his first look at the place. He was disappointed. A letter to his mother describes Port Essington as the 'most useless, miserable, ill-managed hole in Her Majesty's dominions' (Huxley, 1848). He recorded greater detail in his journal:

> ... We dropped anchor opposite a high cliff on the left bank of the harbour, on the top of which was perched a ruinous-looking block house with a few pieces of cannon mounted on its top, the firing off of which would I verily believe have blown down the whole concern. A diagonal road ran down the side of the steep, to a stone pier terminated by a crane, which as I afterwards found was decidedly the chef d'oeuvre of the colony, having occupied the whole disposable force for some seven months. Beyond this on the other side of the road was the Hospital, a low building with a white face and a wide veranda, behind the various stores and huts of the marines peeped through the trees ...

> ... Presently the Commandant's gig came off bringing the sergeant-major of marines with a note from Captain McArthur apologising for the non-appearance of himself or the officer of the day on account of sickness. We further learnt ... that there were not more than ten healthy men in the settlement (Huxley, 1848).

Exploring the town, the next day, Huxley met Lieutenant Lambrick, who invited him to lunch. The lunch was 'most acceptable' and, in particular, the locally grown pineapples impressed him greatly, for they were of 'very fine flavour and grow like weeds'. But 'as to the

---

* Huxley was called 'Darwin's bulldog' when he became one of the staunchest supporters of Charles Darwin's theories of evolution. He was also the author of the word 'agnosticism', and the father of Aldous Huxley.

Decline and departure

Figure 49: HMS *Rattlesnake*, by Oswald Walters Brierly, 1822.

Figure 50: HMS *Rattlesnake* leaving Port Essington Nov. 17th, 1848
(Oswald Walter Brierly. SLNSW)

place itself, it deserves all the abuse that has ever been heaped upon it. It is fit for neither man nor beast' (Huxley, 1848).

John MacGillivray had enjoyed his four months visit to Victoria in 1845, but now he was equally appalled at the conditions:

> ... We found the settlement in a ruinous condition. Even the hospital, the best building in the place, had the roof in such a state that when rain come on some of the patient's beds had to be shifted, and the surgeon found it necessary to protect his own bed with a tent-like canopy (MacGillivray, 1852).

The hospital was indeed the best building in the place. McArthur evaluated it in his report in March 1848 and called it a 'fine building' (see Appendix 5.2). But, even better for convalescents, was the 'resort' over in Coral Bay, where invalids were sent to recover in hospital tents. The Assistant Surgeon, Richard Tilston, was there much of the time looking after them and MacGillivray made him a visit:

> ...During our stay at Port Essington, I made an excursion in the decked boat of the settlement (which Captain Macarthur [sic] kindly allowed me the use of) to Coral Bay, a station for invalids very pleasantly situated on the western side of the harbour, twelve miles from Victoria. We found there my old friend Mr. Tilston, the assistant-surgeon, with some convalescents under his charge. This is a much cooler and pleasanter locality than the neighbourhood of the settlement, still the heat was at times very great (MacGillivray, 1852).

In a lengthy letter to the editor of the *Sydney Morning Herald*, MacGillivray outlined the history of Victoria, and described the ruinous state he found it in. Government buildings were 'very paltry and insecure edifices', infested with white ants, with hollowed out beams and supports. The men were 'lodged in small huts, most of which are constructed of reeds, and are very uncomfortable in wet weather' (MacGillivray, 15 October 1845).

Oswald Walters Brierly* was one of the keenest observers of the Iwaidja. As the expedition's artist, he was enthralled by all native people, and recorded everything he could learn of their lives, such

---

* O.W. Brierly, 1817–94, later Sir Oswald Brierly.

Decline and departure

Figure 51: From Keppel's journal, a 'Native Bier' in Port Essington. Page 526, Oswald Brierly (Keppel, 1853).

as their arts and crafts, corroborees, and what they ate. He was particularly intrigued with how they disposed of their dead in a bier:

> ... the body is carefully wrapped in grass and bark and laid upon a small stage or platform formed of branches, one end resting against a tree the other being supported by forked branches which raise it about five feet from the ground—on this the body is placed and left exposed to the action of the weather until the bones whiten ... the bones were then collected and ... carried from place to place ... (Brierly, 1848).

Dr Archibald Sibbald had noticed people carrying bones around—especially women carrying bones of their lost children. Eventually, they were discarded, sometimes by being buried under a pile of stones. Sibbald also discussed infanticide, stating that one of a set of twins or 'diseased' children would have their heads crushed with a rock, because the mother could not carry or suckle two children (McKenna, 2016).

The 'sombre, dismal and monotonous'* (Jukes, 1848) life in the

---

* For literate members of the community there was a very small collection of books to relieve the monotony. There may have been others, but these were listed by McArthur in his notebook: *The Last of the Mohicans* (Cooper,

settlement, sweaty humidity, poor food and physical illness created yet another problem: depression. The mental state of the men in the garrison was becoming desperate. McArthur wrote that it was high time they went home, and hoped they would be relieved in the new year (McArthur, 15 November 1848). Nearly everyone wanted to go:

> ... With few exceptions, everyone was dissatisfied, and anxiously looked forward to the happy time when the party should be relieved, or the settlement finally abandoned. The unhealthiness of the place, so often denied, had now shown itself in an unequivocal manner; everyone had suffered from repeated attacks of intermittent fever, another fever of a far more deadly character had occasionally made its appearance, and, operating on previously debilitated constitutions, constantly proved fatal. (MacGillivray, 1852).

In Huxley's opinion, the illnesses among the community were caused by poor management, overwork and bad food:

> ... the people at Sydney appear to have sent them things they could not get rid of elsewhere, bad peas, bad biscuit, bad everything, and though they had a good many cattle, yet for months together they never tasted fresh meat ... (Huxley, 1848).

McArthur would not let a beast be slaughtered unless there was a ship visiting. The extra people would be able to then 'divide the spoil'. McArthur did not want to see food go to waste. 'So, the oxen live, and the men die!' wrote Huxley. He blamed Captain McArthur for much of the ills of the community. McArthur was 'with all reverence, one of the most pragmatical old fogeys I ever met with, (he) contrives to keep the people under his command continually in hot water' and he was 'a litigious old fool, always at war with his officers, and endeavouring to make the place as much of a hell morally as it is

---

1826); *Slave King* (Victor Hugo, 1833); *Trevelyan* (Scott, 1834); *St Clair of the Isles* (Helme, 1825); *Tom & Jerry* (probably the 'operatic extravaganza in 3 acts' by Moncreiff, 1821); *Mr Ledbury (The Adventures of Mr. Ledbury and His Friend Jack Johnson)* (Albert Smith, 1844); *Tales of an Antiquity* (no information found); and *Heroine of the Fern Isles* (Reynolds, 1839).

physically' (Huxley, 1848). James Cameron concluded McArthur was a 'pettifogging martinet' (Cameron, 1989).

Among the officers, there was 'as much petty intrigue, caballing, and mutual hatred as if it were the court of the Great Khan'. Within two days of arriving on the *Rattlesnake*, Huxley and his mates knew everything that was going on. The gossip was intense:

> ... I can't say more for Port Essington that it is worse than a ship, and it is no small comfort to know that this is possible (Huxley, 1848).

Huxley and MacGillivray agreed that the settlement would surely be abandoned soon. They were there for only five days. Huxley suffered badly—he spent much of his time lying on his bed complaining of the heat. He was not enjoying any of his journey very much. He had hoped that the break in Port Essington would be a pleasant diversion, but:

> ... Since our leaving Cape York the cruise has been as monotonous and tiresome as I can well imagine any voyage to be. We called at Port Essington and remained there for five days only to give our ship's company a little more sickness and if possible make what was sufficiently unpleasant already still more so ... (Huxley, 1848).

Like most of the garrison, McArthur desperately wanted to be recalled, especially after a recent bout of malaria, but his was a duty he could not forsake. He may not have thought about it, but there was a new technology on the horizon that would finally prove the end of his little settlement. Steamships were fast overtaking their predecessors of sail in other parts of the world, and Australia was keen to be involved. Governor Charles Augustus Fitzroy was already on task by November 1846:

> ... As the ready adoption [of a steam technology plan] affords a convincing proof of the anxiety felt in this Colony that the great advantages of Steam Navigation should be extended to it, and as I cannot conceive that Her Majesty's Government could confer a greater benefit on the Australian Colonies, generally, than by acceding to this request, I venture

earnestly to recommend it for favorable consideration (Fitzroy, 1 November 1846).

The original thought was that a monthly service would begin with 'iron vessels of from five hundred to six hundred tons, and from one hundred and fifty to two hundred horse-power' (Jack, 1922), travelling from Sydney via Torres Strait and Port Essington to Singapore. These would connect with the existing line of steamers to the last port.

> ... A steamer of moderate power, to ply between Port Essington and Ceylon, would ... suffice to complete a direct line of communication with England, for letters and passengers from New South Wales. Batavia might afford a half-way depot for coals ... (Arden, 1 October 1843).

Naturalist, J.B. Jukes, of HMS *Fly*, suggested that very soon there would be another settlement like that at Port Essington, on Cape York, because of the need for coal stores for the new steamships. Captain Stanley of the *Rattlesnake* and Lieutenant Yule of the *Bramble*, both promoted Port Albany, which lies just south of Cape York, as a suitable site (*Herald*, 30 June 1838). Captain Mackenzie of the *Heroine*, predicted that such a settlement would speedily become 'another Singapore' in an article for *The Nautical Magazine and Naval Chronicle* of February 1847 (Jack, 1922). The argument for strategic settlements in the north was appearing again. Sir Roderick Murchison, the president of the Royal Geographical Society in 1845, was a keen supporter of Port Essington:

> ... the establishment of a continuous chain of steam communication between Great Britain and China, by the Straits of Malacca, suggests the possibility of a branch line of packets from this great trunk line to Sydney... the most eligible line for such branch would seem to be from Singapore through Torres Straits ... (Murchison, 1845).

Others supported the establishment of a new settlement on Cape York, arguing that there was no advantage gained to steamships calling in at Port Essington, as they would be 300 miles off their direct course (Bogue, 1848).

The same thoughts drove the desire for an overland route across the country. If there was enough arable or pastoral land found, there would evolve a series of settlements that would serve the northern port. Murchison—without ever visiting the continent—looked at the blank map and swore there must be an inland sea in the interior. As we have seen, he was not alone in his ideas, and many were brave enough to venture into the deserts to look for it, such as Eyre, Sturt, Mitchell, Kennedy, Leichhardt, Gregory, and later Burke and Wills, McKinlay and Stuart.

However, as the technology developed and increased, economics dictated a safer route via the Swan River Colony (Fremantle) and Port Adelaide. This became the route of choice. Then the British Colonial Secretary, Earl Grey, double checked with the India and Australia Steam Packet Company and asked them if it were likely they would ever use Port Essington. Their reply was that the settlement lay well off their routes and the company would not need it for any purpose at all (Spillett, 1972). Port Essington was just too isolated, and its original reason for existence, claiming the whole continent for Britain and protecting it from foreign settlers, was no longer an issue. For a final year, the settlement limped along to its doom.

In January 1849, a shipment of 20 '*Bali sapi*'—banteng cattle*— arrived from the Dutch Consul in Bali. They replaced the bull and cows that had come from Sydney and not coped with the climate. Unfortunately, they were difficult to care for: and they needed constant 'tailing' and handling to stop them running wild. Many of the cattle sent in 1845 had easily slipped off into the bush and, despite much searching, had never been seen again (McArthur, 1 December 1846).

Part of the cargo from Bali—which was more to the liking of the men—was a supply of ale, spirits, and wines. They arrived just as the wet settled in to a period of heavy monsoon rains, and then— almost inevitably—the fever returned. One young man, Private James

---

* The irony of this is that nowadays, Cobourg Peninsula is home to one of the last remaining wild herds of banteng cattle in the world.

French, died in February 1849. Assistant Surgeon Tilston had only recently recovered from illness himself and returned from Coral Bay.

From Leichhardt's journal we learn that:

> ... the treatment for Dr Tilston was Mercury (calomel) until salivation took place, which required a remarkably long time (Webster, 1986)

Tilston then had five others under his care in the hospital, with others visiting him every hour for medicines. Then, the surgeon in charge, Doctor Crawford, fell ill and became delirious in his fever.

Tilston and Leichhardt were able to have long discussions and Tilston had time to draw the brightly coloured grasshopper Leichhardt had collected in the tablelands. We know it as Leichhardt's grasshopper (*Petasida ephippigera*). Leichhardt was pleased with the drawing: 'I shall attach it to the publication of my expedition', he wrote (Webster, 1986).

Tilston had a nervous breakdown in mid-February and he needed constant watching. Suddenly the hospital was full, and the epidemic appeared to be as bad as that which had ravaged the community in 1843. McArthur fell sick too, as did Lieutenant Dunbar, and the only officer left to arrange for the nursing of the sick and manage the affairs of the entire settlement was George Lambrick.

Richard Tilston died on 4 March, to everyone's shock and grief*. Another marine private died a few days later and Crawford remained sick and delirious, though in lucid moments, he could advise Lambrick on what to do. There was one private whose symptoms were different from the rest, and Crawford diagnosed cholera. He died on 24 March†.

---

* Dr Richard Tilston's last will and testament can be seen online at The National Archives, (Reference PROB 11/2123/). He had a collection of birds (from Port Essington?) he bequeathed to 'Elizabeth', and a silver ring, that was still on his finger, to a brother. The will was prepared and written by George Lambrick and says, in part 'In the name of God, Amen, I Richard Tilston, being in bodily health and sound mind ...' but I defy anyone to decipher Lambrick's writing and read the complete text!

† The diagnosis of 'cholera' cannot have been correct, as there was no source of the bacterium, and no one else had caught it.

All but essential work in the community was put on hold. The only important occupation for some of the men was digging graves.

When the wet season drew to a close, Lambrick and two privates were the only men untouched by the epidemic. Everyone else belonged to a 'garrison of yellow skeletons' (Browne, 1871). There were 26 others who needed constant care and were capable of light duties only—if any. Only three men were well enough to be night guards (Spillett, 1972). Crawford recovered, but was now the only doctor, so convalescents could no longer be sent to Coral Bay when the dry season arrived. Instead, McArthur sent a prefabricated building to Spear Point in the outer harbour, where it would catch the sea breezes. Dr Crawford set up a recovery camp and it was close enough for him to visit and not be too long away from the hospital.

By mid-May the fever had left the community. But death and decay hung over it like a black cloud. The population was 'dispirited and lifeless' (Spillett, 1972). The buildings had suffered badly during the wet season, and the gardens had been neglected for months. The *Freak* arrived with provisions—including ten hogsheads of porter, and 50 sheep. However, as Spillett wrote, 'not even the temporary enjoyment of beer could erase the mark that death and sickness had left on the remaining little band of settlers' (1972).

Captain McArthur tried his best to restore a normal routine to the community. The men cleared the gardens and undertook the most urgent repairs. 'Doctor Sir William Burnett's solution of chloride of zinc' was poured onto the termite-infested structures, and it seemed to work for a while.

Six more privates were invalided out—probably on the *Freak*—leaving the garrison at just over half its original strength (MacGillivray, 1852). With the cooler weather of the dry season—known to modern Top Enders as the most pleasant in the world—the men's health improved once again, though many remained weak. As the year progressed and clouds once again built up on the horizon and the air became sticky with humidity, they resigned themselves to having to

Figure 52: HMS *Meander* under Captain Keppel removed the garrison from Victoria on December 1, 1849; Oswald Brierly, Mechanical Curator Collection (Keppel, 1853).

endure another wet season, and a sense of futility and despondency pervaded the settlement. But then, on 13 November, a new sail appeared in the port. It was the warship HMS *Meander*[*]. She dropped anchor well off the pier, and time must have slowed for the settlers. They watched Captain Henry Keppel and his officers climb down to a boat. The oars dug in the water and they were rowed slowly ashore. McArthur led them to his house and the men followed, eager to hear the news. Captain Keppel took refreshment and quietly handed over the dispatches to the commandant. A letter from Colonel J. Owen was the one everyone had been waiting for.

[*] Serving on board the *Meander* was a young gunner named John Henry Brookshaw. In 1824, Brookshaw was still a baby when his father, Corporal John Brookshaw, R.M., boarder the *Tamar* and sailed with Captain Bremer to begin a new settlement in north Australia. Promoted to sergeant at Fort Dundas, his father served with the Royal Marines until 31 December 1826, when he died of an illness (erroneously recorded as cholera). In 1849, Gunner Brookshaw may not have known that, in Port Essington, he was about a day's sail from his father's last resting place (Brookshaw, 2013).

Adjutant-General Owen, of the Royal Marines, had ordered the marines to withdraw from the settlement—it was to be abandoned entirely, and immediately. This was a shock—most had expected a timely warning announcing their replacement, not abandonment, and suddenly there was much work to do. The next monsoon would soon arrive, and the *Meander* needed to be on its way before the change in winds. Even as it was, she would have to sail north around New Guinea, rather than risk the Torres Strait. But it was the news the settlers had waited so long to hear. The *Meander* would take everyone to Sydney. Keppel recorded the event in his log:

> ... We came to, on the evening of 12th November, in the outer anchorage; and immediately communicated with Captain McArthur and the party of Marines the unexpected and acceptable intelligence that we were come to remove them. While the garrison however rejoiced, the natives, especially the women, showed their grief by cutting their heads and faces with sharp flints, and otherwise disfiguring their already unprepossessing persons (Keppel, 1853).

It took three weeks to evacuate the settlement. The men needed to transport all the stores from Victoria to the holds of the *Meander*. Beasts were butchered for a supply of fresh meat on board, 300 gallons of beer was carried to the ship's sick room, together with the patients from the hospital and all the medical equipment and supplies. Whilst dodging regular storms and heavy rain, carpenters' tools, guns and gunners' stores, barrels of salt beef and pork, peas and rice, and everything else that belonged to the government, had to be carried down the sunken road to the jetty. It was then placed in boats and rowed out to the *Meander*. On board, cabins were built on deck for the women and children, and their private belongings were loaded. The Iwaidja helped carry and load and were paid by McArthur with the unusable tobacco and old flour. He also gifted them the kangaroo dogs, and the cattle and horses that had to be left behind. Many Iwaidja had been friends and companions of the marines for five years, and McArthur had been there for 11 years. Friendships were genuine and warmly felt, and more than one child had been born to Iwaidja women after liaisons with the Royal Marines. In the terminology of the time, Oswald Brierly called them 'half casts' (Brierly, 1848). Few of the diarists mentioned these children. Brierly said several were living in the camp, but according to Keppel, children of different colour were 'generally destroyed by the natives' and that 'only one was allowed to attain any degree of maturity, and was so overfed by both Europeans and natives, that the removing of the settlement has most likely been the means of the child's escaping death by apoplexy'. This child seems to have been so cherished by everyone it casts doubt on Keppel's claim of regular infanticide (Keppel, 1853).

Captain Keppel took advantage of his time in the port to do a little hunting. He was very impressed with an Iwaidja man who escorted him:

> ... When riding through the jungle on a shooting excursion, I gave my gun to a naked savage to carry. I was rather astonished at his addressing me in very good English, with. "Should an opportunity offer, Sir, I shall fire!". This man was frequently with me afterwards. One day he said to me, "If you English could thrash Bonaparte whenever you liked, why did you put him on an island, and starve him to death?" (Keppel, 1853).

He was equally impressed with his own man, Hutchings, who proved himself a hunter of such skill even the Iwaidja must have been in awe. He was a 'huge fellow' who would hunt alone, and return with geese, ducks, and kangaroos strung around his neck, and 'handkerchiefs full of small birds ... his face smeared with perspiration and blood' (Keppel, 1853).

In the *Meander's* hospital the patients continued under care of the settlement's doctor. Keppel wrote:

> ... During our stay at Port Essington we lost our surgeon Mr. John Clarke. His remains rest in the bush in a shaded picturesque spot where also are deposited the remains of an amiable lady, the wife of one of the officers, and her two children. Poor Clarke contracted a disease at Hong Kong from which he never recovered (Campbell, 1916).

On the final day, at 9 A.M. on 30 November, Captain McArthur led Captain George Lambrick, Lieutenant Sheddan Dunbar, Surgeon John Crawford and 33 N.C.O.s and Royal Marines out of Victoria Square for the last time. Together they followed the *Meander's* military band and marched down to the pier. A 21-gun salute was fired from the ship as a final farewell. The flag was lowered for the last time, and the settlers were ferried to the ship in small groups.

On December 1, 1849, at last, McArthur and his marines and their families were safely on board the *Meander*, and they sailed away to Sydney, never to return. As they left, there was genuine sadness among the Iwaidja, tempered with a little avarice—a few had come down to the pier to see them off and there were women on the beach wailing, and cutting their heads with sharp rocks. Others were too busy salvaging anything of value in the deserted settlement. According to the *Meander's* journal, one of the last acts was to blow up the decked boat, which had done so much over the previous decade, and set fire to the old buildings, even though they were already rotten and collapsing. Keppel thought destroying them would save Iwaidja lives, as the buildings which 'could have been of no service to the natives … would have probably been the cause of bloodshed between [the Iwaidja] and the other tribes' (Keppel, 1853).

The *Meander's* crew had spent much time with the Iwaidja during their short stay and were taught many things during 'corobories [sic] and dances'. As they sailed on, Keppel reported that the 'kangaroo dance was as well performed on the main-deck of the *Meander*, many thousands of miles from the place where it originated, as we'd seen on that spot' (Keppel, 1853).

John MacGillivray, writing his journal during his stay in Port Essington with the *Alligator*, had been critical:

… the natives of Port Essington have little to thank the white man for. The advantage of being provided with regular food and other comforts enjoyed by such as are in service are merely temporary, and, like the means of gratifying two new habits, the use of tobacco and spirits, to which they have become passionately addicted, will cease when the settlement is abandoned. The last importation of the whites was syphilis, and by it they will probably be remembered for years to come... (MacGillivray, 1852).

But perhaps the British presence there had not been all bad: Don Christopherson, a modern historian from the Muran Clan of Western Arnhem Land, said:

'... There are some amazing stories of Aboriginal people and the British treating each other with respect... If people are going to stand on the beach and cry for you, and have sorrow in their hearts, they must have had a good relationship ...' (Moodie, 2019).

The *Meander* took 10 weeks to arrive in Sydney, finally dropping anchor in Sydney Cove next to the *Alligator*, which had arrived two days earlier. After 12 weeks in Sydney, McArthur, Lambrick, Dunbar, and most of the marines, travelled home to England on the *Rattlesnake*, via New Zealand and Cape Horn. They finally arrived in England on 9 November 1850 (Jack, 1922).

None of McArthur's official writings show any emotion regarding his return, but some of his poetry survives (see Appendix 7). He had been away from his wife, Mary Elizabeth, and their family for 12 years: 'Does not affection—parted from those loved—at length from its own isolation draw its greater strength?' he wrote in his notebook (McArthur & McArthur, 1849).

Young John McArthur also wrote in the notebook, and several of the poems are his. Captain McArthur's second son spent years by his aging father's side, writing and re-writing the official dispatches and records, and running the commissariat. He was clearly looking forward to seeing his mother and his brothers again when he wrote:

> And am I then once more to see,
> The land of my Nativity,
> To visit scenes of boyhood's bliss,
> And greet my mother with a kiss,
> And meet those Brothers, who then were,

> Children, grown youths now, tall, and fair,
> Find others who were there at home
> Now absent, and to manhood grown.
>
> Oh! Yes, again I yet may be,
> Happy in meeting all of thee,
> Tho' ten long years have now rolled round,
> Affection still remains as sound,
> Tho' persons change with time and clime,
> Absence adds to a love like mine,
> Oh, may I then in joy soon meet,
> Those who I long have sighed to greet.
> March 10, 1848.

Captain McArthur had served with stoic devotion to duty for 11 years in the north of Australia. Sadly, his efforts are now mostly forgotten in today's Northern Territory. There is a 'McArthur Park' in Palmerston, and a stream that runs into Knocker Bay named after him—but that is all. Perhaps this is the price of failure, worse for McArthur, as it was through no fault of his own. In fact, as MacKnight eloquently put it:

> ... This is the classic example of failure and defeat in northern Australia. The common problems of insufficient information and an inadequate technology produced, after initial careless optimism, bitter frustration, and despair (MacKnight, 1969).

Captain McArthur's career in the Royal Marines continued, and he saw action in both Africa and France, gaining promotions to brevet* major in 1852. He retired as a brevet colonel in 1853 and died in 1862 at the age of 71 (Street, 1990).

George Lambrick and his daughter Emma, both survived the Port Essington ordeal, and Lambrick's career carried on brightly. On 1 August 1848 he was promoted to captain whilst still at Port Essington. After that, he was sent on another isolated posting, to the British island of Ascension, in 1855. He eventually became a General (*London Gazette* 5 February 1878) and an *aide-de-camp* to

---

* The term 'brevet' means that he worked at a higher rank than that for which he was paid.

Queen Victoria. He died on 30 January 1903 (Allen and Corris). His daughter, Emma, outlived him, and died a wealthy spinster aged 82 in March 1925. Lambrick has an avenue named after him in Palmerston*.

Captain Stanley led an adventurous life, only part of which involved the settling of Port Essington. He was in Port Essington in command of the *Britomart* when the settlement began, and 11 years later, was back, in command of *Rattlesnake,* when Victoria was nearly abandoned. In the time between the two events, he had become quite famous through the quality of his art, his survey and exploration work around Cape York and New Guinea. He played an important role in the founding of Auckland as the capital of New Zealand. He also fought, with distinction, in the *Britomart* in Burma. As a result, he was promoted and given command of the 28-gun frigate, *Rattlesnake*. The Owen Stanley Ranges—through which the Kokoda Trail passes—are named after him.

Stanley died in Sydney, on 13 March 1850, after an 'epileptic paralytic fit' in his cabin on the *Rattlesnake*. He fell on his head and never regained consciousness, dying in Huxley's arms a little later (Lubbock, 1967). The *Sydney Gazette* reported: 'the gallant officer, having been seized with an epileptic fit on Wednesday morning, died about eight o'clock' (*Gazette*, 16 March 1850).

---

* Numerous other place names commemorate the Port Essington settlers, such as Tilston Avenue, Dunbar Street, Dunbar Park and Confalonieri Park in Palmerston, and Earl Place in Milner.

Chapter 10
And then?

The British never came back. However, within two years of the abandonment of Victoria, the *General Palmer*, under Captain Thomas Beckford Simpson, visited the port. Simpson was looking for Ludwig Leichhardt. The famous explorer disappeared on his third journey and was never found. In Port Essington, Simpson met Jim Crow, Confalonieri's assistant. Crow gave him a guided tour of the settlement site, and Simpson noted that every house in Victoria Square had been destroyed and the hospital burned down:

> … all the buildings with the exception of the Commandant's house (which was gutted) and the Officer's cook house had all been destroyed … the various roads and pathways through the settlement were scarcely discernible… (McKenna, 2016).

Thomas Baines was the artist attached to Augustus Gregory's North Australian Expedition (1855–57). Sailing past Port Essington in 1856, he met two men in a canoe who spoke some English:

> … This fellow who was uncircumcised and naked as Adam in his blessedness spoke a few words of English picked up no doubt from some whaler as he seemed to apply to us some word like Americaan … Holding up a stick of tobacco I pronounced its name and the bowman immediately answered 'Yes, berry good, tabacca me want him' … (Carruthers & Steibel, 2012).

The earliest photographs of the Northern Territory were taken during the first civilian expedition to settle the north coast in 1865. They came from Adelaide and settled on Escape Cliffs, near the mouth of the Adelaide River. The expedition was led by Colonel Boyle Travers Finniss* and officially named 'Palmerston', although it was always called 'Escape Cliffs'.

Troubled by poor management and under-resourced, the colony lasted just two years from 1864. Many Iwaidja from the time of the Victoria settlement were still alive then, of course, but there is no record of them visiting the colony. It was too far to visit and meant travel across potentially hostile territory. Nevertheless, some Iwaidja had contact with mariners from Escape Cliffs who passed by Port Essington and Croker Island during those years. In February 1865, Captain Frederick Howard, on the *Beatrice*, was hailed by an Iwaidja man in a canoe, asking him if he had come from Sydney. Four men and a woman then came along side and boarded the boat. The woman was 'Flash Poll', now much scarred by smallpox (Webling, 1864–66). She and the leader, 'Bob White', could both speak English well, and mentioned names of the settlers at Port Essington and Raffles Bay. Bob White and several of his countrymen worked for the Malays in the trepang fisheries, so they could also speak Malay. They stayed on board for several hours, smoking *bacca* and drinking the sailors' grog. Bob White then agreed to travel with Captain Howard for a few days, in the search for John McKinlay's missing party, and when he left them, Howard gave him letters to deliver to McKinlay, if he should meet him. His photograph was also taken by Lieutenant Guy but, unfortunately, it has been lost (Pugh, 2018a).

After the failure of the First Northern Territory Expedition to Escape Cliffs in 1866, the next British ship to appear in northern waters was an old wooden steamer named the *Eagle*, under Captain Francis Cadell. Cadell spent almost 12 months exploring and mapping the coast. His discoveries were few: the most important was the Cadell River in central Arnhem Land. He spent weeks touring the Arnhem Land bush on 20 horses he brought with him and unloaded on the banks of the Liverpool River. He travelled west to Mountnorris

---

* All the early photographs are reproduced in my book *Escape Cliffs* (2018).

Bay and Cobourg Peninsula, looking for 'White Bob', who had been so useful to the crew of the *Beatrice*. Cadell's expedition reads like a *Boys' Own Adventure*, full of excitement and sometimes laughable incompetence. For example, several sailors shot themselves, or one of their mates—a seaman named Frazer killed himself after he picked up his loaded gun with its muzzle pointing at his chest. Another blew his own fingers off (Napier, 1876).

On board the *Eagle*, one of the men had stored some emu eggs in a drawer, and the men were surprised to find one hatch. The baby emu stalked about the deck for a day or so but was quickly killed and eaten by the ship's rats.

The *Eagle's* crew never found Bob White, but they did find thousands of buffalo tracks near Cobourg Peninsula, where:

> ... The country was very clear of timber and easily penetrated. No mosquitoes, no flies, no bugs, no mangroves; in fact, as compared to the Liverpool River, a perfect paradise (Napier, 1876).

Where the Iwaidja were, whilst their visitors were shooting ineffectually at the plentiful buffaloes on their land (because they killed none), is unknown. Eventually the mate met two men, one of whom was dressed in a Malay shirt, who said that 'White Bob' would arrive by sunset. The man in the shirt accepted a glass of rum, but it 'was refused by his nude companion, who was probably a teetotaller' (Napier, 1876).

Cadell then took his party back to the Liverpool River and continued his search for new rivers, but that was not the last time he visited Cobourg Peninsula. Cadell was back in 1877, operating as a 'freeloader outside the law' (Cross, 2011). He had two ships in the area, the *Trois Amos* and the *Gem*, and was making a living whaling, trepanging, collecting pearls, and turtle shell. To crew the ships, he recruited native labour from across the Top End, but particularly from Port Essington. They were ill-treated and underfed and complained to the authorities in the Queensland port of Somerset*. They were

---

* As a result of Cadell's poor management and behaviour, Inspector Foelsche, in Port Darwin, convinced the Government Resident to bring in a law prohibiting the removal of an Aborigine from the coast without police permission.

Figure 53: In 1877, the older Iwaidja people here on the beach below Adam Head would have remembered Victoria Settlement in the 1840s. The building behind the camp was constructed by Foelsche and used as his photographic darkroom (Foelsche 1877, NLA PH1060-0057).

Figure 54: Three visitors pose with Iwaidja people in front of a mango tree planted in Victoria about 30 years earlier (Foelsche 1876, SLSA PH1060-0051).

hungry and wanted to go home. In August 1878, the Iwaidja mutinied whilst the *Gem* was in the Torres Strait. Cadell was away in a small boat when the ship's mate, Henry Brown, was stabbed. He managed to shoot four of his attackers with his pistol before jumping overboard and swimming to an island. The *Gem* was then trashed by the Iwaidja. Led by a man named Wandy-wandy, they seized the long boat, and ten men and four women sailed it back to Port Essington*. Captain Cadell was left without a crew.

Perhaps wisely, Cadell never returned to Port Essington after that. However, he did try to secure a monopoly on the gathering of pearls and trepang from the north coast in 1878. He was refused and was sent instead to Macassar to report on the trepang trade there. He found that the whole industry was under the control of three Chinese businessmen, and that 23 proas had sailed to Australia that year, with 1000 crew. Astonishingly, he also said that a 'colony' of Aborigines lived at Macassar and were employed as menial workers (Cadell, 23 December 1878). No one ever followed this up, and Cadell was not available for confirmation, because he was never seen again. It is thought that he was murdered by his crew because they were never paid, and that the *Gem* was scuttled in seas unknown.

In 1874, three men sailed to Port Essington in an open barque named *Wild Duck* (*NTTG*, 20 February 1874). Captain and owner, James Miller, a Mr Sinclair, and James Robertson had gone to the port looking for new fishing prospects but had not returned after a month. In the new settlement of Palmerston in Port Darwin, their friends were worried. The Government Resident, Bloomfield Douglas, allowed his Government cutter, *The Flying Cloud*, under Captain Marsh to be used to search for them†.

---

* Wandy-wandy became a political activist and tried to drive away the Macassans and Europeans from Port Essington in the late 1880s. He thus ran afoul of the law, and Inspector Foelsche reported that Wandy-wandy was hanged in 1893, and left hanging in a sacred meeting place in Port Essington (Cross, 2011).

† Marsh had been the mate on Captain Sweet's *Gulnare* during the settlement of Port Darwin.

Marsh sailed directly to the anchorage opposite the abandoned settlement. There he dropped anchor and waited for Iwaidja people to contact him. He had seen their fires at night, and knew it was only a matter of time for someone to come calling. One of the crew wrote the story for the *Northern Territory Times and Gazette*:

> ... Having come to anchor at the settlement, the captain and others went ashore and spent a few hours in looking round. We landed on an old jetty formed of pieces of rock and stone which the settlers who were there more, than 30 years ago had collected and rolled together, thus with the assistance of wooden piles and cross pieces making a very useful boat jetty. Portions of the wood still remain and are apparently as sound as when the settlers left the place in 1849. They then remarked upon the durability of the timber; and there it is still in a good condition after the expiration of a quarter of a century. This wood was apparently obtained from the ironbark tree, which grows on the Peninsula, where there are also paperbark trees, white gum trees, cabbage palm trees (in great abundance), and various others ...
>
> Leaving the jetty, we walked up a rather steep cutting to what used to be the town or place of settlement. There is still standing in a state of excellent preservation the stonework of houses and cottages, built for the officers and men of the garrison that was stationed there. The masonry is very solid and well put together. Portions of outbuildings and workshops are also still standing; and at a short distance inland there is the cemetery, which contains the tombstones and monuments erected over the graves of several officers and men who were interred there. The garden is also close by, and a part of the wooden fence still remains. We saw pineapple plants growing there and various trees of handsome appearance, which had evidently been planted and cultivated.
>
> One could not help regretting that a place where so many improvements had been made should have been completely abandoned, after all the money and trouble which had been expended upon it (*NTTG*, 20 February 1874).

The Aborigines soon turned up. The first man who could speak any English was Jack Davis's son, a skinny young man named 'Fat

Jack' and, in a few minutes:

> ... Jack Davis, who is the chief, and many others came on board. We asked him about the missing boat, and he said that three white men had been there, that their boat had been smashed on the rocks, and that they had since obtained two canoes from the natives, by which they hoped to get back from the Peninsula to Melville Island and thence to Port Darwin.
>
> We asked the name of the white men, and, after a considerable pause, one of them said, 'Sin-sin-clair'. This of course set all doubt at rest ... Jack Davis was a very intelligent man. He remembered the officers and men of the old settlement; he had been to Singapore and China with a Captain Bisset; and he said he could speak Malay as well as English. He and the other natives had several articles which Sinclair had given them, and he said that after the boat was lost he offered to build a hut for the white men; but they persisted in trying to get back to Port Darwin, so he gave them two canoes, and sent two natives to assist in managing them; but he advised them not to leave the coast unless the weather was fine. He thought, therefore, that they might still be on the Peninsula in the neighbourhood of Trepang Bay or Cape Don ... (*NTTG*, 20 February 1874).

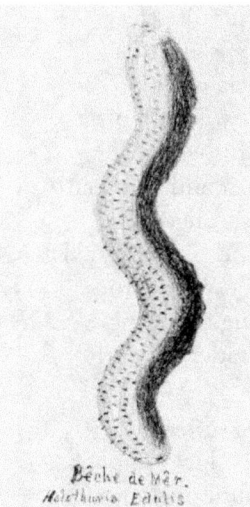

Figure 55: Trepang (Napier, 1876).

Marsh then attempted to set off at once to find the men but was beaten back by contrary winds. Instead, they moored for a few days and spent the time hunting cattle, for they saw no buffalo. Then, out of the bush, an Iwaidja man led three sorry-looking white men:

> ... On Wednesday morning the captain was considering the desirability of trying to sail round to Trepang Bay again, when we heard a loud shout from the natives who were camped on the beach, and presently we saw a blackfellow and some white men coming out of the bush.
>
> These proved to be Smike, and the three castaways—Sinclair, Robertson, and Miller. They were immediately brought on

Figure 56: John Lewis, from 'Fought and Won' (Lewis, 1922)

board, and it was then quite clear that they had not been sent for a bit too early. Mr. Sinclair had no clothing but a waistcoat, and a piece of canvas tied round his waist. He was without hat, shoes, and trousers; and his arms and legs were covered with deep scratches and partly healed wounds, the result of exposure to a broiling sun and long travelling through the prickly underwood of the bush.

The other two had not suffered so much, as they had been lucky enough to preserve some amount of clothing. It appeared that they had been living ashore some weeks. On leaving Port Darwin early in January they touched first at Melville Island, then at Trepang Bay, and then at Port Essington; and it was on their return from the latter place that they got their boat knocked to pieces near Vashon Head. This compelled them to take to the bush, where the natives were very kind to them, and Jack Davis built them a hut, where they remained some time… (*NTTG*, 20 February 1874)*.

During the same year, Edward Oswin Robinson arrived to fish for trepang, find pearls and hunt buffalo on Cobourg Peninsula, using his boat, the *Northern Light*. He was still there in November 1874, when a party led by John Lewis (1844–1923)† arrived. Lewis came to Port Essington in the lead of a search party looking for two lost gold miners—Thomas Permain and Edward Borradaile—who had gone exploring for gold on five Timor ponies east of Port Essington. They were never seen again and are thought to have been murdered by Aborigines near Tor Rock in Arnhem Land. Lewis's rescue party

---

* James Miller also wrote his story for the *Northern Territory Times and Gazette* (*NTTG*), and it is reproduced in Appendix 7.
† Lewis was a son of the explorer James Lewis, who travelled with Charles Sturt, and he was the father of Essington Lewis (1881–1961), who was named after the port. Essington became the general manager of BHP in 1921.

Figure 57: John Lewis's Homestead, Port Essington from 'Fought and Won' (Lewis, 1922).

included Charles Levi, Trooper J. Miller, a 'black boy' named Prince who was originally from Cobourg Peninsula, a Chinese cook named Ling Ah Loo, George Reid, Neddie Lewis and Jack Crossman (Lewis, 1922). John Lewis was pleased to volunteer 'his services gratuitously' for the search (*NTTG*, 3 October 1874)*.

While on the peninsula, Lewis noted huge numbers of buffalo and wild cattle. He developed a plan to harvest them, and when he returned to Palmerston he started the Cobourg Cattle Company and leased a large slice of the Cobourg Peninsula (Lewis, 1922). Lewis and Levi then moved to Port Essington to start hunting buffaloes. Ling Ah Loo, Reid, Neddie Lewis, and Crossman were retained as the staff. The journey there was fraught with danger—they were attacked with 'showers of spears' several times during their transit through the East Alligator River region.

Lewis built his homestead just south of the ruins of Victoria settlement:

> ... We built two rooms, twelve by twelve, placing the timber horizontally between posts, and covering it with a paperbark

---

* Lewis's story of the journey was sent to the *Northern Territory Times and Gazette* by Inspector Foelsche and published on 7 August 1875. It makes for good reading.

roof. We put a veranda front and back and made a floor with bricks from some of the old buildings (Lewis, 1922).

Lewis sent a test consignment of buffalo horns and hides to Adelaide in 1876. They sold for 10 shillings per horn and 23 shillings per hide. Lewis was satisfied, and started to process as many beasts as he could get (*NTTG* 22 April 1876)*.

Lewis's diary shows that he met 'Flash Poll' 'Bob White' and 'Jack Davis' soon after arriving. 'Jack Davis' was working for E.O. Robinson:

> … November 1. — Port Essington. Left camp this morning at half-past six, and after travelling a mile west came to a stony rise, from whence we could see the harbour of Port Essington. At nine o'clock arrived at the old settlement, but, as there was no water, sent the horses back about two miles to camp. Saw four Timor ponies, but they were very wild and galloped off.
>
> During the stay of the party at Port Essington, Mr. Robinson, of the *Northern Lights* pearling schooner, came to the camp (5th November.) He had been out with Jack Davis, the native chief, getting trepang, and as soon as it was made known that Lewis and party had arrived, Mr. Robinson and the natives came across to the camp from Trepang Bay.
>
> The party included Bob White and 'Flash Poll.' This black woman is sixty years of age, but she does not appear to be more than forty. Her hair is but just getting grey, and she is as active as a girl of fifteen. The natives are great smokers and would give anything for tobacco. Among the men who came to the camp on the 5th is one who seems to be the terror of the country. His age is about twenty-seven years; he is six feet high, and well made. The natives of Port Essington say that he has killed five of his own countrymen at East Alligator. He has just been over to Trepang Bay to see if the Malay prahus were there. These natives trade with the Malays to a considerable extent, and many of them can speak both English and Malay. 'Flash Poll' can say the Lord's Prayer correctly. The Port

---

* At the same time Fred Dewar, Daniel Munro, William Leslie and an employee named Marshall (who later sued Dewar for breaking his jaw) leased land between Raffles Bay and Mountnorris Bay (Bauer, 1964) for a buffalo station. Their homestead was built on the old Fort Wellington site.

Essington and East Alligator natives visit each other and seem to be on good terms… (Wildey, 1876).

Lewis employed a number of Iwaidja:

… We gave the men working for us half a stick of tobacco and a pannikin of rice daily, with a little tea and sugar (that is, the men who were doing the fencing and clearing). We often employed an old man and his two gins getting yams, and another party gathering native honey … another out fishing … we always had a turtle, and sometimes two on the shackle. Another party were out with a gun, and brought duck, or geese or jungle-fowl, with often jungle-fowl eggs (Lewis, 1922)

Just after Christmas in 1874, an unnamed Palmerston correspondent to the *Northern Territory Times and Gazette* wrote from the new colony of Palmerston in Port Darwin, of a sailing tour to visit Port Essington, 33 years after it was abandoned. The tourists were met by 'Jack Davis' and 'Flash Poll' and they were guided by Edward Oswin Robinson*, who took over the management of the Cobourg Cattle Company in Port Essington from John Lewis or Charles Levi† (who managed the station in 1876). The visiting 'correspondent' was most impressed by the station and how well the Aborigines worked for the manager:

Great praise is due to the latter gentleman [Levi], for the work done and improvements made on the station (of which he is part owner), the amount of which cannot be realised unless actually seen… A Palmerstonian going to Port Essington would be astonished at the amount of work that Mr. Levi gets out of the natives. Besides the cook there are only two Europeans on the station—all the rest of the work being done by the natives, who work as well as most white men.

There is no begging or grumbling on their part. If they are told to do anything, they must do it at once and take their pay in tobacco, &c., at the end of the week. Laziness or refusal to work entails immediate discharge, a proceeding which happily

---

* Robinson spoke both the language of the Macassans and Iwaidja, and, in the 1880s, set up a camp in Bowen Strait to regulate and collect tax revenue from the trepang fleet.

† Lewis Close in Jabiru, and Levi Street in Milner are named after these men.

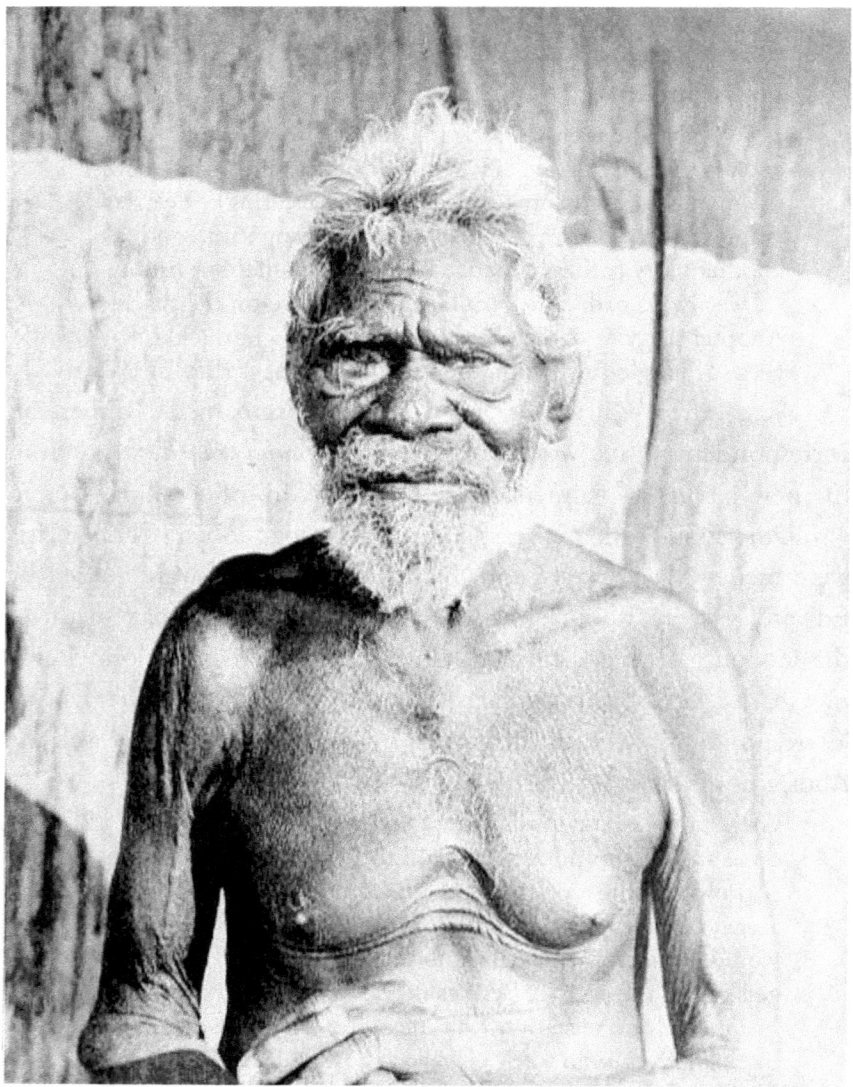

Figure 58: Mildun 'Jack Davis', photo from 'An Untamed Territory' by Dr Mervyn John Holmes (the Chief Medical Officer) (Masson, 1915).

the captain has seldom found necessary to adopt. During our short visit to the station, the obliging manager conducted us to the spring well, by the side of which is a fine large mango tree, thence over part of the land fenced in, showing us the mobs of buffaloes and Timor ponies, on the old settlers' garden, in which there are some fine tropical fruits—notably mango and jack fruit—thence past the cemetery, which we were pleased to see had been carefully fenced in to keep sacred and undefiled the 'God's acre' set apart by the old settlers, whose monuments are still to be seen.

The old township of Victoria is situated on a cliff commanding a fine view of the harbor, and from the nature of the soil we cannot understand how it can be otherwise than healthy. This must also have been the first impression of the settlers, for they appear to have built very substantial stone houses, the walls of which are still standing, and are apparently as strong now as on the day they were first raised, and are a lasting memento of the persistent but unfortunate attempts of the mother country to extend her power and to colonise the then remotest regions of the earth (*NTTG*, 16 December 1876).

'Flash Poll' and 'Jack Davis' could both speak excellent English and they continued to work as 'tour guides' and interpreters for any visitors who came to Port Essington during the next few decades.

'Jack Davis' real name was Mildun. He was about four years old when the settlers arrived at Victoria in 1839, so he grew up surrounded by Royal Marines and sailors. He could swear as well as the best of them and would imitate their drilling on the parade ground. In 1846, Mildun travelled to Sydney with four other Iwaidja and was on the *Heroine* when she was wrecked on 4 April. The next year, Mildun and two other boys, Mijok and Aladyin, were taken on a merchantman to Hong Kong. They became stranded there after the death of the captain. Luckily for them, Crawford Pasco, who had been stationed at Port Essington in the early years, recognised them, and arranged passage home. Then, as a young man, Mildun was employed in the crew of a merchant ship, and he sailed the seas of the world for several years. When he returned to port Essington, he was an elder of his clan.

In 1898, an unnamed buffalo hunter sold his story to the *Northern Territory Times and Gazette*. The story was serialised over a half dozen editions. The author told of his visit to Victoria with his mates:

> ... Leaving Mr. Robinson's at daylight, we pushed along to reach the old settlement, Victoria, which we managed to do after a long and tiring ride of about 50 miles or it seemed that distance on account of the thick timber that we had to ride through.
>
> We arrived at the old settlement just at dark and being too tired to do any prospecting we were soon in the land of Nod. After an early breakfast we went up to the site of the old town.
>
> We could trace the street by the look of the timber. When we got on top of the small ridge, the first thing we struck was the powder magazine, and considering the time that it had been built, and the heavy wet seasons it has stood, it was in splendid repair. It is a stone building, very small, and is the nearest tenement to the cliffs.
>
> The next were two houses, or rather the remains, the walls of which only are standing. the wood of some of the windows was as sound as a rock and defied the ravages of dry rot and white ants; the timber used was ironwood. After a little while we found the old cemetery and two grave stones still standing; but we could not decipher the names on them.
>
> Traces-plough furrows, very faint, could still be seen of the old garden.
>
> Heavy timber of all kinds has grown on the one-time clearings, and one must look keenly to notice the difference between the old and the new forest. After a few more years all traces of the settlement will be a thing of the past (*NTTG*, 10 March 1899).

The hunters found many buffaloes, and mobs of wild horses not far from Victoria, and were surprised when an old man arrived to tell them the stock and horses were his:

> ... There are a few English cattle here, but they are very small and weedy. The ponies, cattle, and buffalo were left here by the first settlers, and are claimed by an old blackfellow named Jack Davis. Old Jack was a boy when Port Essington was deserted by the English settlers. He has had a trip to the old country and can remember several things which occurred when the settlement was in full swing. Jack says that 'big fellow boss been gib it me all about pony, bullock and buffalo; and suppose white fellow shoot him buffalo, him gib it me

tobacco, me no more growl'.

If old Jack had had one stick of tobacco only for each buffalo shot, he would have had over forty thousand sticks to his credit, for there has been fully that number of animals shot, since buffalo shooting started. On our return to camp we decided to continue on overland to Glencoe Station, of which more anon (*NTTG*, 10 March 1899).

Soon after Captain Marsh*'s rescue of the *Wood Duck* trio in 1874, the crew of the *Victoria* made a visit to Port Essington and noted a cool reception from the Iwaidja.

In a series of critical letters about his ex-colleague Sinclair, written to the editor of the *Northern Territory Times and Gazette*, James Miller thought he knew why:

To the Editor,

Sir—My opinion of the cool reception of the *Victoria* boat party by the blacks at Port Essington was owing to the presence of Robinson; and not to any promises made them by the officers or the gentleman forming the search party in the *The Flying Cloud*.

On one occasion when I visited the blacks' camp, Mr. Sinclair said to me, 'the blacks are very good to us, and I will send them many presents from Port Darwin'.

All this time the head chief, Jack Davis, was sitting on the grass between the two white men, and within two feet of them. the chief understands English well and listened to the promises as they fell from the lips of Mr. Sinclair. The chief, looking at me, said, 'I believe Sinclair speaks the truth, saying he will tell Captain Douglas to bring these presents, and his orders will be obeyed', at the same time calling my attention to Sinclair's sores, saying, 'I am healing them, and I and my wife are feeding them', pointing to the two white men.

At this moment Robinson handed me a leaf taken from Sinclair's book, and I read from it the list of the presents to the tribe for saving their lives. This list I afterwards read in presence of several men on board the *Flying Cloud*. Sinclair promised to send or bring to the chief the undermentioned

---

* Marsh Street in Milner is named after the Captain of the *The Flying Cloud*. He was also mate on the *Gulnare* with Captain Sweet in 1869.

articles—one box of tobacco, one gun, six pounds of shot, four pounds of nails for their fish spears, one knife, one axe, one bag of flour, one bag of sugar.

Now Robinson was implicated in these false promises of which accounts for his cool reception this time by the natives. Now, Mr. Editor, within my hearing many times Sinclair told the chief, and led him to understand that he himself was a great white chief, and next in command to Captain Douglas, and would be sure to send the presents.

By inserting the foregoing remarks in your valuable paper, you will oblige a friend of the Port Essington blacks.

I am, Sir, &c.,

JAMES MILLER.

Shackle, May 25th, 1874.

Jack Davis probably never received his presents, or the 40,000 sticks of tobacco owed to him by the buffalo hunters, but he survived for many more years in Port Essington. A portrait of him, 'Old Jack Davis', by the Chief Medical Officer, Dr Mervyn Holmes, was published in 1915 by Elsie Masson (Masson, 1915) (see Figure 58). Jack Davis was in his seventies when the photograph was taken, and some of the things he said showed his experience in the settlement had not been forgotten, as Masson wrote:

> ... Nearly seventy years ago, Jack was an eager, agile little black boy, something of a pet of the regiment, who loved to run messages for the officers, to strut alongside a squad of marching men, and imitate their stiff movements at drill. Still he mumbles out the story of the regiment, beginning when 'Siggem Bemmer' (Sir Gordon Bremer) first sailed into the harbour, and repeats the names of the officers, dwelling on the wonderful feasts at Christmas. Then his back straightens, a curious change comes into his voice, and he feebly attempts to shout the old words of command—'Shon! Eyes right!'
> So do the long-forgotten tones of some Cockney Sergeant-Major linger ghost-like for a few more years in the voice of an ancient North Australian aboriginal (Masson, 1915).

'Flash Poll' was Memorimbo, the girl who lived with the

Lambricks for two years. It was she who climbed on board the *Beatrice* in 1865. She became good friends with Alfred Searcy, a customs inspector who had an annual camp in Knocker Bay. Searcy waited there at the beginning of each trepanging season, for the Macassan trepang fleet to arrive. Memorimbo, Searcy said, used to tell him amusing stories of the officers in Victoria, though he never recorded them. She died in Port Essington in 1907, and apparently willed her skull to Searcy, which he never collected (Harris, 1990). Searcy's recollections of Memorimbo are worth repeating:

> ... I must tell you about an ancient black lady, called 'Flash Poll', I met, who took me under her wing and professed the greatest regard for me. I expect grog and tobacco had a lot to do with her affection. This dame was a young woman when the soldiers were stationed at Port Essington, and a fine woman she must have been, judging from her appearance even when I saw her. Many a good yarn I had with her about the old days, and some funny stories she told. The old woman remembered the Officers well, particularly the chaplain. Poll could still repeat like a parrot a prayer and sing a psalm; but I am bound to say Singing was not her strong point. She had a great command of a certain sort of language, which she did not hesitate to use when her liver, for instance, was out of order. As sure as she said the prayer and sang the psalm, she wound up with 'Give it tobacco, give it nobbler,' both of which she got at times. Whenever I said good-bye, Poll always rattled off a list of things she wanted. They would have fitted out a decent bush shanty.
>
> Once a year I did send her Turkey-red, tobacco pipes, and a bottle of medicine of a sort. Flash Poll thought a lot of me; in fact, she promised me her skull; but I am afraid that interesting relic will never come my way. Her pet way of showing her grief at my departure was to ask for a knife to cut her head. Poll was a great hand at making hats out of leaves of a palm-tree. The amount of work in one was enormous, and generally occupied six months. I have to this day one of the hats that Poll made (Searcy, 1909).

Mildun 'Jack Davis' lived until at least 1914, when Elsie Masson

met him (Harris, 1990). Looking back over his long life of travelling, Mildun may have had some regrets. John Lewis asked him in 1873, whether he should take a boy named Nanyenya with him to Adelaide.

And then?

Figure 59: An Iwaidja corroboree in 1877 in the Victoria Settlement ruins, that was probably performed for tourists and Inspector Paul Foelsche (Foelsche, NTL PH1060-0063).

Mildun's advice was:

> ... If you take him to Adelaide always call him 'Nanyenya'*,

---

*   Nanyenya did travel to Adelaide with Lewis and had some interesting adventures, which Lewis recounted in *Fought and Won*, but he 'developed the lung trouble

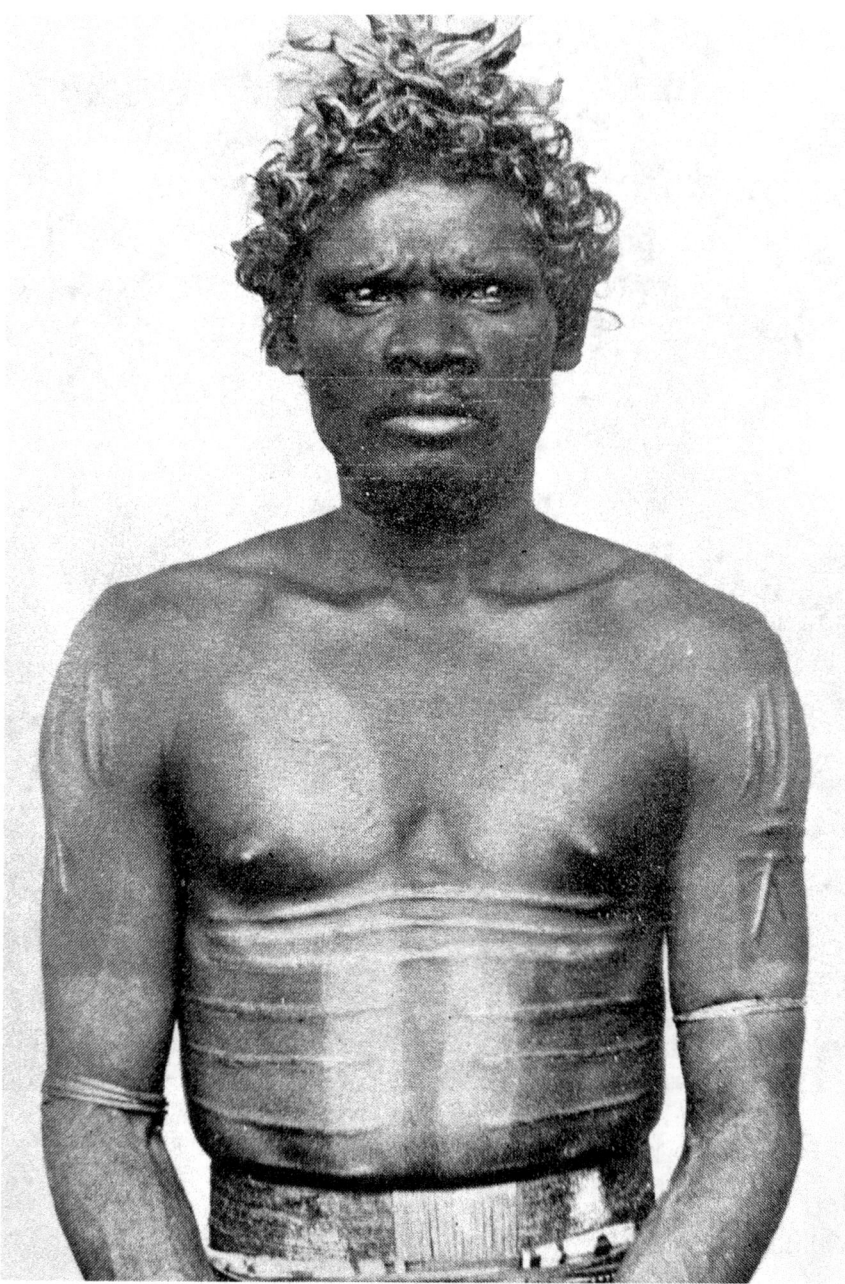

Figure 60: An unnamed Iwaidja tribesman from Port Essington. From 'Fought and Won' (Lewis, 1922)

never call him any other name, because when I went away my name was [Mildun] and when I came back I had forgotten a great deal of my native language, and went by the name of Jack Davis; and my people did not believe that I was the king or heir to the throne" (Lewis, 1922)

Alfred Searcy also knew Mildun as 'Jack Davis' and 'Flash Poll's' brother. He was a regular visitor to Searcy's camp and, according to Searcy, he was a cook of some skill:

Old Jack Davis, Flash Poll's brother, an aged Port Essington nigger, was preparing a real good meal. A lot of Alligators' eggs had been brought in, the contents of which Jack proceeded to extract—in the same manner we have been told that we can't teach our grandmothers—and to deposit in a basin; these, when the basin was full, were fixed up in a manner peculiar to the natives, I suppose. This plan may have been followed to make certain that the eggs were all good (Searcy, 1909).

In 1875, the Government Resident lent the schooner *Woolner* to a party of five well-equipped men. It was led by Joseph Lorence and they were searching for gold. They picked up Mildun and seven other Iwaidja and asked them to guide them to a rumoured place of gold. The Iwaidja had no idea, but the jaunt was like a holiday and a source of free victuals they weren't likely to pass up. Lorence and the *Woolner* returned to Darwin enriched only by the experience.

Succeeding Government Residents: Bloomfield Douglas, George Byng Scott, and Edward Price, all visited the port during their times in office. Douglas was there twice, in 1872 and 1873. When he first met the Iwaidja, he was impressed, particularly for their modesty, because the women wore wooden 'fig leaves'. Everyone called him 'Commandant', which appealed to his ego (Douglas, 7 November 1872). In 1873, he took a 10-day cruise in *The Flying Cloud*, a small Government schooner he treated as his own, and spent time talking to the leaders of the Macassan trepang fleet. His experience with the Iwaidja that time was marred when he was affronted by several drunks

---

which some of the natives get, and after four months in hospital the poor little fellow passed away' (Lewis, 1922).

who had sourced some *arak* from the Macassans. Douglas discovered that the Iwaidja traded their labour and their womenfolk for rations, tobacco, and alcohol (Cross, 2011).

Inspector Paul Foelsche—who usually accompanied the Government Residents—took photographs of Iwaidja in the settlement ruins in 1875, 1876 and 1877, including some of a 'corroboree', which was possibly a dance performance for Edward Price's party, paid for by presents. Price was there to inspect John Lewis's Cobourg Cattle Company's buffalo operation (O'Brien, 1990). Port Essington clearly interested the South Australian government. John Lewis saw its potential, as did other travellers, such as William Brackley Wildey in 1876:

> … The Near Future of Northern Australia: The durable timber of the old jetty at Port Essington, the varied vegetation indigenous and foreign around that former settlement, the herds of wild cattle, the turtle and trepang on the coast, and the success which is known to attend regular fishing operations there, combine to prove that within about three days' sail from Port Darwin, and thence onward to the east, as far as the Gulf of Carpentaria, where Queensland enterprise meets that which radiates from the Northern Territory, there are the natural materials of future wealth—& productive soil and convenient harbourage. To those who are attracted to Port Darwin by the goldfields in that part of the country and fail to realise their expectations there, other modes of enriching themselves will be available. Whether fostered by the Government of the two colonies concerned or not, there can now be no doubt that the natural development of colonial enterprise will in a few years result in a chain of settlements along the whole of the Northern coast, and vessels will be employed from Somerset round to Perth, in transferring to the chief ports the produce of many settlements (Wildey, 1876).

Chapter 11

And now?

Five of us paid about $200 each for a daytrip to Victoria from Black Point. For our money, we had a seat in a sleek, fast, 10-seater launch that ate up the kilometres across the flat harbour water. We had our own guide and boat driver, whom I will call Bob. He was an excellent boatman, and, as a guide, he knew something about the history of the site. He had read Peter Spillett's excellent 1972 book, *Forsaken Settlement*, so he could answer some of our questions and point out the pertinent historic sites.

Bob paused the boat off Point Record and told us how Bremer read a declaration of possession here in 1824, in the name of the King. He had buried a bottle somewhere close to make sure that the whole world, particularly the French, knew that the British had ownership of

Figure 61: Headland, Port Essington.

the land all around. Perhaps the French found the bottle and took it, but Bob seemed to think it was a hidden treasure, still there, waiting for someone. I wondered if he had ever scratched around in the sand himself. I thought the bottle was more likely washed from the sand by cyclonic tides or dune movements over the last 195 years.

Whilst at Point Record, I wish Bob had told us in graphic detail how Captain Yule had scuttled the *Bramble* there. He could have given us vivid images of millions of cockroaches spreading across the sea like an Exxon Valdez oil slick, and let us imagine the smell of them, until it clogged in the back of our throats. He missed the opportunity and took us instead into the inner harbour and across to the beach next to Adam Head.

It was a beautiful, albeit standard, cool dry season morning in July, just like every other day four weeks on either side of it. The sea was calm, the air warm. Fish were jumping. Occasional swirls of water indicated something large beneath the surface.

We saw the white cliffs of Adam Head from a long distance. It was the obvious place for a settlement, although the residents used to complain it was too far inland for the sea breeze to reach them, and fever was so easy to catch there.

We landed on the beach at high tide and jumped onto the sand. Bob could not risk the boat being beached by the tide, so he took it out and anchored 50 metres off shore. He then swam back to join

Figure 62: Like every tour group since the National Park opened, we gathered behind the sign for a photograph.

us, unconcerned about the possibility of becoming breakfast for any large reptiles in the area. If he had, we passengers would have had to draw straws over who would risk becoming dessert, because one of us would have to swim out to the boat to get help. The water was so clear we could see his feet kicking as he swam. Nelson, the huge Newfoundland dog and hero of the wrecking of the *Heroine*, had met his demise in the jaws of a crocodile in these very waters.

We gathered behind the Victoria Settlement sign, and Bob juggled three or four cameras to take the obligatory arrival photograph. A crocodile stole a marine's blanket as he snoozed in his hammock somewhere near here.

We then we marched into the forest towards the settlement. There was a well-trodden trail up the slope, but the first ruin we came across lay just behind the beach's thick line of vegetation. It was not a ruin of Victoria Settlement at all. A small sign at our feet told us it was the remains of John Lewis's cottage, but there was no other information about this extraordinary man, who loved the place so much that he named his son after the port. The ruin was little more than a few straight lines of rocks and flagstones. Here Lewis, and his partner, Charles Levi*, sat their 'homestead'. It has changed a lot: in 1876 a correspondent to the *Northern Territory Times and Gazette* described how it looked then:

> ... Substantial fencing extends for miles in different directions, enclosing paddocks for various purposes; besides which there are large mustering and branding yards for cattle, stockyards, and buffalo enclosures.
>
> The head station is situated a little south of the old settlement of Victoria, on the Coburg Peninsula, and consists of a neat log house, surrounded by a veranda, with storehouse, men's rooms, workshop, and all the necessaries of a compact model

---

* Charles Levi was later the 'outdoor manager' in the Delissaville sugar plantation experiments on the Douglas (now Cox) Peninsula in 1882. Levi had a team of 'Port Essington natives', who, according to the *Northern Territory Times and Gazette*, were 'devoted to him' and who worked 'most industriously' (*NTTG*, 1 April 1882).

station in its immediate neighborhood. The whole is encircled by a strong fence at gun-shot distance from the centre building, leaving a clear space, over which no natives are on any pretence allowed to pass after sunset without having first received permission. Owing to this restriction, and the excellent tact and firmness of the manager, the head station is remarkably free from intrusion, and apparently from attack (*NTTG*, 16 December 1876).

The trail started to rise from here, through an open, dry *Eucalyptus tetradonta* forest that indicates to naturalists that the soil is deep and sandy on the Victoria peninsula. The forest was liberally dotted with another tell-tale sign of sandy soils, the magnificent palm, *Gronophylum ramsayi**. When young, this palm has an edible 'heart', like the 'cabbage palm', *Livistona humilis*, and both were harvested by the settlers in Raffles Bay and Victoria.

Soon we passed by a brick kiln. This was where Private William Handy, the brick-maker, had cooked his first bricks. He must have been good at it, and taught others well, as there were thousands lying around the site that still looked like they could be used.

One of the most impressive ruins was that of the magazine. It was restored by Peter Dermoudy and a team in 1984—some of the stones were reset and the whole structure waterproofed (Dermoudy, 1984). To us, more than 30 years later, it still looked solid and serviceable.

The magazine was dug into the ground beside where the fort had stood, on top of Adam Head. I stepped down and bent double to enter a small rectangular room. Its interior walls were dotted with the mud nests of solitary wasps, and scratched by World War Two soldiers, suggesting there were more stories to learn about Port Essington. Who were these people?

---

* This palm has a very limited distribution. It is common on Cobourg Peninsula, and there is a good stand near Gochan Jiny-Jirra, south of Maningrida. A single giant grows off the old road to Jimarda, in central Arnhem Land. This single palm is the 'Devil-devil Tree' that found its way into the title of my memoir, *Turn Left at the Devil Tree* (Pugh, 2014).

And now?

Figure 63: The magazine on Adam Head.

I.R. Nichols 1st A.A. ... P.Calvin Garrison 1940 ... J. Leng BOMBO ... BWILLIAMS 1917/YO.

The fort was a 'block house', upon which several cannons pointed out across the harbour. Its timber had been a delight to the termites, and the regular earth tremors that were felt by the residents, cracked, and weakened its structure even more. As Huxley said, if the cannons had been used, the whole fort might have come tumbling down. There was nothing left of it, but it was never a grand design:

> ... The little fort ... was only a temporary structure, sufficient until the time when the colony had developed further and could build a citadel capable of defending it. In fact, however, this construction was not without a certain solidity; though it is unlikely that it would ever be of any great use. One would need a strange situation indeed before any power could think of coming to attack a settlement whose success was still so much in doubt, and long before this tiny colony had grown large enough to inspire any apprehensions, these few cannon could have been replaced by more respectable fortifications (d'Urville, 1839).

Government House was a little inland of the magazine. The remnants of its pylons are celebrated as the Northern Territory's first

Figure 64: Remains of McArthur's house, a small steamer in the background, from 'An Untamed Territory' (Masson, 1915).

elevated house—all the better for air flow, and apparently above the termites. The house was blown off its pylons by the 1839 cyclone, but the marines had managed to manhandle it back into place. This was where the dinner party was held by the English for the French officers of *d'Astrolabe* and *Zélée*. It was the last event of the Frenchmen's visit and 'nothing was spared to make it a magnificent spread and the most unrestrained merriness was in evidence' (d'Urville, 1839).

The merriment in part stemmed from a liberal supply of the best Bordeaux wines from the ships' stores for the table. Parts of these same bottles were found by Jim Allen and his team of archaeologists 130 years later, when they dug up the rubbish tip behind the site of the commandant's house (Allen, 1973). 'In general', wrote Allen, 'it would seem that the rubbish was merely thrown immediately outside or towards and over the cliff ...' (Allen, 1973).

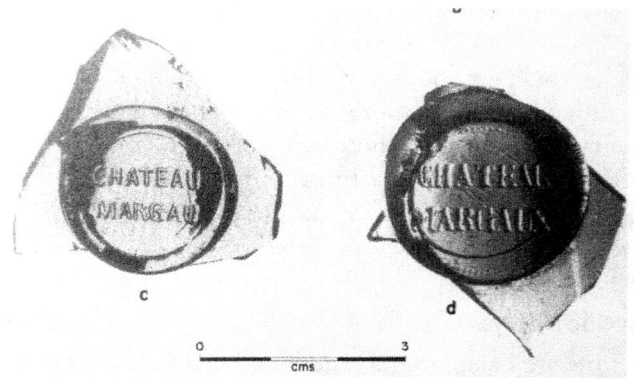

Figure 65: Glass stoppers from French wine bottles (Allen, 1973).

And now?

In fact, they found 6,275 pieces of glass behind the house, including the French pieces. There were also 475 shards of pottery. These included plates with the famous 'willow pattern', which is still in production. There were also 11 metal buttons, a crown and anchor insignia, several percussion caps and lead musket balls, collar studs, brass hinges, and copper and iron nails. A few heavy bases of bottles were found, and some of them had been modified into implements and tools such as scrapers or knives. In number, 827 pieces of glass appeared to have been 'worked'.

After the settlement closed, and probably even during its time, the local Iwaidja used the rubbish as a resource. As the Englishmen routinely threw their rubbish out of their doors and windows, much of it may have been immediately salvaged by resourceful men and women. Glass was traded south, and probably still lies far and wide across Cobourg Peninsula, Arnhem Land and beyond; discarded and forgotten.

From Government House we followed the trail as it wound through the bush and then arrived at the most famous of the Victoria ruins. A row of five round 'Cornish chimneys' stood there and marked the site of the married quarters. Here, the wives of the marines swept the hearths and beat the rugs, whilst their husbands tended the small plots of land behind them, growing private bunches of bananas, and the best pineapples* in Australia. Mary Ann and Eliza Mew and several other children spent their days here, running between the huts, or playing knuckles in the dust. Their homes were small huts with huge fireplaces, which suggests that they must also have had verandas or a place outside to escape the kitchen heat when anyone was cooking. Baby Margaret Mew leaned to walk here, and the nearby cliff must have been a source of terror for her mother, and others with toddlers.

Beside the trail, a variety of useful plants grew. If the settlers only knew how useful they could have been, things might have been

---

* The pineapples were great survivors. John Lewis found pineapples, 'a few bananas, jack fruit and guavas' growing in the gardens in 1873 (Lewis, 1922) and Walter Campbell saw a small pineapple plant in 1913 (Campbell, 1916).

Figure 66: The round 'Cornish' chimneys of the married men's quarters. Map ref: 11° 21' 51.02"S, 132° 09' 10.95"E.

Figure 67: The blacksmith's forge.

different. *Planchonia coreya*, the cocky apple, was fruiting when we were there. This plant has edible fruit, and the bark and leaves can be used as a bush medicine for a variety of ailments—from boils to leprosy—and as a poultice for sores and even spear wounds. People also used the bark to make ceremonial string belts, pubic tassels, string bags, and fish poison (Brock, 1993).

There was also plenty of *Terminalia ferdinandiana*, the billy-goat plum, growing nearby. This is famous as a fruit containing one of the highest concentrations of Vitamin C. It was a scurvy beater but was unknown to the British in the 1840s.

As we moved on, low rock walls marked the storehouse and the officers' mess. Then we saw a solid construction that was the blacksmith's forge. Near it were the remnants of the little prison, and an overgrown well, mostly collapsed or filled in. Remarkably, it was close to the cliff's edge, and must have been a handy source of water. To the west from here the bush closed in. A thick *Acacia* understory laced with 'wait-a-while' vines (*Smilax* sp) filled in the old town square. In fact, I saw no sign that a town square had ever existed there at all.

The access to the jetty was cut down through the cliff at this point. The jetty still ran out to sea, but it was just a pile of rocks, capped with the occasional small mangrove seedling. A large dead stump stood alone about halfway along the jetty. The rocks almost looked natural, as if they had been there forever. A small pile of broken glass gathered by visitors lay on the rocks nearby.

In the 1840s, the most imposing and most used public building was the hospital. Most of the residents spent time there at one time or other, and nearly a quarter of them died there. It was a wooden construction of four wards on a row of low stone foundations. The ground where they lay had been cut flat into the slope. Behind the foundations, reached by a short rise of steps, were the impressive ruins of the cookhouse. A metal sign read, 'Restored by NT Command Sept 68'. A large chimney with two large renovated ovens looked like it could

Figure 68: The hospital foundations, and the ruins of the kitchen. Map ref: 11° 21' 41.72"S, 132° 09' 12.61"E.

Figure 69: One of the ovens in the hospital kitchens, with broken glass.

And now?

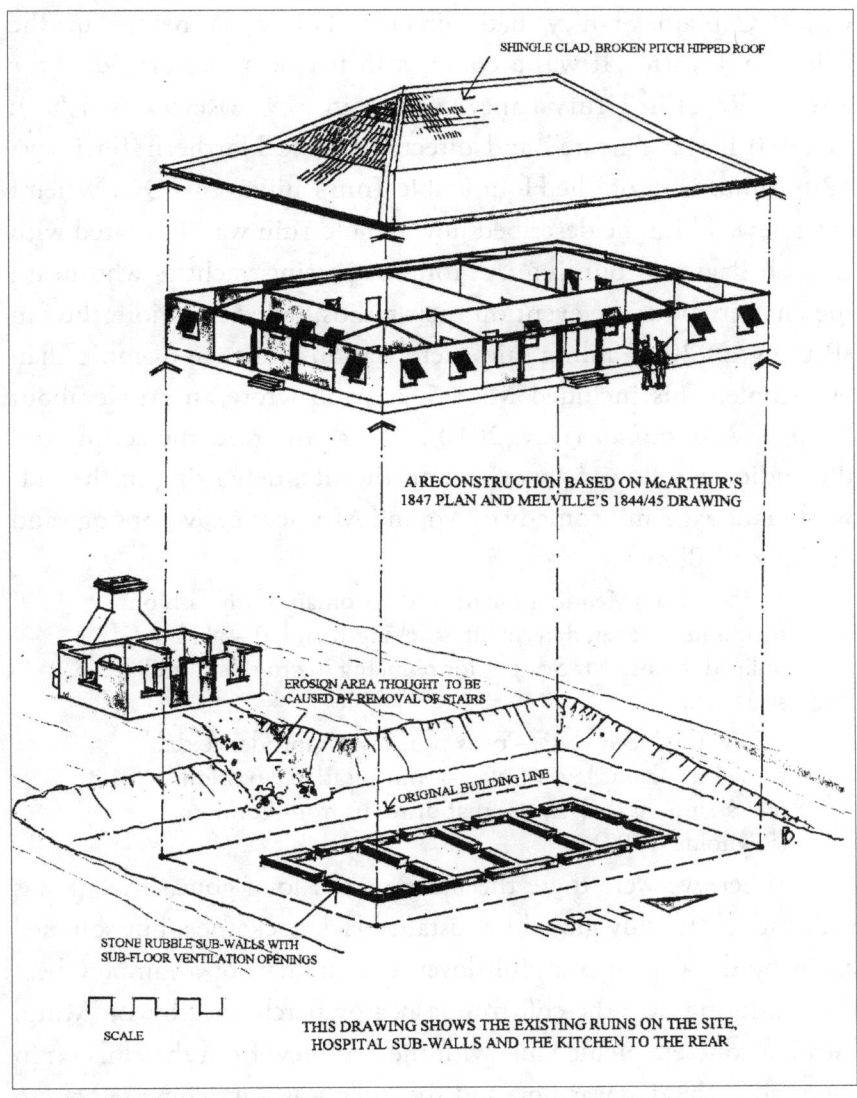

Figure 70: An architectural sketch of Victoria Hospital (by Peter Dermoudy: with permission).

still cook good food. It would not look out of place in any modern pizza shop, I thought. More broken glass was lying in one of the ovens.

In 2010, the hospital witnessed a resurgence of life. A working party, there to clear the cemetery, re-staged the play *Cheap Living* which Captain Stanley had directed 171 years before in the 'Victoria Theatre'. It was a comedy, in five acts, performed at the Theatre Royal in Drury Lane, London in 1797 (Reynolds, 1797). In 2010 it was narrated and directed by the Northern Territory's 18th Administrator, the Honourable Tom Pauling AO QC. When I interviewed him, he described how the old ruin was decorated with English flags and bunting. A group of passing yachties who heard the chatter about the event on their radios, sailed in to join the fun (Pauling, 2020). Pauling said there was an audience of more than 30 people. This included Mark Day, who wrote an article about it for *The Australian* (Day, 2010). The actors read the script, and the audience followed them around the site, delighting in the old-world language and comedy of Mr and Mrs Scatter, Mr Sponge and Sir Edward Bloomly:

> MRS SCAT {Mending linen] And a woman of my fashion turn housekeeper, dairymaid, stocking-mender!—ah! I'm obliged to you, Mr Scatter, for reducing me to this humiliating situation.
>
> SCAT. I reduced you?—'twas your own imprudence that ruined us—your love of play—your insatiable passion for cassino, hazard, saro—that drove us from London...
> (Reynolds, 1797).

When we were there the bunting had long gone. The air was still, though harshly grated by distant black cockatoos, but softened again by the coo of peaceful doves and the flap of a rainbow bee-eater, hunting over the cliff from a nearby perch. Nearby, on Minto Head, a concrete picnic table with the best view from the cliffs sat in the shade. The day was hot, and the table was a welcome refuge, so we rested and enjoyed the view. Several trees clung to the very tip of the cliff edge, doomed. A brave *Jacksonia*, in full flower, had such a precarious grip, the slightest breeze might have pushed it to its death on the beach below.

From Minto Head the trail crossed to the western side of the site and entered a different type of forest. We saw it, when we stopped at the low foundations of the officers' mess, near the centre of the peninsula, as those low walls backed into an encroaching jungle. The *Eucalyptus* forest that grew close to the cliffs was replaced by a thicket of tropical monsoon vine-forest—the local equivalent of rainforest—and it dominated the centre of the small peninsula. Almost certainly, it was not there prior to settlement. The detritus of the community—broken glass, bricks, rocks, and gravel, still lying across the land—has had a long-lasting effect. From aerial photos you can see that the uniform greys of the open sclerophyll forest suddenly change to the darker colour of higher density foliage (see Map 3).

When the British abandoned the site, they left bananas, mango trees, lime trees and other exotics, as the most common plants—although, in the artwork of the day—several large shade trees which were left growing to shelter the marines can be seen. All the exotic trees were long gone.

We entered the forest and, as the vegetation closed in on the ruins, the shade got deeper. Colourful songbirds flitted between the branches. On the ground, orange footed scrub fowls scratched at their nests. In fact, the quartermaster's store, which lay in the thickest part of this forest, contained the growing mound of a scrub-fowl nest (Figure 71). It is likely that the rainforest tree species arrived because the fire regime was changed by the settlement, and the less fire-tolerant species were able to establish themselves on the site. Their seeds were probably brought in by birds from fruiting trees in a dense patch of rainforest just west of Victoria. Other, typical Northern Territory rainforest species then arrived, perhaps carried in the fur of agile wallabies, or flying foxes. For example, *Smilax* 'wait-a-while' vines took hold and climbed to great heights in the trees. They are so-called because when you pass too close to them, you have to wait a while, whilst you unhook your clothing from their vicious barbs.

A large kiln next to the path on the way to the cemetery is thought to have made enough charcoal for the blacksmith's fires, and to supply ships' galleys. It was in excellent condition, and a testament to the stone

Figure 71: Quartermaster's Store with the huge mound nest of a pair of orange-footed scrub fowls (Pastmasters).

Figure 72: The monument of Mrs Emma Lambrick and her two children as it was in 2016.

masons who built in. We carried on passed it and reached what is the most poignant site of the tour—the Victoria Cemetery.

Rangers kept the vegetation here cut back, so the graves lay in a sunny clearing, with the jungle pushing in on all sides. Among the black wattle trees (*Acacia auriculiformis*), other monsoon vine-forest trees and vines such as *Denhamia obscura* and *Opilia*

And now?

Figure 73: The Memorial Board in Victoria Cemetery, erected in 1990, lists the names of the dead.

amentacea, grew well. It was clear this area had not been burned for many years.

It was a lonely cemetery, just as it was in McArthur's painting (see Figure 76) and it kept its secrets well.

However, Peter Dermoudy*, a Darwin based 'heritage architect', returned in 2010 with a ground-penetrating radar. He wanted to discover, once and for all, the number of graves that lay in Victoria's graveyard. It was a question that had puzzled historians for years. Estimates had ranged from 45 to 110 graves, but as only five tombs or headstones existed, no one had an accurate count of the occupants of the cemetery, and there were never any accurate lists. Dermoudy's radar uncovered 54 graves (Day, 2010).

On the memorial board erected in the cemetery in 1990, there were 59 names, but some of those were incorrect. For example, John Armstrong, is known to have died in Timor, and the Normans were

---
* Dermoudy famously lived in a 'flying saucer' house, named *Futuro*, in Darwin, before it was destroyed by Cyclone Tracy in 1974. It was hit by pieces of his neighbour's house (Dermoudy, 2020).

buried at sea. There were others, unnamed, as well. The board was as confusing as it was useful.

The Northern Territory Government Secretary, H.E. Carey, visited the cemetery in 1912. He was dismayed enough by its degradation to write to George Lambrick's son, the Reverend George Lambrick, to tell him that the inscription on the obelisk above the grave of his father's first wife had been obliterated.

When Elsie Masson visited the cemetery in 1913, guided by Mildun, she wrote that there were no readable inscriptions on any of the tombs at all. However, visitors today can spend time deciphering ancient inscriptions on each tomb. Publicity from the early 20th century visitors roused the conscience of the government. As a result, a contractor named Tom Stiles was sent to Victoria to renovate the graves. Four of the tombs were in reasonable condition, though the fifth was small and broken. Poor Tom did the best he could, despite his apparent inability to spell, and lack of care for historical truth. Walter Campbell visited the cemetery in 1913 and:

> ... found that the cemetery has been put in very good order, fenced in, and cleaned up. The graves were hilled up; and the three tombs renovated ... (Campbell, 1916).

Emma Lambrick's monument has now stood proudly in the forest for nearly 180 years. In an attempt to ensure it remains standing, the monument was taken apart and rebuilt in 2018. It had a slight lean, and there was concern that it was in danger of falling over. Peter Dermoudy was outraged. He had sketched every rock and measured every angle of the monument and was convinced it was safe. He was already affronted by the 1913 renovation by Tom Stiles, because when visitors stand and read the semi-literate inscription, they are standing on one of Lambrick's children. Their graves, Dermoudy points out, can be seen in McArthur's painting of the cemetery (see figure 77). The inscription should have been placed 90 degrees around the obelisk where flowers were once placed on the shelf provided (Dermoudy, 2020). Recent photographs of the memorial show the inscription was

And now?

Figure 74: Mrs Lambrick's monument in 2019 after a controversial restoration using white concrete (ABC).

cleaned and is easier to read, and white modern cement now holds the rocks firmly together. But, says Peter Dermoudy, its renovation was 'vandalism', and 'absolutely criminal'. I have some sympathy for him—it looks as good as new, which is disappointing for a history buff, but in a hundred years who will know?

The wording of Stiles' inscription is unchanged, but it is now more legible:

IN MEMOERY
OF
MRS LAMBRICK AND CHILD,
DEARLY BELOVE WIFE OF
LUTIENT LAMBRICK 47 REGMT
HOBART
DIED PORT ESSINGTON
1838–48

The other tombs in the cemetery could have belonged to any of the settlers who died there. We could have chosen to believe Stiles'

Figure 75: The tomb's plaque was probably installed by Tom Stiles in 1913.

Figure 76: McArthur's painting of the Victoria Cemetery, 1848. Mrs Lambrick's two children lie on either side of her obelisk grave monument. Perhaps the uniformed soldier standing near Mrs Lambrick's grave is her husband, George (John McArthur, NLA PIC R245 LOC1981/nla.obj-135264415).

Figure 77: Detail of Mrs Lambrick's grave monument (John McArthur, NLA PIC R245 LOC1981/nla.obj-135264415).

inscriptions, except that the names, dates, and military information in them were all wrong. A few metres from Emma Lambrick lay a tomb that had an inscription to 'Captain Crawford' of the 47th Regiment. There were two Crawfords at Port Essington. The first was

And now?

William Crawford, who was the mate of the *Pelorus*, but he died in 1843 long after the ship had left, and, anyway, he was not a captain. The second was Doctor John Crawford, who survived and went home in the *Meander*. Also, there was nobody from the 47th Regiment in the settlement at all—they were Royal Marines. Instead, this grave probably belonged to Captain Phillip Chetwode R.N. of the *Royalist*. The inscription read:

> SACREAD TO THE MEMOERY OF CAPTAIN CRAWFORD
> 47 REGIMENT HOBART DIED PORT ESSINGTON 1838-49.

The third tomb belonged to an unnamed doctor. It must therefore have been the final resting place of Doctor Richard Tilston. Its inscription simply said:

> SACREAD TO THE MEMOERY OF THE DR OF THE
> SETTLEMENT DIED PORT ESSINGTON 1838-48.

The last of the tombs was inscribed to a German missionary. It clearly belonged to the Italian priest, Don Angelo Confalonieri:

> SACREAD TO THE MEMOERY OF FATHER VON ANSLOWE,
> GERMAN MESSONER, SMITHS POINT
> DIED PORT ESSINGTON 1845.

Understandably, 'Don Angelo' could easily be scribed as 'Von Anslowe', but the priest died in 1848, not 1845. Some of Darwin's Catholic community occasionally seek to exhume Confalonieri's bones and relocate them to Darwin's Catholic Cathedral, perhaps to treat them like the relics of a saint. The *Pastmasters* team run active research programs and an excellent website on Northern Territory history. They argue that the remains of the Port Essington settlers should stay exactly where they are. Removal, they say:

> … would diminish Port Essington as an historic site. It would be contrary to world best practice to remove the artefacts from their context. Darwin didn't exist when Confalonieri chose to dedicate his life to the Aboriginal people of Port Essington and it is thanks only to the inept, semi-literate, ill-informed & slipshod renovation contractor Tom Stiles that they have survived in the place where they have most meaning—for which we gratefully salute him (Pastmasters, 2016).

Dermoudy agreed—it would be another act of vandalism. Another problem is that we cannot be sure which of the graves is Confalonieri's. They were inscribed 63 years after the settlement was abandoned, and Tom Stiles was not a reliable archaeologist. Of course, Confalonieri could be identified as the skeleton with a missing shoulder blade, as one of his was sent to his sister in Italy, for their church's ossuary.

The similarities in the writing style, the spelling and wording of the four inscriptions confirms they were written by the same person, no doubt Tom Stiles. Spillett (1972) thought he probably sourced his information of the graves' occupants from Mildun, who was quite elderly by then.

It was time for us to go, and with the heavy hearts that isolated cemeteries always engender, Bob led us out of the monsoon vine forest, across the site of the old gardens, and back among the *Eucalyptus tetradonta* of the peninsula. There had been a fire here earlier in the year and the ground was clear, but fire had not entered the settlement for many years, probably protected by the rangers' design.

I reflected that it was a strange experience walking through the failed settlement that John McArthur had tried so hard to make work. But did it fail? Jim Allen, an archaeologist who studied both the ruins and the records believed it served its purpose well (Allen, 1980). As Allen wrote:

> ... For the puppet-masters in Whitehall, Port Essington was an important but temporary strategic dot on the map of Australia. For the unfortunate marines whose job it was to show the flag, immediate problems of survival quickly dissipated the arrogance of imperialism (Allen, 1980).

It was only after the British were no longer afraid of foreign powers arriving in the north that they were able to leave Victoria to rot in the bush (Conner, 1988). Perhaps the British presence on the north coast really did keep the French and the Dutch away.

The ravages of disease knocked the Royal Marines and their families around as surely as the termites and winds destroyed the wooden buildings. The forces against the residents were just too great—'they were confronted by an environment foreign in the extreme' (Allen, 1980). They were incredibly isolated and fed second-rate preserved victuals that were sometimes years old. Their food was left over from the battles of the Opium Wars in China or, it was sent from Sydney because no one else wanted it. The marines knew little about tropical agriculture and less about the local native foods. It is no wonder that their health suffered.

The British were welcomed by the Iwaidja. They saw them not as the invading harbingers of doom and purveyors of disease that they became, but as friends, suppliers of resources and trade items they could share throughout the tribes of the north. They were also protectors against other tribes and the Macassans. No doubt, they also provided unlimited novel entertainment.

The British had other long-term effects on the land apart from the change in forest type in the town area. The descendants of the settlers' buffaloes, cattle and pigs still roam the bush. Banteng cattle look like other domestic cattle, but prettier, with white patches on their rumps and lower legs. The largest population of wild banteng in the world now lives on the Cobourg Peninsula, and they cause tremendous damage to the native vegetation of the forests, the wetlands, and the sand dune ecosystems. Unfortunately, they are listed as vulnerable to extinction in their native South East Asia, so they are managed by the rangers and traditional owners of Cobourg Peninsula, rather than removed.

The numbers of buffaloes are increasing in Arnhem Land, with rare management efforts, such as aerial shooting programs, or ad hoc hunting, barely denting their population.

We arrived back on the beach and Bob waded out to get his boat—the water was shallower now at low tide. He brought the boat closer and we climbed on board, and we motored away from the cliffs.

The British in North Australia: Port Essington

Figure 78: A 'Bali sapi', or banteng cattle (*Bos javanicus*). A healthy population of banteng cattle, which are otherwise endangered, still lives on Cobourg Peninsula (Sandbunny 2010, Flickr).

Figure 79: A buffalo (*Bubalus bubalis*) near Vashon Head, Cobourg Peninsula (Sandbunny 2010, Flickr).

I reflected—as McArthur must have done in 1849, on the British folk who remained behind—men, women and children, almost a quarter of the settlers that came were buried in that little cemetery, so far from home. Theirs was an extraordinary story, and it took place in an extraordinary part of the world.

Figure 80: Heritage in isolation.

Appendices

Appendix 1: Lists

1.1: List 1: Members of the Victoria Garrison and their families*

Garrison and families	Arrived	Departed
HMS *Alligator* ex Plymouth		
Captain John McArthur	27 Oct 1838	Nov 1849
James H. McArthur	27 Oct 1838	Sept 1841
Lt. Phineas Priest	27 Oct 1838	March 1843
Sgt John Edgecumbe	27 Oct 1838	Died 5 March 1843
Pte Daniel Rees	27 Oct 1838	Nov 1844
Pte Robert Williams	27 Oct 1838	Nov 1844
Pte Richard Barker (fifer)	27 Oct 1838	Nov 1844
Pte John Allen	27 Oct 1838	Nov 1844
Pte Francis Bathurst	27 Oct 1838	Nov 1844
Pte Walter Bell	27 Oct 1838	Nov 1844
Pte William Best	27 Oct 1838	Nov 1844
Pte John Bray	27 Oct 1838	Died May 1843
Pte Henry Brown	27 Oct 1838	Died 15 Sept 1843
Pte Samuel Butler	27 Oct 1838	Nov 1844
Pte Thomas Clarke	27 Oct 1838	Nov 1844
Pte John Cocking	27 Oct 1838	Nov 1844
Pte George Fox	27 Oct 1838	Sept 1844
Pte Edward Gidlow	27 Oct 1838	Nov 1844

* Sources (Spillett, 1972) (Keppel, 1853) (Powell, 2016) (Cameron, 1999).

Appendices

Garrison and families	Arrived	Departed
Pte James Barber	27 Oct 1838	Nov 1844
Pte William Hatch	27 Oct 1838	Nov 1844
Pte Joseph Hooper	27 Oct 1838	Nov 1844
Pte John Jordan	27 Oct 1838	Nov 1844
Pte Robert Male	27 Oct 1838	Nov 1844
Pte William Prince	27 Oct 1838	Nov 1844
Pte William Pryor	27 Oct 1838	Nov 1844
Pte John Weeks	27 Oct 1838	Nov 1844
HMS *Alligator* ex Adelaide		
Ass Surgeon F. J. Whipple	27 Oct 1838	Aug 1843
Unnamed Royal Marine	27 Oct 1838	Died 3 June 1844
Pte Joseph Chandler	27 Oct 1838	Sept 1844
Pte Henry Graves	27 Oct 1838	Sept 1844
Cpl Richard Mew	27 Oct 1838	Nov 1844
Mrs Margaret Mew	27 Oct 1838	Nov 1844
Mary Ann Mew (child)	27 Oct 1838	Nov 1844
Eliza Mew (child)	27 Oct 1838	Nov 1844
Margaret Mew (child)	Born 7/1/1841	Nov 1844
Pte Richard Seagar	27 Oct 1838	Nov 1844
Mrs Susan Seagar	27 Oct 1838	Nov 1844
Unnamed Seagar (baby)	Born Nov 38	Died at birth
Pte Joseph Mountain	27 Oct 1838	Nov 1844
Pte Robert Wesson	27 Oct 1838	Nov 1844
Pte William Wheeler	27 Oct 1838	Died July 1844
Pte Joseph Davis	27 Oct 1838	March 1841
Mrs Kaziah Davis	27 Oct 1838	March 1841
Josiah Davis (child)	Born 7/2/1841	March 1841
Pte Samuel Davis	27 Oct 1838	July 1843

Garrison and families	Arrived	Departed
Pte James Fawkes	27 Oct 1838	March 1843
Pte James Fish	27 Oct 1838	March 1843
John Armstrong	27 Oct 1838	Nov 1840
George Windsor Earl	27 Oct 1838	Sept 1844
HMS *North Star* ex China		
Pte John Allum	March 1843	Nov 1844
Pte Amos Barber	March 1843	Nov 1844
Pte Robert Beck	March 1843	Nov 1844
Pte John Donoughue	March 1843	Nov 1844
Pte Joseph Sheppard	March 1843	Died Jan 1844
Lt Henry Timpson	March 1843	Nov 1844
Pte John Willcocks	March 1843	Nov 1844
HMS *Britomart*		
Pte Edward Dawson	Sept 1841	Nov 1844
HMS *Fly*		
Surgeon Archibald Sibbald	August 1843	Nov 1844
HMS *Alligator*		
Pte Robert Nicholls	March 1840	Nov 1844
Pte John Durwood	June 1839	Died Feb 1843
Sgt James Kingdom	June 1839	March 1843
Pte Isaac Coolen	June 1839	March 1843
Pte William Elford	June 1839	March 1843
Pte Stephen Grant	June 1839	March 1843
John McArthur (Jnr)	1841	Nov 1849
HMS *Enchantress*		
Father Confalonieri	13 April 1846	Died 9 June 1848

Appendices

Garrison and families	Arrived	Departed
HMS *Cadet*		
Lt George Lambrick	9 Nov 1844	Nov 1849
Mrs Emma Lambrick	9 Nov 1844	Died Oct 1846
Ms Emma Lambrick	9 Nov 1844	Nov 1849
George Lambrick (Jnr)	Born Oct 1844	Died 1845
Baby Lambrick	Born 1845	Died Nov 1846
Lt William A.G. Wright	9 Nov 1844	Aug 1846
Ass Surgeon Richard Tilston	9 Nov 1844	Died 4 March 1849
Sgt John Copp	9 Nov 1844	Nov 1849
Sgt William Masland	9 Nov 1844	Nov 1849
Sgt Hugh Isaacs	9 Nov 1844	Nov 1849
Mrs Jane Isaacs	9 Nov 1844	Nov 1849
Cpl John Conway	9 Nov 1844	Died Jan 1846
Cpl John Quinn	9 Nov 1844	Died early 1849?
Cpl James Brooks	9 Nov 1844	Died early 1849?
Pte William Bagguley	9 Nov 1844	Died early 1849?
Pte William Baldwin	9 Nov 1844	Nov 1849
Pte George Bartlett	9 Nov 1844	Nov 1849
Pte William Beauchamp	9 Nov 1844	Died April 1845
Pte Charles Carey (fifer)	9 Nov 1844	Oct 1847
Pte George Carter	9 Nov 1844	Nov 1849
Pte James Clark	9 Nov 1844	Nov 1849
Pte George Clalford	9 Nov 1844	Nov 1849
Pte James Coppock	9 Nov 1844	July 1849
Pte William Coye	9 Nov 1844	Nov 1849
Pte George Craton	9 Nov 1844	Nov 1849
Pte Henry Crowden	9 Nov 1844	Nov 1849
Mrs Mary Ann Crowden	9 Nov 1844	Nov 1849

Garrison and families	Arrived	Departed
Pte Mark Curthoys	9 Nov 1844	Died June 1845
Pte William Easy	9 Nov 1844	Nov 1849
Pte Robert Eyre	9 Nov 1844	Nov 1849
Pte James French	9 Nov 1844	Died Feb 1849
Pte Henry Gillett	9 Nov 1844	Oct 1847
Pte Thomas Hammond	9 Nov 1844	Died early 1849?
Pte George Haskell	9 Nov 1844	Died early 1849?
Pte Henry Heades	9 Nov 1844	Died Aug 1846
Pte John Holmes	9 Nov 1844	Nov 1849
Pte Thomas Hutchings	9 Nov 1844	Nov 1849
Pte Richard Jarvis	9 Nov 1844	Nov 1849
Pte George Jefferies	9 Nov 1844	Nov 1849
Pte David Kirk	9 Nov 1844	Nov 1849
Pte George Larner	9 Nov 1844	Died June 1845
Pte James Lee	9 Nov 1844	Died July 1844
Pte William Mansifield	9 Nov 1844	Nov 1849
Pte William Milstead	9 Nov 1844	June 1844
Pte John Nicholls	9 Nov 1844	Died May 1846
Pte William Norman	9 Nov 1844	Nov 1849
Mrs Esther Norman (died at sea)	9 Nov 1844	Died May 1844
John Norman (son)	9 Nov 1844	Nov 1849
Baby Norman	Born April 1844	Died April 1844
Pte Stephen Oborne	9 Nov 1844	Died March 1846
Pte Charles Pole	9 Nov 1844	Nov 1849
Pte Charles Rowe	9 Nov 1844	Nov 1849
Pte William Sargeant	9 Nov 1844	Nov 1849
Pte Robert Skuse	9 Nov 1844	Nov 1849
Pte Charles Swan	9 Nov 1844	Died March 1845
Pte Thomas Tapley	9 Nov 1844	Nov 1849

Appendices

Garrison and families	Arrived	Departed
Pte James Taylor	9 Nov 1844	Died early 1849?
Pte John Thomas	9 Nov 1844	Nov 1849
Pte Joseph A. Thorpe	9 Nov 1844	Died June 1845
Pte William Webb	9 Nov 1844	Nov 1849
Pte James Wescott	9 Nov 1844	Died early 1849?
Pte Henry Whitford	9 Nov 1844	Nov 1849
Pte William Wilson	9 Nov 1844	Nov 1849
Pte John Wiltin	9 Nov 1844	Nov 1849
Pte Thomas Wood	9 Nov 1844	Died early 1849?
HMS *Freak*		
Lt George Sheddan Dunbar	Oct 1847	Nov 1849
Surgeon John Irwin Crawford	Oct 1847	Nov 1849
Pte John Davies	Oct 1847	Nov 1849
Pte James Tossell	Oct 1847	Nov 1849
Mrs Martha Tossell	Oct 1847	Nov 1849
Pte James Wright	Oct 1847	Nov 1848
Pte Thomas Sampson	Oct 1847	Nov 1848
Unnamed private	Oct 1847	Presumed died
Unnamed corporal	Oct 1847	Presumed died

1.2: List 2: Prisoners of the Crown loaned to the settlement, Nov 1844–Feb 1845*

These men were aboard the survey ships, as stonemasons, to build a 13-metre stone beacon on Raine Island, which marked the entrance to a passage through the Barrier Reef. Skilled men like these were not already present in Victoria, so McArthur borrowed them for a few months to build the stone-walled kitchen and ovens of the hospital (Powell, 2016). It still stands today, (albeit with some renovation in 1968).

Ex HMS *Bramble*

- Daniel Maude
- Richard Payne
- Will Redpath
- Patrick Russell
- John Sullivan
- Will Weston
- Zacharias Williams

Ex HMS *Fly*

- Will Brown
- John Fox
- Robert Hastings
- Michael McDonald
- James Monaghan
- John Moore
- John Percival
- Thomas Picken
- George Rolling
- Charles Shepperd
- Henry Stockwell
- George Whitehurst

---

* Source (Spillett, 1972).

1.3: List 3: Others who died at the settlement who were not part of the garrison*

Peter Dermoudy's team discovered 54 graves in the Victoria Cemetery in 2010 (Dermoudy, 2020) using ground penetrating radar. Names are gathered from previously published lists (Spillett, 1972) and the Port Essington journals and dispatches, but the list is probably not complete. Note that Spillett counted 43 deaths, but at least 11 more graves are in the cemetery, unmarked and unnamed. Some of them were probably not of the garrison.

Transport			Cause of death
HMS *Britomart*	Pte Henry Dance	10 Nov 1838	Consumption
HMS *Pelorus*	Gunner John Kelly	25 Nov 1839	Cyclone
HMS *Pelorus*	Armourer John Bond	25 Nov 1839	Cyclone
HMS *Pelorus*	Able Seamen John Taylor	25 Nov 1839	Cyclone
HMS *Pelorus*	Ship's Boy David Bayliss	25 Nov 1839	Cyclone
HMS *Pelorus*	Pte John Kennedy	25 Nov 1839	Cyclone

---

* Sources (Spillett, 1972) (Keppel, 1853) (Powell, 2016) (Cameron, 1999) (Campbell, 1916).

Transport			Cause of death
HMS *Pelorus*	Pte Patrick Davis	25 Nov 1839	Cyclone
HMS *Pelorus*	Pte John Handcock	25 Nov 1839	Cyclone
HMS *Pelorus*	James Meldrum	10 June 1840	Fever
HMS *Chameleon*	Thomas Hogg	June 1843	Fever
HMS *Chameleon*	Henry Foyle	July 1843	Fever
HMS *Royalist*	Lt Phillip Chetwode	15 Sept 1843	Fever
HMS *Royalist*	Pte Mick Reardon	July–Aug 1843	Fever
HMS *Royalist*	Pte Leon Marcutt	July–Aug 1843	Fever
HMS *Royalist*	Pte James Deveraux	July–Aug 1843	Fever
HMS *Meander*	Surgeon John Clarke	Nov 1849	Fever?
HMS *Meander*	Able Seaman James Bartlett	Nov 1849	Fever?

Appendix 2

Letter: Sir George Gipps to Lord Glenelg, 1838

(Despatch No. 147, per ship *Marinus*; acknowledged by Marquess of Normandy, 26th February 1839).
Government House, 22nd Sept. 1838.

My Lord,

I have the honor to report to Your Lordship that the Departure of Expedition under Captn. Sir J. Gordon Bremer of the Royal Navy sailed from this harbour for Port Essington on the 18th instt. The Expedition consisted of Her Majesty's Vessels of War, Vessels 'Alligator' and 'Britomart', accompanied by the '*Orontes*', a Barque of about 400 Tons, which had been taken up here at the moderate freight of 14s. 11d. per ton per month to convey a portion of the Stores required for the intended settlement.

Six houses framed in wood and weather boarded have been shipped, as well as numerous other stores, obtained either from Her Majesty's Magazines or by purchase at this place; and I have the satisfaction to report to your Lordship that the Expedition has started as well equipped for the object it has in view, as could possibly be desired; at the same time, it is only justice to add that in my opinion no unnecessary or useless articles have been taken, or any expense incurred by Sir Gordon Bremer that could reasonably have been avoided.

I am greatly gratified in having to inform your Lordship that a very neat Church, framed in wood and weatherboarded, was presented to the persons engaged on this interesting expedition previously to their sailing by the Lord Bishop of Australia, on the part of the Diocesan Committee in Sydney of the Societies for Promoting Christian Knowledge and the

Propagation of the Church provided for new settlement. This Church, capable of holding 300 persons, is very neatly executed, and will be, I trust, considered an object of great interest in the Settlement, not only on account of the purpose to which it is dedicated, but from the manner in which it was acquired. The cost of it is, I understand, upwards of £300.

In consequence of this large addition to their equipment, it was found that the accommodation afforded by the three vessels I have already named was insufficient for the whole of the Stores, and it became necessary to put a portion of them into a schooner, which has been fitted out in this harbour by Mr. Watson, a Sydney Pilot, for the purpose of being the first to open the trade between Port Essington and this place.

This schooner, which has been named the 'Essington', sailed a few days before the rest of the Expedition, and will visit Murray's Island at the entrance of Torres Straits, where (as I reported to your Lordship in my Despatch of the 25th Augt. last, No. 131) the Master of her will endeavour to ascertain whether any persons from the wreck of the 'American Transport' are yet in existence. The schooner 'Essington' is not engaged as a part of the Expedition, but Mr. Watson, her Master, is to be paid £150 for the freight of the Stores which he has taken on board.

The supplies for the Expedition have all been obtained through the Ordnance or Commissariat Departments in the way that is usual at foreign stations, so that the whole responsibility for the agreements under which, and for the prices at which they have been furnished, rests upon the officers of these Departments; but payment has been made by Bills drawn on the Military Chest (under my authority) by Sir Gordon Bremer, and the Vouchers are to be transmitted direct by the Deputy Commissary General, Mr. Miller, to the Accountant General of the Navy. I enclose for your Lordship's information an abstract of the whole expense which has been incurred, exclusive however of the value of the articles which have been supplied from the Ordnance or Commissariat Stores without purchase.

Sir Gordon Bremer arrived in Port Jackson on the 23rd

July last; his stay therefore with us has been of eight weeks' duration. Agreeably to the directions contained in Your Lordship's Despatch No. 66 of the 25th Jany. last, I have issued to Sir Gordon Bremer a Commission in the name of the Queen, and under the Great Seal of this Colony, constituting him Commandant of the Settlement.

I have also given to Sir Gordon Bremer, and the undermentioned Officers of the Expedition, powers to act as Magistrates of this Territory, and also as Commissioners of Crown Lands, under 228 s38 of the Local Act of the Governor and Council of New South Wales …

The officers are: Lieutt. Stanley, R.N., Commanding the '*Britomart*'; of crown lands Lieutt. Kuper, R.N., 1st Lieutt. of the '*Alligator*'; Captn. McArthur, Royal Marines; Lieutt. Priest, Royal Marines.

I cannot, My Lord, close this Despatch without congratulating your Lordship on the prospects which are opened, not only to this Colony but to the British Merchants in general, by the Establishment of this Settlement on the Northern Coast of Australia.

I have, &c, GEO. GIPPS. (Glenelg, 22 Sept 1838).

Appendix 3

Log of the *Essington*: first of the fleet to arrive in Port Essington

Oct'r 13th Lat 10°-52 S Long 132-57 E Ch Daylight steady trade wind with fine clear weather. land made from the Masthead bearing S. At 10 AM hauled up to S.S.W. At noon New Grass[?] Island bore E.S.E Cape Croker WSW. Bore away under all sail to round Croker Island. (There is a long reef extending from this island in a NE direction 7 or 8 Miles, upon which HM Brig *Brittomart* [sic], struck on her passage to Port Essington).

Inside this reef there is a good passage. At 3 PM saw a Canoe to the Southward with 4 Natives rounded to and they came along side. We wished to know if there were any Vessels at Port Essington, but we could not make them understand us, they gave us some of their spears and Baskets without requiring anything in return, but we made them a present of some Knives. Bore away and at sunset came to off a small Island name unknown 6- or 7-Miles E of Port Essington, in 7 Fathom water dist 2 Miles.

Oct'r 13th At daylight weighed anchor and bore away for Port Essington, at 9 A.M. found the Long. by Chronometer to be 132°-10-30 E. Point Smyth bearing ESE dist 2 Miles. Saw several large Water Snakes, bearing a strong resemblance to the Diamond Snake. At 11h 30m AM brought up in 5 Fathom Water, on the Westside of the Harbour between Curlew Point and Oyster Head, and to our disappointment found ourselves the sole Master of the Harbour not even a Native to be seen. After dinner we took one of the boats down the bay at the entrance of which we were Anchored to explore for fresh water, in the excursion we met with several salt water Creeks or small rivulets, one of which was laid down in the Chart, up this one we proceeded in the hope that somewhere upon its bank we should meet with what we were in search of; we found, however, that it was through its whole course thickly overgrown with Mangroves and underwood so much so as to prevent a passage into the interior of the Country. We observed great numbers of tropical Birds, of various kinds amongst others were Black and Coloured Cockatoo's, Pigeons, Wild Ducks, and also two large Pelicans at which I fired; of quadrupeds the only one that we saw was the Kangaroo. As it was getting late, we returned on board, not having found any fresh water. We found that the other boat which had been out on a fishing excursion had returned equally unsuccessful.

Oct'r 14th We are anxiously looking out for the arrival of the *Alligator* and *Brittomart* [sic] to form the New Settlement since we cannot discharge the Church we have on board until their arrival, gave the crew liberty to go on shore, and also allowed each man to take his Musket with him. After dinner I went on shore and walked about two miles inland, saw many traces of the Natives, Viz quantities of the Shells of fishes upon which they had fed, and also the remains of Baskets [etc] but saw not a single native. Large droves of Kangaroo's were to be seen running in all directions, but not sufficiently near to be shot at. The Country round about Port Essington partakes of very little variety the highest elevation scarcely being perceptible; throughout its whole extent it appears to be thickly crowded with trees but owing to the destructiveness of the innumerable insects found here, the timber is of little value. The soil appears to be a thick black lume, [loam] and might most probably be made to produce anything which has hitherto been found in a tropical climate, in most places it is well clothed with fine grass of luxuriant growth. In the Evening returned on board found that the men had discovered a small lagoon of fresh Water.

Oct'r 15th Employed variously about the rigging repairing sails [etc] Struck our Main Top Mast. In the afternoon sent one boats Crew out fishing, and also to kill Kangaroo's.

Oct'r 16th No appearance of the *Alligator*, People

employed in the rigging [etc] as yesterday, In my rambles on Shore I found amongst other trees which are indigenous a species of Nutmeg; indeed I question whether it is not the real Nutmeg (*Myristica moschata*) its odour and flavour are the same, but it is somewhat less in size. The Mace produced by this fruit is quite equal to any I ever saw, and I have no doubt, will become an article of great value to the Colony. I also saw a kind of wild vine, which produces a very palatable fruit of the vegetables kind, the only productions I found were the Wild Cucumber, and a root very much resembling Yam or Coco.

Oct'r 17th The lagoon of fresh water discovered by the people being too far in the bush, this morning we again commenced our search, After wandering some time we found a place which we thought would afford water, and we accordingly dug a well; this was on Spear Point, just round Oyster Head.

Oct'r 18th At daylight a watering party went on shore and filled two casks at the well we had dug yesterday. At 3 PM weighed Anchor and rounded Oyster Head, to be nearer the watering place; came to off Spear Point in 4 Fathoms Water. People employed in the rigging [etc] We have seen several large Alligators since we came into the Harbour, and today I followed the track of one for a considerable distance into the bush; in following this track I fell in with great numbers of land Crabs, and also several large Snakes.

Oct'r 19th We are still anxiously expecting the arrival of the *Alligator*. At daylight, a Party went on shore to get Wood and Water, they dug another hole near the former, brought off two Casks of Water, and a boat load of Wood. People employed dismantling the Foremast [etc] We have not yet fallen in with a single Native since our arrival, which has rather surprised me, since any of the Points round the Harbour afford in abundance all the requisites for their subsistence, Water is plentifully produced as we proved, and the Harbour abound in fish of all sorts, both shell fish and others, it is also very probable that the soil produces many eatable Vegetables [sic], which we have not discovered and I should therefore say that any of the points is admirably calculated for a Native Settlement.

Oct'r 20th The Watering party on Shore filling Casks, and procuring Wood, The People on board refitting rigging [etc] as per days past.

Oct'r 21 Gave permission to the Crew to go on Shore with their Muskets, in the evening they returned having killed only a few Birds, The *Alligator* not yet arrived.

Oct'r 22 Having now waited a considerable time for the arrival of the *Alligator*, and being anxious to lay my Vessel on Shore in order to examine her bottom, towed over to Point Record on the East side of the Harbour, and prepared to land the Materials for the Church. Another reason for choosing Point Record was that we might have a more plentiful supply of Water.

Oct'r 23 People employed landing Materials for the Church. Watering party on Shore filling Casks.

Oct'r 24 At 6 AM hauled the Schooner on Shore, and at 12 N being low water the Carpenter surveyed her bottom as far as he could, the water not entirely leaving it, Patched a little about the Stern, which the Chain had rubbed, being the only repair wanted as far as I can see at present. At high water, this afternoon got the Schooner afloat again, this morning we observed a Canoe push off from Middle Point with three natives, they landed about ½ Mile from us, and then walked along the beach to where our people were employed. Each of them carried a Spear, they also had with them some small pieces of Tortoise Shell, which I purchased off them after having been with them some time on Shore I got them to pull me in their Canoe to the Vessel, where after remaining some time, and partaking of something to Eat [etc] they again embarked for Middle Point [later known as 'Middle Head].

Oct'r 25th Not being satisfied as to the state of the Vessel's bottom from the examination made the other day, I determined again to lay her on the Shore; and for this purpose, we have been occupied in lightening her by breaking out her hold.

Oct'r 26th The *Alligator* has not yet arrived, still employed preparing to lay the Schooner on Shore, filling Water [etc]

Oct'r 27th This morning hauled her ashore to ascertain if possible what damage was done to her bottom, by running on the Reef in Torres Straits. At low water we discovered that there was a considerable portion of copper off her stern post, this appeared to have been off for a long time; and the tide not ebbing sufficiently to enable the carpenter to make his repairs, we were obliged to abandon the project. Making about the same water as when we left Sydney. I find since I left Sydney that the Schooner which was originally called the '*Isabella*'. had been aground previous to being purchased by myself and others, but of this circumstance we were not informed, and she was therefore sent out on her present trip without undergoing any repairs, I have no doubt that the principle damage to her keel was sustained whilst she was the '*Isabella*' and prior to our purchase. At 2h-30m P.M. we discovered a ship at a distance in the offing which supposed to be the long looked for '*Alligator*' and shortly after a second ship was seen. Made them out to be the '*Alligator*' and the '*Orontes*', Merchantman, with stores for the settlement, Lowered a boat and went on board the 'Alligator', found she had left Sydney on Sept'r 17th Ult. Reported to Sir Gordon Bremer the whole of my proceedings at the different Islands in Torres Straits, when in quest of the supposed survivors of the '*Charles Eaton*'; and was gratified to find that my whole conduct had met his unqualified approbation, Our men having complained several times on the passage, about their provisions, but more particularly today, I am induced to take notice of it, and more especially since their allowance has been much more liberal than they had any right to expect, The allowance has been since we left Port Jackson: Beef 1½ lbs with a fair proportion of Flour, and Pork 1 lb with Pease Soup on alternate days, besides this they have had Tea and Sugar Night and Morning and other small stores not stipulated in the Articles.

Oct'r 28th Sunday—Gave the men permission to go on shore with leave to take their Muskets.

Oct'r 29 & 30th Employed filling up our water, stowing it, and otherwise as most necessary. Weather very hot. The Natives have increased in numbers since the Ships arrived, they resemble the New Hollanders on other parts of the Continent, both in their average size and form, they wear no covering whatever, saw none of the females.

Oct'r 31st Finished taking in Water, went on board the *'Alligator'* to make arrangements for supplying the settlement with Cattle. It was also arranged that Mr Earl should accompany me to the various Islands at which I propose to trade, that Gentleman being able to speak the languages of those parts, at 5 PM returned on board the Schooner, accompanied by Mr Earl found men intoxicated by spirits given to them on board the *'Orontes'*. At midnight light Airs and variable. Weighed Anchor and made sail.

Nov'r 1st At daylight saw a Brig rounding Point Smyth, supposed it to be the 'Brittomart', hoisted our colors, on approaching we found our supposition to be correct, and noticed that she had a large launch towing astern for the use of the New Settlement at Port Essington. At about 10h-30m A.M. cleared the heads and bore away WNW. The second officer went off duty today—through an attack of illness.

Nov'r 2nd Lat 10°-19 S Long 131°-29 E Ch Light Airs with fine clear Weather. Heading to the W saw numbers of Snakes, and various kinds of fish.

Appendix 4

Journal of the French Explorer Captain d'Urville

On 5 April 1840, the French explorer, Captain Jules Sébastien César Dumont d'Urville, and his two corvettes, *d'Astrolabe* and *Zélée*, visited Victoria just five months after its establishment. The officers were taken on a grand tour of the settlement.

The expedition included the marine artist, Louis Le Breton, who spent a few days painting watercolours of the settlement, some of which are included as images in this book. A section of d'Urville's journal follows, as it is a useful outsider's perspective on the new settlement. Note that d'Urville's visit fell during the last weeks of Captain Bremer's residence in Port Essington and he doesn't mention Captain McArthur at all (d'Urville, 1839).

> Wishing to take advantage of the cool of the morning to tour the new settlement, I set out at six A.M. in the whaler. An hour later I came alongside an attractive jetty about six metres long, built with care and solidity and furnished with ladders to help getting up. A flag pole stuck up on the end of the jetty and from it there waves the flag of Great Britain. An English officer M. Stewart, whom we already knew, was waiting to receive us, and he obligingly offered to lead us to the governor's house.
>
> Victoria Town is situated on a flat piece of ground about ten to twelve metres above sea level. A wide road with a very gentle slope had been cut in the cliff beside the beach and runs down to the jetty; we followed it. We soon met Commodore Bremer, who, already informed of our arrival, was coming out to receive us. He is a man about fifty-five

years old; his expression is pleasant and kindly, and his manner civil and engaging. He received us with perfect cordiality and politeness, and we were made to feel as if we were meeting old friends. He led us first to his dwelling; it is placed on the highest point of the plateau and the view extends over the whole roadstead, in the middle of which the vessel, the Alligator, lay at anchor. This pleasant situation allowed quick and easy communication between the governor and his vessel. Commodore Bremer, without leaving his house, was able to watch the movements in the harbour and at the same time the work going on shore. The house, completely built of wood, had been made up at Port Jackson, and had every comfort that could be desired. All the rooms were arranged with good sense; drawing room, bedroom, study, washroom, bathroom, office; nothing was lacking.

We had hardly arrived there when the sun began to rise quickly above the horizon, and we hurried to set out on a tour of the settlement. M. Bremer wished to be our guide, and he led us first to the fort placed on the end of a small promontory about thirty metres from his house and about fifteen metres above sea level. It consisted of a single battery placed on top of the cliff overlooking the roadstead. It was built of strong, wooden planks and a few ship's timbers from the wreck of the '*Orontes*'. The battery is in the shape of a semi-octagon and is pierced by four openings, of which three had cannon. This little fortification was completely open on the landwards side but covered the jetty and roadstead that it was meant to defend against foreign invasion.

As for the natives, the English seemed to worry very little about them. In the six months since they had set up their tents on the shore, the inhabitants had shown only the most peaceful intentions. Normally they roamed around the settlement observing the work without taking any part in it. However, a few days before our arrival, a quarrel had broken out between these savages and the Malay fishermen who had come to collect trepang in the bay. The two camps had come to blows and one man had been killed. Since then, the natives, worried by the consequences of the quarrel, had vanished into the interior and the English did not expect to see them again until the end of the trepanging season. Until then, more

Malay praus might arrive in the harbour at any time. A camp of Bugis fishermen had been set up at the bottom of Port Essington. Like those who had come to visit us in Raffles Bay, they collected the trepang as quickly as possible in order to continue on their way and get back to Macassar.

The little fort we were inspecting was only a temporary structure, sufficient until the time when the colony had developed further and could build a citadel capable of defending it. In fact, however, this construction was not without a certain solidity; though it is unlikely that it would ever be of any great use. One would need a strange situation indeed before any power could think of coming to attack a settlement whose success was still so much in doubt, and long before this tiny colony had grown large enough to inspire any apprehensions, these few cannon could have been replaced by more respectable fortifications.

We left the fort to tour the flat area selected as the site for the town. Raised up above the level of the sea, the air renewed itself easily enough to make one hope that perfect health could be enjoyed there. We visited the hospital where there were only four patients, three had been wounded and the other was homesick. It was a wooden building raised on piles about a metre from the ground and taking the shape of a rectangle. It was capable of holding eight or ten beds. We then visited some of the houses of the soldiers of the permanent garrison. These men, thirty-seven of them, commanded by a captain and a lieutenant, had built their own dwellings. All these houses were tastefully constructed, and everything was arranged with the greatest neatness. In front of each house was a small square of fenced and cultivated ground. Four soldiers' wives had followed their husbands to these distant parts: the couple lived in small cottages which they had built. The unmarried soldiers had been mostly paired off to build the dwellings which then provided their shelter. Each of these men kept their weapons beside them; at the least signal he could rush to defend his home against any rash attack on the part of the natives. During the day, the men busied themselves with the general work of the settlement and with the cultivation of their own gardens. The barracks and buildings meant to house the military officers had not yet been completed and the men were hard at work on them.

Like the soldiers, each of the officers had built a small temporary house; certainly, one of the most attractive was that of the young M. Bremer, a young man of intelligence and vigour [Captain Bremer's son, Edward].

Finally, we went to pay a visit to M. Priest, the lieutenant of the marines. As we approached, this officer was busy tidying up the small cottage he had built for himself. M. Priest spends all his leisure in the study of natural history; in the course of his residence at Port Essington he has already collected a large number of specimens which were of great scientific value on account of their rarity and in some cases were new altogether. He did us the honours of his house with the utmost courtesy and was eager to show us his little museum which already possessed a large number of objects ...

Leaving M. Priest, we went to make a visit to the Malay camp; we arrived just as the fishermen were preparing to weigh anchor and came back by way of the livestock yards. About twenty buffaloes, a few goats, a few sheep, and several draught horses were to be seen there. The English had brought with them a great number of fowls, but after a few days these had all taken into the bush where one still came across some of them in their wild state. The settlers were so afraid of their livestock escaping in the same fashion, that they never allowed them out of the yards where they were kept. Every day the animals were brought the grass necessary to feed them, but they were never permitted to graze freely.

This part of Australia is the home for a host of snakes; one comes across great numbers of a type of boa; the English have often seen them slithering around their houses and M. Priest had killed an enormous one at the door of his hut a few days before our arrival. The presence of these dangerous reptiles which fill the English with fear for the preservation of their herds, is another reason compelling them to keep a very close watch, particularly around the livestock paddocks.

We still had to visit the governor's garden where the colony's attempt at agriculture was to be found. M. Armstrong, the botanist attached to the settlement, did the honours. It is large and well cultivated; among numerous plantations of the most useful plants M. Armstrong particularly drew our attention to several coconut palms to which he attached the greatest value. It is indeed the staple food tree of the tropics; Australia is completely without it, whereas the neighbouring lands are so rich in it; we also noticed banana plants, areca nut trees, etc; in short, all the plants which grow so quickly in the torrid zone. I went away expressing my sincere good wishes for the success of these useful undertakings on which the fate of the colony so much depended. But I confess that I did not entirely share the hopes of M. Armstrong, who seemed to see already in the appearance of his garden the realization of that wonderful vision of making fertile this great land which appeared so dry and lacking in production.

One of the greatest scourges that the English have to contend with is the continued invasion of their gardens, and even of their houses, by the ants. In a short space of time, these destructive mites have turned over the soil and consumed all the seeds entrusted to it. The largest trees cannot escape their unceasing activity; they are pierced in a thousand different places, their growth checked and their maimed trunks often lacking soundness, rendered useless for shipbuilding.

The shores of Port Essington, just like those of Raffles Bay, offer no easy watering place. Nowhere does one even come across a stream where the traveller could quench his thirst. This complete absence of water, which is so essential for agriculture, particularly in the torrid zone, will always be a check on extensive plantations. It is true that there are some marshes near the settlement in which the English hope to grow rice, but it still has to be discovered whether the water, always a little brackish in these swamps, will not rather be an obstacle to the cultivation of this plant. It is only at considerable depth that one comes on sweet water. Five wells more than 10 metres deep have been dug by the English; four are completely finished and plastered inside; they supply plenty of good quality water and provide for all the needs of the colony. Victoria is already quite able to supply fresh water to ships that put in there.

We had come to the end of our tour and we had visited

all parts of the settlement. Beside the sea at the bottom of the cliff we also saw the carpenter's and blacksmith's workshops, which seemed to be in full operation. Two hundred men directed by a leader who knew how to win their confidence by being as efficient an administrator as he was a good officer, had completed all these undertakings in the space of six months; when we returned to his house where he led us to sit down, I could compliment Commodore Bremer without reserve on the happy outcome of his perseverance and excellent administration. The remainder of the day passed quickly listening to the lively and interesting conversation of this excellent officer. I was full of admiration for this white-haired gentleman who had left his country and his family to come to this unpromising spot and undertake a laborious and difficult task. He appeared happy in the midst of the little colony of which he was both founder and father; one thought alone seemed to concern him above all others, to see Victoria prosper, and although we could not entirely concur in the vision of the future that he held for his settlement, none of us had the courage to try and destroy his illusions with which this happy father seemed to surround the cradle of his child.

At four o'clock the officers of the two corvettes and most of the English officers repaired to the governor's house where we sat down for dinner. Nothing was spared to make it a magnificent spread and the most unrestrained merriness was in evidence. The young M. Bremer showed us the rich collection of objects of native art which he had already been able to amass. This young officer who has a wonderful talent for imitation, showed us how each thing was used. The most deadly weapons of the Australians are a type of spear made of very light wood which they throw with the aid of a piece of wood about a metre long, one end of which is held in the hand while the spear lies on the other. Young M. Bremer had become very proficient in the use of this weapon and wished to give us a display of his skill. Then taking a long flute of the natives, pierced with a hole into which they blow with the nose, he undertook to perform all the ludicrous dances of the savages to the accompaniment of the noise of this instrument. This performance was highly amusing, and all heartily applauded the actor's talent. Eventually night came on suddenly and it was unhappily necessary to take our leave of the others, who promised to come and see us again next morning on board the *d'Astrolabe* (d'Urville, 1839).

Appendix 5
Reports, an Advertisement, and the McArthurs' Diary

5.1: Sir J. Everard Home's report on the Victoria Settlement: 1843

... It stands upon a rising ground on the west side of the harbour, elevated about 50 feet in the highest part, above high water mark, the soil being a conglomerate of red stone and sand, which, from its dryness, evidently conduces to the heat thereof for which it is remarkable.

The extent between the northward most building, which is the hospital, and the Government House which stands southward of it, is 590 paces, and from the water's edge to the west 570 paces. The settlement called 'Victoria' stands upon partially cleared ground, and consists of the Government House, which is built of wood and has a shingle roof; the hospital which is a building of the same description, with a kitchen behind built of stone but unfinished; there is a mess room, to which is added the quarters of the second officers. There is another building also of a similar description, the upper part of which forms the quarters of the store keeper and linguist, the lower part of which is the spirit room. There are three good storehouses, one of which is the ordnance store, the foundation being of brickwork, the sides of wood; the roofs of all these buildings are shingles. There is another store house or building used as such, having a thatched roof which is supported by wooden posts, the sides are formed of the same material as the roof. There is a house also made of wood and thatched with reeds, formally occupied by Captain Stanley, and used by him as an observatory. There are also the ruins of a church which was built of wood. It was blown down by the hurricane and had never since been repaired. The rest of the buildings are small huts, formed for the most part of reeds—29 in number; the greater number of these are occupied by the marines; gardens are attached to each of them which are productive and very well kept. These huts form a square, in the centre of which is a well.

At a distance of about half a mile southward from the square, there are two gardens, one near the beach, the soil of which is sandy and in the wet season saturated with moisture; the other stands more to the west on higher ground, and it is a better soil. They are about an acre and a half in extent each and are extremely well kept by three of the marines. The contents of the two gardens ... [include]: The pineapples (part of one I have tasted) are esteemed the best, and are improved as is the cotton, by being transplanted hither. The lemons are of thick skin, and without juice. The orange trees are evidently from a state of nature, and the guavas are not of a good kind, but all appear to grow in the most luxuriant manner and appear in the highest health. Bamboo for every purpose, sago for feeding pigs, guinea grass for the cattle should be procured and cultivated, but I think it highly advisable that another piece of ground should be cleared, to be cultivated as an Arboretum, or orchard, so that the trees may be by themselves, and the herbaceous plants in a garden by themselves, for as they stand at present, they will very shortly be crowded.

Of the breed of stock, cultivation of the land, and amount of produce, nothing can be said, for no land is cultivated, excepting the public and private gardens, the produce from which it appears is sufficient to keep the marines' health with the fish they procure, during the time that fresh meat is not served out, and they have nothing to spare. Of stock, there is one English cow and a bull; two Indian cows, and two heifers, about fifty goats, and a few fowls, of which one cow and several of the goats are the property of Sir Gordon Bremer. Another cow and the bulls, with the heifers, are the property of Government. There are, besides, six working oxen, thirty buffaloes, and six pigs, the property of the Government. Five ponies and twenty greyhounds for catching kangaroos complete the account of livestock. These last are private property ... (Home, 19 April 1843).

5.2: McArthur's Report on the Buildings, 18 October 1847

HAMILTON TO UNDER SECRETARY MERIVALE.

Sir, Admiralty, 18th March 1848.

I am commanded by My Lords Commissioners of the Admiralty to transmit to you, for the information of Earl Grey, a copy of a communication which has been received from Captain John McArthur, Commandant at Victoria, N. Australia, relative to the state of the Public Building at that place.

I have, &c, W. A. B. HAMILTON.

[Sub-enclosure.]

CAPTAIN MCARTHUR TO -----------

Sir,

Victoria, North Australia, 16th October 1847.

In reply to your letter of the 6th February, 1847, I beg to state that, from long detention of Mails and consequent accumulation of letters producing considerable pressure of business during the short visit of a vessel, I have not been able to execute their Lordships' order as communicated by you in a manner satisfactory to myself, but the general correctness of my statements I can vouch for.

The Buildings may be classed thus:

First, those which were framed, and all the materials prepared at Sydney, shipped, and brought on in Freight Ships with the expedition to this Port.

Secondly. Those which have been erected with materials on the spot.

Of the first, there were six in number, besides the Church; Government House being larger than the other five. In the map, they are distinguished by the letters,

The British in North Australia: Port Essington

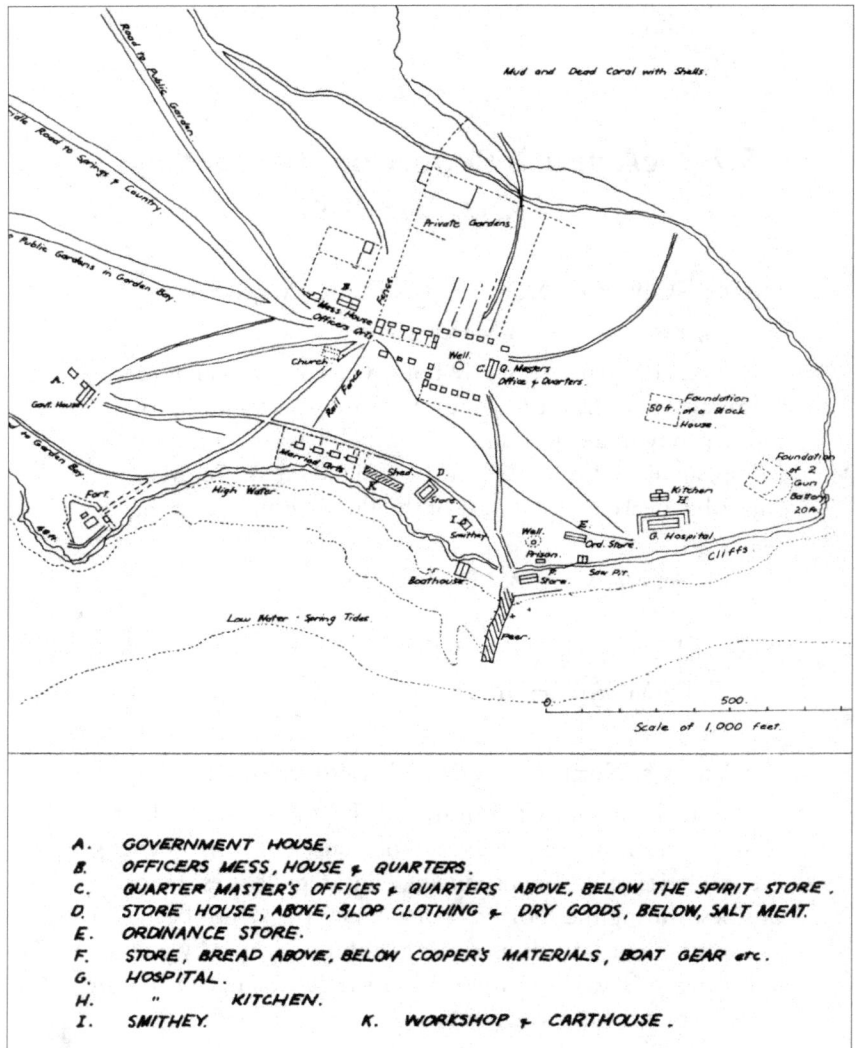

A. GOVERNMENT HOUSE.
B. OFFICERS MESS, HOUSE & QUARTERS.
C. QUARTER MASTER'S OFFICES & QUARTERS ABOVE, BELOW THE SPIRIT STORE.
D. STORE HOUSE, ABOVE, SLOP CLOTHING & DRY GOODS, BELOW, SALT MEAT.
E. ORDINANCE STORE.
F. STORE, BREAD ABOVE, BELOW COOPER'S MATERIALS, BOAT GEAR etc.
G. HOSPITAL.
H. "   KITCHEN.
I. SMITHEY.   K. WORKSHOP & CARTHOUSE.

Map 9: McArthur's map of 1847 as he labelled it (Spillett, 1972).

A. Government House:

B. Officers' Mess House and Quarters.

C. Quarter Master's Offices and Quarters above, below the Spirit Store.

D. Store House, above Slop clothing and dry goods, below Salt Meat.

E. Ordnance Store.

F. Store, bread above, below Cooper's Materials, Boat Gear, etc.

G. The Hospital sent from Sydney complete in 1840. This is a fine Building. I regret I cannot possibly complete an elevation of it.

The Church was opposite the Officers' Mess House, a good building, but unfortunately was blown down in the Hurricane. The Wreck of it has now been nearly all worked into the other Buildings as they have required repairs.

The Buildings, marked A and E, stand on dwarf pillars of Stone and Wood about two feet from the ground or more.

Those marked B and F, the former on piles 8 feet high forming a complete under store and the latter on similar piles but not enclosed.

Those, marked C and D, were originally also built upon piles of eight feet, but in time C was completed in solid masonry and formed an admirable Spirit Store, whilst D was completed with Bricks in a substantial manner. The dotted lines in the elevation denote the brick work.

This temporary method of piling in order to raise the buildings has proved very useful. Had they been fixed on the ground in the usual manner, they must have been destroyed long since by vermin. Then the capacity of every house so raised was doubled.

As to their present condition, I regret to say that the Store 0, standing on Masonry, will need extensive repairs before the rains set in; the Stone Walls harbour the white ant, and we have long since been obliged to move the coping and clear the Masonry of the Wood work so as to intercept these invaders. Lt. Lambrick has always succeeded in extirpating them, but they first effect much mischief; the framing and roof have been undergoing frequent repairs. None of the buildings have suffered like this from the same cause, but all without exception are now beginning to decay; the shingle covering readily saturates when the rain falls, and thus Water is constantly deposited on the rafters. E upon the beach has suffered less than any other; the Ant cannot reach it.

The second Class of Buildings are the Blockhouse, Smithy, Hospital Cook House and the general quarters and accommodation for the People, consisting of Messing houses and dormitories. The Map shows their positions.

The Blockhouse and Fort are particularly infested by the White Ant; having so much solidity in the construction, it is not possible to reach the destructive creature, and ultimately it must be destroyed by them; it requires a new roof now; the Magazine, constructed by solid Masonry and arched over, had been lined with thin plank, ventilated in the usual way, but we discovered that the whole of it had been destroyed, ere we suspected any evil.

The Hospital Kitchen stands well, Walls Masonry. The Smithy consists of a solid stone Chimney, strong framing of timber throughout and covered roof and walls with bark. I have taken some pains to make it complete, and it is a respectable workshop. This was finished about Eight Months ago, I think.

The Men's quarters comprise two kinds; the thatched roof with reeded walls and the entire bark covered. I prefer the first as being most cleanly; they will not last more than two or three years. We are just now actively employed about them. The long shed is covered with bark and includes Carpenters, Wheelwrights and Coopers' Workshops, Cart House and various Marine stores are lodged here. The whole of this Class of building will soon be in order.

All the buildings have been considered by me to be under my own charge, and I uniformly required of those, who had duties connected with them, immediately to report the appearance of the White Ant. Nothing can be done but to rip open every place where they are found, invariably at the angles, or else some of the principals. The lower plates are seriously damaged, but the upper parts are yet good though not sound.

I shall immediately commence and complete plans with details of scantling used in all the buildings and forward them by the first conveyance, as I must repeat, Sir, the present has been too hasty a performance.

I beg leave respectfully to assure their Lordships that I will not fail in my duty bestowing every care and attention upon the public property under my superintendence.

I have, &c,

JNO. McArthur, Captain Royal Marines,

Commandant (McArthur, 16 October 1847).

5.3: McArthur's Advertisement for Land: 1845

McArthur informed the Macassans about the forthcoming opportunity to lease land at Victoria in April 1845, and he also wanted Chinese and Malay farmers to take up the opportunity. He sent a public notice to Singapore on the *Fly* in June, offering 'Town Allotments' and 'Country Allotments', but he was underwhelmed by the response. When prospective tenants read the conditions, they tended to withdraw their interest:

> Her Majesty's Government have been pleased to authorise the Commandant at the settlement of Victoria on the coast of North Australia to encourage the immigration of a limited number of Chinese and Malays who may feel disposed to adventure there.
>
> They will be received on the following conditions.
>
> They must bring with them a sufficiency of rice and other food to sustain them until they can raise crops.
>
> The land will be let upon annual lease and is to be distinguished as being of two descriptions—Town allotments and Country allotments.
>
> Town allotments of one acre, or of half an acre are included within a section of land at present immediately under protection of the garrison, and will be let (excepting such portions as may and will be required for public works, roads &c hereafter to be determined upon), and may be occupied on an annual rental of from twenty to thirty shillings per acre, as shall be agreed upon, according to the conveniences enjoyed, such as harbour frontage and superior landing places; portions of an acre to pay at the same rate. According to dimensions.
>
> The country allotments will comprise all lands beyond the boundary of the town allotments, and will be occupied upon annual lease, and on extremely moderate terms.

If the position selected has no harbour frontage, no rent will be demanded for the first year of occupation; if the lease is renewed for a second year, then one shilling will be demanded per acre per annum for that year.

If the lease is renewed for a third year, then two shillings will be demanded per acre per annum for that year.

And after the third year of occupation, the rent shall remain fixed at three shillings per acre per annum for as many distinct yearly leases as the Commandant or Governor for the time being shall so annually determine, and the parties shall agree to.

When country allotments have a harbour frontage, rental shall be paid upon first occupation, at the same rate as above mentioned.

It must be understood that the settlers bring with them a sufficiency of provisions for six months' consumption, as no assistance can be promised with regard to provisions.

The only description of persons intended to be benefited by this encouragement are those who understand the modes of cultivating rice, cotton, sugar, and vegetables, and fruits generally, and, as the resources of this country are at present but limited, the Commandant will not receive more than fifty men, women and children collectively until experience shall prove that such a number can maintain themselves with every certainty of permanent benefit.

The coasts furnish an abundance of fine fish; turtles are taken in the harbour and are numerous in the vicinity of it.

A considerable number of prahus from Macassar visit Port Essington every year and return in the course of three or four months laden with trepang. The harbour itself supplies sufficient to load several of them.

By labor at home and traffic with the Islands, it is anticipated that articles of commerce can be immediately collected at Port Essington sufficient to support a trade that will maintain a few families and ultimately extend itself to more general benefit and encouragement.

There being a European garrison at Victoria must not lead those who may desire to settle here into any false and erroneous expectation of what may be derived from this source. Employment for the few attendants who are capable of cooking, serving in the house, and of washing linen, will be offered, provided good testimonials are produced from respectable authority.

It should be observed that no bamboo or cocoa-nut is yet to be procured on the spot, but for building purposes this defect is remedied by an abundance of timber and bark.

Dated at Victoria, 9th day of June 1845

Jno McArthur

Captain Royal Marines, Commandant.

P.S. No family consisting of more than two parents and two children will be received unless the children are of an age to be capable of doing some work sufficient for their maintenance.

5.4: The McArthurs' Notebook: Diary entries

A notebook was used both by Captain McArthur and his son John, during the years 1843 to 1849. On many of the pages are lists of accounts, wages and provisions from the stores, accounts payable by members of the community and hundreds of calculations (additions and subtractions) of currency. From the lists we can tell that McArthur enjoyed coffee and bought supplies of it regularly. We also know about the clothing he bought from his brother Hannibal, in Goulburn N.S.W. There are also about 80 sketches of ships, faces, and dogs etc, some of which are reproduced in this book, and 15 poems written by the McArthurs, all except one of which are reproduced in Appendix 7. What follows here are the complete diary entries made by one of the men, probably the younger John. They are valuable as they are the only diary notes we have from the McArthurs. They deal with a variety of subjects, including the cutter named *Gipsy*, with details of her sea trials and a week's excursion out of Port Essington to the Croker Island area. (McArthur & McArthur, 1849).

> [p63] April 10th the Sue sailed on the 13th. Rumpah brought me the boat for which I paid 12 rupees on the same day hired Salajah the Carpenter is employed at the cutter and the two Manila men digging a well—got from the store ten feet of rod from ¾ and 4/8—April 28th advanced salary two rupees to get himself some clothing—Have been able to get no pots for boiling yet—or anything else as the *Nokodas* will part with nothing till they sail. May 3rd—the last of the salt meat I had left issued today. Mr Selby and the Manila men busy making rope. The cutter sails are all finished. The well carried twenty-nine feet down—Went over the water this afternoon for the first time since Sue's sailing and I certainly was astonished at [p64] the work that has been done there these

last three weeks. The internal work of the cutter is finished, and the well is a credit to the men who have dug it. It is about four feet in diameter and twenty-nine deep, accomplished by two men in about three weeks with one mattock. There has been some disturbance between Stucky and Mr Selby, but I think I left them in better temper with one another—It will be some time yet before the cutter is ready. The work is very heavy for one man—May 3rd Advanced Salajah 1 ½ rupees to purchase a fishing line for himself. May 5th Mr Selby came over this afternoon and laid up about 60 yds of rope and informed me to my great disappointment that there was thirteen feet water in the well but all salt [p65]. The fact is they have gone too deep with it and the only chance of doing anything with it now is to empty the water out and fill it up again to above high-water mark level. The fresh water was in about thirteen feet down. May 6th All the meat being out and only about ten pounds bread left and no appearance of *Heroine* it is arranged that the people shall be victualled weekly by Mr Lambrick on those species at the same allowance as the detachment. Paid today sixty-five rupees for thirteen piculs rice / the Sue landed 11 bags, 9 of which are left very little more than 7 piculs / I must take care not to be short of this commodity.

[p66] Arranged with the Nakoda to have four pots at eight rupees each and also the house at eight rupees—got from the store one-gallon stock Yar [?] and three gallons coal.

May 7th supplied one case of soap between Mr Selby, Stuckey and English—May 8th Hired the Macassan lad Soowan at four dollars per month he is in debt forty rupees to his Nakodah Ramali to whom I have paid fifteen rupees in advance with a promissory note to pay him twenty five more on his return next year the whole to be deducted from Sooman's wages. I was in hopes of getting a third Macassar man but see no chance of it now.

May 9th Paid Hassan thirty-two rupees for the pots and eight for the house and two rupees [p67] for a picul of salt got from the store + 14 fathoms of 3 1/3 in rope and 30 pounds of pitch. The rope left for shrouds being useless—drew 26 ¼ pounds of salt pork from Mr Lambrick for the first time. The last prahu Hassam sailed this evening. May 16th drew from stores 26 ¼ lbs Pork & 25 lbs Bread and [blank] lbs old for making pintles and gudgeon for sudden meats [?] across the water this morning before breakfast. The carpenter has been sick all the week and done scarcely any thing.

May 10 went across this evening. Carpenter much better deck will be laid by tomorrow morning.

[p68] May 20th Mr Selby came over today drew from the store 18 lbs ¾ inch round [illegible] and 25 fathoms ¾ rope weighing 5¾ pounds and got four planks for upper works. They are now at work on the keel of the cutter.

May 23rd Purchased twenty-five pounds of four-inch rope from '*Enchantress*' at -/6 per lb for a forestay for the cutter. Recd from Lieut Lambrick one cask beef 304 lbs one cask pork lbs. Five bags Bread five hundred today lbs. Issued six pieces pork more [?] pieces beef twenty-four and a half lbs bread purchased from '*Enchantress*' five gallons vinegar at 3/-6 per gallon. May 26th got from the stores one hundred

[p69]and four pounds sheet lead six lbs sheeting nails. Three gallons coal tar and three gallons Stockholm with thirty pounds pitch. May 27th got from Mr Lambrick twenty-five and half pounds five-inch spike nails. May 30 issued four pieces beef and four pieces pork, twenty-four and a half pounds bread. June 3rd Bought from Mr Ray eighty pounds of sugar. Mr Selby and Stuckey have had some occasion for disagreement again about the cutter but situated where I am I can do nothing and it has ended with Mr Selby declining to remain over there as the carpenter positively refuses to obey any orders from him. I can do nothing more than refer the case to Mr Bissex when he comes.

June 6th Saturday [hence 1846] went over the water today and launched the cutter and called her the *Gipsy* about 12 o'clock, brought her over on this side and on Monday shall commence rigging her as all the spars are in hadings [?] having been made over here. June 10th bent sail, and in the afternoon got under weigh with the *Lizard* and *Young Heroine*. There was not sufficient wind to make anything of a trial, but the *Gipsy* will no doubt beat the *Lizard* anytime. Went over to the carpenter, he is getting on well with the small boat. Obliged to ground the *Gipsy* very very leaky.

June 14th Supplied to Mr Selby the case soap and three gallons wine. Supplied the *Gipsy* with five weeks provisions and the Carpenter and Daweor [?] with three commencing from yesterday in the evening sailed for Pt Smith on the way round Cape Don

[p74] Friday 26th Feby [1847] Started from the pier about 8 AM towed out past Minto Head. A very heavy squall of wind and rain about 9 P.M. reached out to and anchored at the triangles, much rain during the night. Saturday 27 got under weigh about 5.30 A.M. as we got out wind freshened to a smart gale with continued squalls of rain arrived at Don Angelo's about 11 A.M. obliged to let go two pigs of ballast to hold the boat the Don says it is the worst weather he has had this monsoon. Last night he expected his house to fall. I dined with him and as he said the worst weather was generally in the night and the boat had already driven considerably, I determined to get out of his place before dark and get anchorage on the weather shore.

Got under weigh to go across to Kennedy Bay a heavy squall came on after starting which caused a perfect calm and we were not able to reach out further than Turtle Point where we anchored very well sheltered.

Sunday 28th Good deal of rain in the night and this morning blowing as fresh as yesterday remained at anchor all day. The weather appears as if breaking up. Caught two fine Cavalho [sic] last night after anchoring—no rain during the day several very heavy squalls passed along to the W and S of M.

Monday March 1st A good deal of rain in the night got under weigh about 5.30 am with a breeze from W.N.W. a heavy swell but wind greatly abated, saw a schooner off Point Smith, ran back to Black Rock and waited until she came in, went up to the settlement with her 'Theresa'

[p87] *Gipsy* took 105 lbs bread being 16 pounds over her allowance. Spirits all out on the 1st Augt found 17 gallons of wine altogether in the cask some of which has been sold—the rest to be taken in lieu of spirits if required.

Aug 2 Sunday, Stuckey did not send the boat over this morning as directed by Mr Selby. He took over the carpenter of the *Bramble* with him last evening and when he came over this evening Stuckey was not sober. I found fault with him but seeing the state he was in refused to say anything more to him tonight. Immediately after leaving me he went on the pier and meeting Mr Selby began abusing him and struck him three times. Mr Selby returned to give him in charge in the meantime. Stuckey took the boat and went away. Tomorrow Mr Selby intends taking out a warrant for him.

Nov 2nd Had the carpenter to look at the *Gipsy*'s bottom and found it necessary to take out the greater part of the main keel which with some of the butt end has become perfectly rotten. Her keel appears to have been much damaged by white ants being nearly hollow throughout the centre.

[p90] Monday June 28th, 1847. Started from the settlement about noon with the Doctor in the *Lizard* to try rate of sailing we went to the opposite side my boat did not appear to do well with her new sail we fired the grass on Middle Head and after bending my boats old sails there appears little difference in the sailing of the two boats. The Doctor left me about 5 PM. I arrived at Coral Bay about 9 PM. Found all well and took Miro on board, got a small? of tortoise shell. Started at daylight for Point Smith a fresh breeze from SE stood past P.S. on the starboard tack beautiful weather smooth sea, with a long swell only. A nice breeze tacked about noon standing in for Raffles Bay. Saw twice some native's fires on Croker Island but could not see the Id.. Three natives in a canoe tried to [p91] speak this morning passing Pt Smith but could not reach me—altho' they got within about a hundred yards—wind fell light in the afternoon and we anchored between the two small islands on the NE of Raffles Bay about 8.30 P.M.

Wednesday June 30th got under weigh about 6.30 A.M. standing through Bowens Straits wind very light from the SE, weather very fine—calm great part of the night with a very heavy dew—about 11 A.M. anchored and went on shore to see a native who proved to be old Bucki-buckie. He told me the natives of Limben Rachienne have killed two of Grants Island for having made them sick—plenty of geese up at the plains but being past them I could not turn back. 12 light winds got under weigh beating through the straits—dead calm for about two hours. Light wind from ENE about 3 P.M. The weather Stanborough's calm has not that sultriness with it which I have felt at times, anchored at [?] the SE point of Cockers Island at sunset very little wind all the afternoon. Three natives came over from the main. They say no natives have died at Limben Rachienne but a good many at Wark / the lakes in the interior.

[p92] Thursday July 1st the boy called me about 4.30 A.M. and said the dingy was gone it appeared when they came off from shore last night, they made her fast with a small rope which carried away from the strength of the tide. The *Gipsy* dragged her anchor a considerable distance as soon as we could barely see we got under weigh standing in the direction the boat had most likely taken and about 6 AM I was delighted at Miro's descrying her about two miles in the offing—picked her up about 7 A.M. Forenoon very light airs from S and E. A tremendous fog bank passed this morning along the Sth side of Bowens Straits shrouding the land from view for about ½ an hour. Made very little progress until the Seabreeze set in the tide being against us all the morning anchored a little after sunset at Valencia Island the wind has been either light all day, had I the wind I had the first day I sho [should] have been to Limben Rachienne before now—the weather appears to me unusually fine and moderated for this time of year—July 2nd Friday, started about 6.30 AM. Beating up to the Id of Valencia Island for De Coursey Head. There is more wind this morning and I think likely to continue.

[p93] 10 [illegible] of wind today blowing stiff from SE dead beat up the bay and strong ebb tides M[illegible]ing out against us the sea is comfortably smooth altho' blowing so fresh upon the plains at Crokers Island is the only place I have as yet learnt from the natives there are any geese at present all the other lagoons have too much water in them—we have caught six fish as yet and although I have been on shore at every place at which we have anchored I have not been able to get so much as a winkle for bait. I never saw such a paucity of shell fish. Anchored about noon went on shore directly with Miro see and get some fresh pray—ut [?] about 5.30 having got no sort of game except one cockatoo and a [illegible] no ducks or other water birds on the lagoons / which are full

I did not see a single kangaroo so much for having a dog with you—there appears to be no natives here, there being no recent traces of them—Saturday 3rd whilst I skinned the Opirrwing [?] this morning I sent Miro on shore with the dog he returned only having seen one which he lost on account of the grass—went on shore for about three hours saw nothing determined on leaving so went on board and got under weigh for De Coursey Hd intending to move over to Grants Id tomorrow. Anchored at sunset.

July 4th got under weigh about 7.30 but was obliged to return about 8.30, found it blowing <u>very hard</u> outside but worst of all a fearful sea running with nasty breaking heads. Lost my dingy [illegible] the second time, I made the natives jump overboard and paddle her in shore and got to an anchorage about twenty minutes before them—about 1 P.M. There ~~before~~ being no natives here or any signs of sport I determined on returning to Bowens Straits and got under weigh for that purpose—the boat behaved very well this morning and the mainsail stood a <u>good trial</u>. Anchored in the straits a little after sunset. Monday July 5th started about 6.30 for Palui Bay grounded for about ten minutes on a sand bank being too near the N. shore Strong breeze again today. It is very cool and fresh weather—about 11 A.M. anchored at Ajimaioko went on shore for about four hours and succeeded in getting a brace of jungle fowls.

Appendix 6
Northern Territory Times and Gazette

6.1: Miller's story after the wreck of the Wood Duck, 1874

James Miller wrote the story of the wreck of his barque, *Wood Duck* on Vashon Head, and his survival in Port Essington with his two colleagues, Sinclair, and Robertson. It was published in the *Northern Territory Times and Gazette* on 20 February 1874:

> … We left Port Darwin, or Fannie Bay, on the 6th of January, and anchored two miles to the east of Cape Gambier on that night. The next morning, we stood to the east and rounded Cape Keith five miles. We there came to an anchor, and we went ashore on Melville Island, taking firearms. There were a great many footprints of natives about, so we soon returned to the boat, and immediately afterwards about 50 natives rushed to the boat, yelling and shouting, and each one carrying a number of spears in the left hand. Fortunately, they were too late. We then rounded Point Fayall six miles and came to an anchor for the night. Whilst there saw a large Alligator pass close to the boat. On the next day (the 10th) we weighed anchor and stood across Dundas Straits; and at daybreak I saw four large Malay proas standing out from under the land and steering east. On that evening we arrived at Trepang Bay, and saw two Malay proas there, each with about 40 men on board. They had not yet begun the season's work. We went on board and took coffee with the captain of one of the proas, and we gave them some biscuits. We then stood to the east and rounded Point Vashon two miles, where we came to an anchor for the night. After dark we heard the wild cattle ashore, bleating all along the coast.
>
> On the 11th we made Knocker Bay in the Gulf of Port

Essington and anchored for the night.

On the 12th we arrived at the native camp, Port Essington, where we saw the natives and gave them some pipes, tobacco, and biscuits. We stopped there four days, looking around and obtaining information. About the 16th we started on our way back. All went well until the 20th when we were near Point Vashon. Mr. Sinclair then went ashore naked, and lay down in the sand, and slept six hours in the broiling hot sun. The next day his whole body was one great blister. On the 23rd the blisters broke, and he was in a dreadful state—shocking to look at. But although Robertson had this example before him as a warning, he went ashore without his clothes for three hours, and also suffered from the effects of the sun.

Afterwards it began to blow hard, and a heavy sea set in. We were on a lee shore, and our anchor was only a temporary one, made of pieces of wood and four pieces of iron as prongs. It was no good for holding. Whenever the sea struck the boat the anchor shifted, and at last she struck the rocks. The next sea filled her, and all was over in a few minutes. She went into a thousand pieces as soon as she struck. We slept at the place that night, and the next day started for Trepang Bay, hoping to find the Malays still there, but they were gone. Now the sun began to tell. Sinclair and Robertson became a mass of sores; they were in a shocking state and in great agony.

That night we fell in with the blacks, one, of whom, Jack Davis, spoke good English. They gave us food and rendered great service to Sinclair and Robertson. I made enquiries what we could get along the coast, and they said trepang and turtle shell; and they gave me a small canoe 9 feet long, 18 inches wide, and 10 inches deep; it was very low in the water.

I went then to the reef, two miles from the shore, and found there three sorts of trepang, black and red and grey, in abundance. The natives caught several turtles, which I helped to eat. Seeing next day that food was scarce, and that Sinclair and Robertson were ill, I took four natives and went into the bush with them. In the evening we killed an Alligator, 10 feet long, which lasted us four days, and I sent some of it to Sinclair's camp.

I then got into the little canoe, taking tortoiseshell, trepang, and small pearl with me, and bade the others goodbye. I intended to cross Dundas Straits and pull along the lee of Melville Island and so reach Port Darwin, and there obtain help. But that night the wind freshened, and the canoe began to fill, which compelled me to throw the things overboard. I nearly reached Cape Don, but as the wind increased and the sea ran high, I was compelled to go to Popham Bay, and arrived at the Heads at 11 o'clock that night. The canoe there filled and capsized, and the firearms fell into the water. I took my wet clothes off and went along the beach and found the natives. They soon came back. They remained the next day, and I saw them make the rope which I have brought back. They made it from the bark of a tree called the Alibanya. The same day they shifted their camp eight miles, as they had not much food to eat.

Out of 25 of these natives only six had their full eyesight; the rest were all more or less blind. I left them the next day, and went into the bush to forage, and continued to do so until Smike arrived from the cutter. I then returned with him and overtook the other two white men, who were 15 miles off in Trepang Bay.

We all then walked to where the cutter was waiting in Knocker Bay, Port Essington (Miller, 20 February 1874).

The story continues through other issues of the *Northern Territory Times and Gazette*. A number of letters to the editor appear from the men involved. James Miller's final letter ends 'and so far as words go, I hope that I am done with the subject for ever'. There was no love lost between Miller and Sinclair (*NTTG* 27 Feb 1874).

6.2: A Tourist Trip to Port Essington, 1874

Just after Christmas, 1874, an unnamed correspondent to the *Northern Territory Times and Gazette* wrote of a sailing tour to visit Port Essington, 33 years after it was abandoned, from the new settlement of Palmerston, in Port Darwin. The tour travelled with Edward Oswin Robinson, who fished for trepang and hunted buffalo in the *Northern Light*. He was later the manager of the Cobourg Cattle Company in Port Essington, taking over from John Lewis.

The article appeared in the *Northern Territory Times and Gazette* on 16 January 1875. A man named Reynolds was the only passenger named, and it was, no doubt, the Honourable Thomas Reynolds, an ex-politician and Commissioner of Crown Lands from Adelaide. He had returned to the Northern Territory as a private citizen hoping to be employed as the Government Resident in Port Darwin. He was unsuccessful in his bid and, in fact, drowned in the wrecking of the *Gothenburg* in February 1875 (Pugh, 2019).

> Mr. Reynolds was persuaded… to explore our solitary Northern Territory ruins. Again, under the guidance of Jack Davis [Mildun], we set out. The first thing we came to was an old well, about 30 feet deep, dug on the side of the rise on which the settlement was built. It has, of course, all fallen in, but still contains water. The site chosen for the settlement was not only a most suitable, but a very pretty one, commanding a view of the whole harbor. It is on some rising ground which gently slopes off on either side, terminating in front of a perpendicular cliff. Just on the cliff their defence works were thrown up and their guns mounted. The solid powder magazine is in a perfect state of preservation, except that the door has been burnt away.
>
> About a hundred yards back is the site of Captain McArthur's house—one of the principal ones in the settlement. It had evidently been a wooden house, built on stone piers about two feet high. Every vestige of woodwork was gone, but the substantial stone piers, each with its coping of solid cut ironstone, remained intact. Farther along the rise there had been a row of cottages, singularly built with one end of stonework, in which was a small chimney: the rest of the cottages had evidently been of wood and had wholly disappeared; the concrete floors remained. Further in we saw the ruins of more houses. One was pointed out as the doctor's -others as belonging to married people. The barrack site was also pointed out, but not a vestige of it could be seen. Of course, in between the houses the trees, bushes, and shrubs had quite grown up—so completely, indeed, that it

was difficult to imagine them to be the growth of 30 years. The soldiers' garden was close by; the remains of a few solitary posts of the fencing were standing. The cleared site was easily discernible, but hardly the remains of a cultivated plant could be seen. On our way down to the second and larger garden, we passed through the cemetery. On looking closely, I fancied I could see indications of mounds, but they were very slight. Two graves there were marked by substantial plain monuments. One, Davis told us, was that of the doctor: the other was the grave of a lady, the wife of one of the officers. It struck me as something unutterably lonely to meet with those abiding memorials of death, shaded over by the wild tangled forest trees. Death must have been exceptionally sad in that remote settlement, so utterly cut off from relatives and friends. The site of the second garden is alongside the cemetery and must have comprised about two acres.

As in the other one very few cultivated plants remain. Conspicuous among the few are some very handsome mango trees, we rested under the thick bower-like branches of one whose stem must have girthed between eight and nine feet. Notwithstanding that the top has been broken off—probably by a storm—it has attained a beautiful cone-like shape. Some mango and pine apple plants were brought over for the garden. We rested for half an hour and then made our way slowly back to the beach: and after promising that we would come and see the grand corroboree in the night, we went on board, washed, changed our clothes, and had an enjoyable lounge till dinner time. Jack Davis was as good as his word—we had scarcely got on board when a canoe with some very fine fish came alongside. The getting of it had been entrusted to Flash Poll—rather a celebrated character. She was servant to Mrs. McArthur, 33 years ago and speaks very fair English with a slight French accent. She was very thankful for tobacco and pipes but would have been much more so for "leetle drop brandy". When leaving the captain gave her some rice, first, for her sister—a woman, I should think, 20 years older than herself. That was put into a basket, and then she had nowhere to put her own share.

After a moment's deliberation, she quietly unshipped her one solitary bit of linen, and with a grin handed it to receive her rice, carrying it off triumphantly.

At dark we went ashore, as promised, to see their corroboree. It was rather a poor affair. There were only about 20 men dancing; and though the night was dark, they had no proper fire. I believe the fact of the matter was, the majority of them were too busily engaged making and eating damper, Mr. Scott having sent a bag of flour ashore to them in the evening, which I believe was "scoffed" during the night. They had many different dances; some of them, from the noise and gesticulations they made, evidently in imitation of native companions. One singular feature about their corroboree was the part the women took in it. They did not mix with the men but stood apart in a row as mute as if they bad been dumb. As soon as the dance commenced, they rose up one by one, standing with their feet close together, and their bodies stooping forward at an angle of about forty-five. A piece of string, about two feet long, was tied to each thumb, and with the hands out above their heads, and as far apart as the string would allow, they kept up a vigorous circular motion with the upper part of their bodies. At the last whoop, with which each dance invariably wound up, they dropped to the ground as if shot. We returned to the cutter about 9 o'clock, quite disposed for rest.

Next morning it was decided to have a cruise round the harbor in the gig. Before we were ready to start, Mr. and Mrs. Davis had come off and of course it was proposed they should accompany us. Eight was found an uncomfortably large number for the gig, and Davis's good missus was set down in the bottom of the boat, between the two sailors who were pulling us, which she found rather an unpleasant position. When the men commenced pulling, she suddenly found Mr. Stroke oars back against her bosom. Shrinking back with native modesty she found her own back come into sharp contact with the bow oar. This was too much for even her placid temper, and as soon as we landed at the old jetty, she stepped ashore. The last we saw of her was taking off her small robe, her only article of attire, carefully folding it up and walking off with it under her arm. We found the jetty of the usual wood and stone construction. Some of the wooden beams within tidal influence were tolerably sound. The ruin would be a substantial help towards a new jetty.

Leaving it, we made across for Middle Point, when we landed and saw the site of a house which Davis told us had been occupied by Manila men. We admired the site very much indeed. Being, as its name implies, in the middle, it commands a view of the open sea as well as of the whole harbor. When Port Essington becomes settled, Middle Point will make a charming place for suburban residences. We walked across it to the eastern arm, and waited there, gathering shells and seeds, till the boat was brought round, when we returned to the cutter. In the afternoon there was a great muster of the blacks on board, which was very near as bad as our introduction to them. Mr. Scott gave Jack Davis, for distribution among his tribe, two or three bags of flour, a bag of sugar and bag of tea, and pipes and tobacco, in [illegible] to all the natives. Davis (was distinctly) given to understand that these things were given them as (reward for) being good to the white (visitors?)[illegible]. Scott impressing on him [illegible] the Alligator blacks, as well, to treat any white fellows they came across in a kind manner, and they would also receive plenty of 'tum-tum', telling him at the same time that if they treated them badly they would be presented with a little powder and lead instead—We made enquiries, but could hear nothing of the unfortunate men, Permain and Borradaile.

All the natives were highly delighted, and (most marvellous circumstance!) none of them asked for more. Poor Robinson evidently felt it was a blue look-out for his trepang gathering for the next three or four days. Of course, the niggers would not budge till they had got through their food. When all the giving and the parting was over, we weighed anchor and stood out with a light breeze. Port Essington is a wide estuary, extending inland between 20 and 30 miles, it is divided into what is called the inner and outer harbor by two points, which run across almost midway, leaving a passage about a mile wide between them.

The old settlement was on the inner harbor, which is the more sheltered of the two. But much shallower than the outer one. The rise and fall of the tide is not so great as in Port Darwin, which is an advantage. Of the neighbouring country

I cannot say much, as we were only a short distance inland. It has the appearance of being much the same, as the general run of the coast. We took two days returning to Port Darwin, having to beat against a stiff headwind and a chopping sea which was anything but comfortable, that we were glad to hail the cliffs of Port Darwin on New Year's morn (Anon, 16 January 1875).

Appendix 7

The McArthurs' Notebook: Poetry

McArthur did not keep a journal, but there are a few diary-style notes written about the settlement by both the captain and his son (John) in a notebook (see Appendix 5.4) held in the Mitchell Library. The notes in the book, his sketches, and the following poetry, allow us to glimpse a side of the commandant that does not come through in his official dispatches. As we might expect, McArthur was homesick, missed his family and the green land of his childhood, and writing these occasional poems may have given him comfort. Several are just sad poems about his missed loved ones. One was written for a favourite dog, Comet; and one particularly clever poem is a humourous take on the boredom inherent to living in such an isolated part of the world. I believe that they are previously unpublished, so include them here.

Not all of them are signed or dated, and two different hands have written them. The second hand is that of John McArthur Junior, who stayed with his father from 1841 through to November 1849. I have noted those I believe to be the latter's poems. Captain McArthur, if and when he signed his poetry, wrote simply, 'JMcA'. Perhaps, some were drafts of poems he later sent to his wife in his letters. One, by the younger John, mentions his mother and brothers. He too, felt the pain of distance.

McArthur was no laureate, but I have included the poems in this history as a tribute to the captain and his son. I admit, I hesitated to do so because they are personal, and by no means brilliant poetry. The McArthurs would not have expected to share them, and probably would never have given permission to publish, so please read them with this in mind.

They are presented in the order they appear in the notebook, but the numbering is mine. One poem is omitted because it was written in 1850, after they had left Australia. Words I have been unable to decipher are included as I see them.

1. (Notebook p9)
Thº I die here I'd be,
Under the shade of the nutmeg tree,
Which by the streamlets crystal bed,
On the north road rears its head,
Where 'neath its sombre shade I've heard,
Oft notes of many a forest bird.
For oh? The land with people fills
A spot like that they'd grant me still
Where yet the weary might retreat
To quench their thirst or stay the heat
Or seek in solitude to find
Some balm to soothe a troubled mind
Such is the place where I'd be laid
Thº poor mortal choose a grave
No house erected there, or shed
Nor plough would e'er disturb the dead
No man would wish 'neath here to dwell
Nor there the soil bear culture well.

2. (Notebook p71)
Land of my childhood, dear to me,
Once more your happy shores I'll see,
Again, mong fields, and woods will stray,
Where I've spent many a happy day.
Again, I'll hear the lark's gay song,
And listen, with affection strong,
To words, from those I love most dear,
Tho' parted many a weary year,
But I to Scotia's coast am bound
[And?] I can tread on English ground.
JMcA

The British in North Australia: Port Essington

By John McArthur Jnr
(Notebook p72)
Oh, was I but gifted with wings like a dove,
I would not be long finding those who I love
To seek near that dear one the happiness wished
By whom like a child I was missed and cherished.
They may tell me I live in a tropical clime
Mid scenes quite as happy as cheerful as thine
But the pleasures of youth, in my heart long enshrined
Turn the thoughts ever homeward and weary the mind.

4. (Notebook p73)
But my mind will still wander—where the violets grow,
O'er meads and o'er meadows—where the Thames waters flow—
To those happy old woods where the sweet songbirds roam—
To the haunts of my youth—to the hearth of my home.
JMcA

5. (Notebook p73)
Does not affection—parted from those loved—at length from its own
isolation draw its greater strength?

6. (Notebook p84)
Oh, where will you e're find a home,
Like the one on which childhood's been passed
Where will joys equal those (if you roam),
Be e're found or yet pleasures that last –
Discontented, should some spend their time,
Or the blessings of youth's home deride,
Let such, seek in some far distant clime,
A home where they'll happier reside.
JMcA

7. (Notebook p87)
Comet, not so fast as you'd suppose,
What's as good he runs by nose
+ when others are in doubt,
He will soon the game find out.
Catch the pride of her race
Always first in the chase
Being nimble and light
She runs only by sight.
Give her but a fair run
Kangaroo's life is done.

Figure 81: McArthur's illustrated poem to his greyhound, Comet.

8. By John McArthur Jnr
(Notebook p88)
Who can tell the mind's emotion?
When far from those most lov'd we roam.
Who can weigh the heart's affection?
When far distant from our home.
Then we think of every Brother,
Of one by nature's ties most dear,
And as our thoughts turn upon our Mother,
Affection yields a silent tear.
All the blessings of our youth,
Then it is the mind broods o'er,
And we think with heartfelt truth,
Perhaps, they ne'er may bless us more,
They can answer, they alone,
Who nine years themselves have been,
Exiles from a much-loved home,
Which may ne'er again be seen.
March 6th, 1847.

The British in North Australia: Port Essington

9. By John McArthur Jnr
(Notebook p89)
And am I then once more to see,
The land of my Nativity,
To visit scenes of boyhood's bliss,
And greet my mother with a kiss,
And meet those Brothers, who then were,
Children, grown youths now, tall, and fair,
Find others who were there at home
Now absent, and to manhood grown.

Oh! Yes, again I yet may be,
Happy in meeting all of thee,
Tho' ten long years have now rolled round,
Affection still remains as sound,
Tho' persons change with time and clime,
Absence adds to a love like mine,
Oh, may I then in joy soon meet,
Those who I long have sighed to greet.
Mar 10th, 1848.

10. (Notebook p98-99)
Not a place in the world like this can be found,
If you search from the Poles the whole earth around,
If to grumble and growl for ever's your wish,
Why come, and reside in a place like this,
If living you'd call't, from the world quite shut out,
Why you'd do well, there is not the least doubt,
And should you not know, how the time you would spend,
I'll soon tell you how if attention you'll lend –
You'd get up at six, walk, breakfast at nine,
And then you might write, read, or sleep till you dine,
That is, if a few thousand flies, and the heat,
Would allow your poor body, or mind such a treat.
At three you'd perhaps dine off (such exquisite stuff)
A slice of Queen's Own, (which she's not known to touch),
After which, if digestion to help was your plan,
You'd go shooting, or riding, (that is if you can),
Or if liking it better, you'd sail on the sea,
You might spend your time thus till you come home to tea.

The tea being over it brings on the night,
The flies go to rest—the musquitoes they bite.
Then three or four hours, spent as you best like,

Brings time for your bed, whence you'd rise with the light.
Thus, having explained the routine for a day,
It'll answer for most of the year I may say –
Unless p'rhaps a ship, some diversion entails,
By arriving at times with the papers and mails -
And if to find out where this place is you're striving,
You'll find it in two lines the problem divining,
To the shape of a rat had this world been subjected,
At the tip of the tail Victoria's erected –
Or if like a bullock it had been in form,
I might have wrote this from the tip of a horn –
That's as much as to say (if you're not clear in mind)
At the end of the world 'Victoria' you'll find.
JMcA

11. (Notebook p100)
O' I have had wants and wishes too,
This place has choked and chilled,
But bless me but again with you,
And half my prayer's fulfilled.

12. (Notebook p101).
Oh, may I see again that land,
The fairest of the fair,
At whose sweet glance, all hearts expand,
For all true hearts are there.
Oh, may I hope my course once more
May to that home be bent,
To land upon its chalky shore
And view again dear Kent
Port Essington 1846

13. (Notebook p145)
Life's Young Day
My years were few, my heart was pure, for via a folly more,
A hideous and disgusting front? In those green days of yore
Destructive dissipation then with her deceitful train,
Had not with their attractive glare confused and teased my brain.

It must have been of happiness a more than mortal dream,
It must have been of heavenly light a bright unbroken beam
A draught of pure unmingled bliss, for to my withered heart,
It doth een now a thrilling glow of ecstasy impart.

The British in North Australia: Port Essington

14. (Notebook p182)

The greeting of friends ever kind
Or a woman's sweet bright sunny smile,
May soften the thoughts of the mind
Or the hours of a wanderer beguile.
By making them lighter pap[?] round
Turn ideas from those lov'd far away
Still, still there a space will be found
Unfill'd in the hearts which yet stray
JMcA

Table of illustrations

Figure 1: Victoria, Port Essington (Thomas Hatfield SLNSW FL3233570).	xxiv
Figure 2: Adam Head, Port Essington.	5
Figure 3: Sir Gordon Bremer	6
Figure 4: The rescue of William d'Orley by the *Isabella* (*Essington*), from Murray Island, Torres Strait, J.W. Carmichael (silentworldfoundation.org.au).	24
Figure 5: HMS *Alligator* log, 28 October 1838 (Bremer (2), 1838).	27
Figure 6: Government House from the battery on the Queen's birthday (Stanley, SLNSW).	35
Figure 7: 'Situation of the Orontes when Abandoned by Her Master and Crew, Port Essington, Decr. 28/38' (Owen Stanley, SLNSW 1837-1843 SAFE/PXC 279).	39
Figure 8: Battery on Adam Head in front of the fort tower (Stanley, SLNSW FL1893215).	41
Figure 9: The fort on Adam Head with the magazine in the ground beside it (Stanley 1847, SLNSW f119).	41
Figure 10: Port Essington, Louis Le Breton, *Voyage au Pôle Sud et dans l'Océanie*, 1839.	47
Figure 11: Artawirr, a bamboo didgeridoo, collected from Port Essington before 1844, now in The British-Museum (Oc1855, 1220.177) (Pastmasters, 2016).	56
Figure 12: A bark painting collected from Port Essington 'before 1868', now in The British-Museum (oc1973-q-17.1) (Pastmasters, 2016).	56
Figure 13: Lt Phineas Priest's cottage (Stanley 1839, SLNSW).	61
Figure 14: Storehouse, Port Essington (Stanley 1839, SLNSW).	61
Figure 15: Owen Stanley's depiction of the Theatre Royal, August 1839 (SLNSW).	63
Figure 16: 'Victoria from the anchorage' (Stokes, 1846).	65
Figure 17: Port Essington, by Captain John McArthur (National Library of Australia).	65
Figure 18: New Victoria in 1839. Lithograph from *Voyage au Pôle Sud et en Océanie* by Jules Dumont d'Urville (Louis Breton 1840, PH1077-0001)	66–7

Figure 19: Éstablishment Anglaise a Port Essington. *Atlas Pittoresque*, plate 120, 69
(Louis LeBreton 1840, SLSA B8964).

Figure 20: Government Gardens (Stanley 1839, SLNSW). 69

Figure 21: Situation of the *Pelorus* the morning after the cyclone 71
(Stanley, 1839, SLNSW).

Figure 22: Barrack Square (aka Victoria Square) after the cyclone 72
(Stanley 1839, SLNSW)

Figure 23: Ruins of Church and the *Pelorus* peoples' tents' 73
(Stanley, Jan 1840, SLNSW).

Figure 24: HMS *Pelorus* at low water (Stanley, 1839, SLNSW). 74

Figure 25: HMS *Pelorus* at half tide (Stanley, 1839, SLNSW). 75

Figure 26: 'Situation of HMS *Pelorus* when pretty righted showing the purchases. 75
Half tide' (Stanley, 1840, SLNSW).

Figure 27: Trepang boilers (Masson, 1915). 83

Figure 28: 'Prow off Port Essington February 13, 1840' (Stanley, 1840). 84

Figure 29: Painting at Malarrak in Arnhem Land, possibly of a Macassan 85
trepang drying shed (Taçon & May, 2020).

Figure 30: Macassan Camp, Port Essington, April 1839. Le Breton, 86–7
Atlas Pittoresque, (pl. 116. NLA).

Figure 31: Macassan Trading Prahu (McArthur, NTRS 3601_p112). 88

Figure 32: The Orange Footed Scrub Fowl (MacGillivray, Zoological Society 92
of London, 1876).

Figure 33: Gouldian Finches are named after Mrs Elizabeth Gould (John Gould, 94
'The Birds of Australia', 1841).

Figure 34: Sugar gliders (Gould: 'Mammals of Australia' 1841). 95

Figure 35: Victoria Hospital consisted of four wards. The hospital kitchen was the 102
stone building on the left of this plan. It was built by borrowed Prisoners
of the Crown (Allen, 1973).

Figure 36: Victoria Square, by H. S. Melville. Four marines lived in each 120–1
thatched hut, and they grew food plants in small gardens behind them.
George Earl and James McArthur, and then Lieutenant Lambrick and
his family, lived above the spirit store on the right (SLSA B-8409).

Figure 37: Monument over Mrs Emma Lambrick's grave at Port Essington 122
Victoria in 1915 (SLSA B-10134).

Illustrations

Figure 38: Two paintings of Middle Head, Port Essington, where *Gipsy* was built (Stanley 1839, SLNSW). 126

Figure 39: *Lizard* and *Gipsy*, sketch probably by John McArthur junior (1847, NTRS 3601_p 107). 127

Figure 40: Sketch by McArthur in his notebook (NTRS 3601_p 129 (McArthur & McArthur, 1849). 127

Figure 41: Regatta at Victoria with HMS *Britomart* (Stanley 1839, SLNSW). 128

Figure 42: Dr Ludwig Leichhardt, 1813-1848 (anon, NLA). 135

Figure 43: Ornithological specimens from the Port Essington Expedition, collected by John Gilbert and carried to Victoria Settlement by Leichhardt after Gilbert's death. Liverpool Museum (www.environmentand society.org accessed April 2020). 139

Figure 44: The McArthurs' notebook, recording Iwaidja spears (McArthur, NTRS 3601_page 35). 147

Figure 45: Neinmal by H.S. Melville (Greenwood, 1863). 152

Figure 46: Aborigines in front of the hospital. According to Olsen, Neinmal is the man third from the left (Herman Melville, HMS Fly, NLA-148363905-1) 155

Figure 47: Father Angelo Confalonieri 161

Figure 48: Captain Owen Stanley 175

Figure 49: HMS *Rattlesnake*, by Oswald Walters Brierly, 1822. 177

Figure 50: HMS *Rattlesnake* leaving Port Essington Nov. 17th, 1848 (Oswald Walter Brierly. SLNSW) 177

Figure 51: From Keppel's journal, a 'Native Bier' in Port Essington. Page 526, Oswald Brierly (Keppel, 1853). 179

Figure 52: HMS *Mæander* under Captain Keppel removed the garrison from Victoria on December 1, 1849; Oswald Brierly, Mechanical Curator Collection (Keppel, 1853). 186

Figure 53: In 1877, the older Iwaidja people here on the beach below Adam Head would have remembered Victoria Settlement in the 1840s. The building behind the camp was constructed by Foelsche and used as his photographic darkroom (Foelsche 1877, NLA PH1060-0057). 196

Figure 54: Three visitors pose with Iwaidja people in front of a mango tree planted in Victoria about 30 years earlier (Foelsche 1876, SLSA PH1060-0051). 196

Figure 55: Trepang (Napier, 1876). 199

Figure 56: John Lewis, from 'Fought and Won' (Lewis, 1922) 200

Figure 57: John Lewis's Homestead, Port Essington from 'Fought and Won' (Lewis, 1922). 201

Figure 58: Mildun 'Jack Davis', photo from 'An Untamed Territory' by Dr Mervyn John Holmes (the Chief Medical Officer) (Masson, 1915). 204

Figure 59: An Iwaidja corroboree in 1877 in the Victoria Settlement ruins, that was probably performed for tourists and Inspector Paul Foelsche (Foelsche, NTL PH1060-0063). 210–11

Figure 60: An unnamed Iwaidja tribesman from Port Essington. From 'Fought and Won' (Lewis, 1922) 212

Figure 61: Headland, Port Essington. 215

Figure 62: Like every tour group since the National Park opened, we gathered behind the sign for a photograph. 216

Figure 63: The magazine on Adam Head. 219

Figure 64: Remains of McArthur's house, a small steamer in the background, from 'An Untamed Territory' (Masson, 1915). 220

Figure 65: Glass stoppers from French wine bottles (Allen, 1973). 220

Figure 66: The round 'Cornish' chimneys of the married men's quarters. Map ref: 11° 21' 51.02"S, 132° 09' 10.95"E. 222

Figure 67: The blacksmith's forge. 222

Figure 68: The hospital foundations, and the ruins of the kitchen. Map ref: 11° 21' 41.72"S, 132° 09' 12.61"E. 224

Figure 69: One of the ovens in the hospital kitchens, with broken glass. 224

Figure 70: An architectural sketch of Victoria Hospital (by Peter Dermoudy: with permission). 225

Figure 71: Quartermaster's Store with the huge mound nest of a pair of orange-footed scrub fowls (Pastmasters). 228

Figure 72: The monument of Mrs Emma Lambrick and her two children as it was in 2016. 228

Figure 73: The Memorial Board in Victoria Cemetery, erected in 1990, lists the names of the dead. 229

Figure 74: Mrs Lambrick's monument in 2019 after a controversial restoration using white concrete (ABC). 231

Figure 75: The tomb's plaque was probably installed by Tom Stiles in 1913. 231

Figure 76: McArthur's painting of the Victoria Cemetery, 1848. Mrs Lambrick's two children lie on either side of her obelisk grave monument. Perhaps the 232

uniformed soldier standing near Mrs Lambrick's grave is her husband, George (John McArthur, NLA PIC R245 LOC1981/nla.obj-135264415).

Figure 77: Detail of Mrs Lambrick's grave monument (John McArthur, NLA PIC R245 LOC1981/nla.obj-135264415).   232

Figure 78: A 'Bali sapi', or banteng cattle (*Bos javanicus*). A healthy population of banteng cattle, which are otherwise endangered, still lives on Cobourg Peninsula (Sandbunny 2010, Flickr).   236

Figure 79: A buffalo (*Bubalus bubalis*) near Vashon Head, Cobourg Peninsula (Sandbunny 2010, Flickr).   236

Figure 80: Heritage in isolation.   236

Figure 81: McArthur's illustrated poem to his greyhound, Comet (McArthur & McArthur, 1849).   291

Bibliography

Aldis, 24 Jul 1844 . *Advertisement*. Page 3 Advertising, trove.nla.gov.au/newspaper ed. Sydney: The Sydney Morning Herald.

Allen, J., 1973. *The Archaeology of Nineteenth-Century British Imperialism: an Australian case study*. World Archaeology 5: pp. 44–60.

Allen, J., 1980. Head On: the Early Nineteenth Century British Colonisation of the Top End. In: *Northern Australia: options and implications*. s.n., pp. 33–39.

Alvis, A. K., 2019. *Biodiversity Heritage Library*. [Online] Available at: https://blog.biodiversitylibrary.org/2019/03/elizabeth-gould.html [Accessed 5 May 2020].

Anon., 1844. *List of the Specimens of Birds in the British Museum*. London: British Museum, George Woodfall and Son.

Anon, 15 November 1845. Penal Settlement at Port Essington. *The Australian*, p. 3.

Anon, 16 January 1875. A Cruise to Port Essington. *Northern Territory Times and Gazette*, https://trove.nla.gov.au/newspaper/article/3143722#(Accessed 1 May 2020), p. 3.

Arden, G., 1 October 1843. Port Essington. *Arden's Sydney Magazine of Politics and General Literature*, Vol 1(2).

Aurousseau, M., 1968. *The Letters of Ludwig Leichhardt*. Edited Vol. 3: The Hakluyt Society by Cambridge University Press.

Austin, K., 1964. *The Voyage of the Investigator*. Adelaide: Rigby.

Barnes, W., 3 Sept 1838. *The New Settlement*. The Sydney Monitor, p. 2.

——, August 5th, 1836. Abandonment of The Northern Settlements. *The Colonist*.

Barrow, J., 13 Dec 1836. *Barrow to Glenelg*. Volume C.O. 201/256.

——, 1824. *Barrow to Horton W (Admiralty)*. London: The National Archives, Kew Colonial Office 201/153, 109028.

——, 1839. *Introduction to a letter by Captain Sir J. Gordon Bremer, Communicated by Sir John Barrow to the Royal Society*. London: JSTOR online.

——, 30 October 1839. *Sir John Barrow to Undersecretary Stephen*. Series 1, Vol. 25, 1841 ed. London: Historical Resources of Australia.

Bauer, F., 1964. *Historical Geography of White Settlement in Parts of Northern Australia, Part*

2. *The Katherine–Darwin Region*. Canberra: CSIRO.

Blackwood, F., 16 September 1845. *Captain Blackwood to Governor George Gipps, Sydney.* in Cameron (1999) p154 ed. H.M.S. Fly: Historical Society of the Northern Territory.

Blyton, G., 2015. Harry Brown (c. 1819–1854): *Contribution of an Aboriginal Guide in Australian Exploration.* www.jstor.org/stable/43687035. Accessed 23 Apr. 2020 ed. Aboriginal History, vol. 39, 2015, pp. 63–82.

Bogue, A., 1848. *Steam to Australia: Its general advances considered.* books.google.com.au ed. Sydney: W. and F. Ford.

Brady, M., 2020. *Macassan History and Heritage: Drug substances introduced by the Macassans: The mystery of the tobacco pipe.* [Online] Available at: https://press-files.anu.edu.au/downloads/press/p241301/html/ch11.xhtml?referer=&page=13#toc_marker-14 [Accessed 15 May 2020].

Bremer, G., 17 September 1839. Advertisement. *The Sydney Gazette and NSW Advertiser*, p. 4.

——, 1838. *Log of HMS Alligator. Sir John James Gordon Bremer Kt. CB K.CH. Commencing May 22rd 1838 Ending January 17th 1840. W.W. Chambers Esq. Capt. Ac.* [Online] Available at: https://www.territorystories.nt.gov.au/bitstream/10070/240726/3/Alligator_Log [Accessed 29 April 2020].

——, 1839. *On the recent Establishment at Port Essington, on the Northern Coast of Australia. Extract from a letter of Captain Sir J. Gordon Bremer, Communicated by Sir JOHN BARROW, Bart., F. R.S.* online ed. London: JSTOR.

——, 4 April 1839. *Captain Sir Gordon Bremer to Secretary of the Admiralty, London.* in Cameron (1999) p. 29 ed. Victoria: Historical Society of the Northern Territory.

——, 7 August 1839. *Captain Sir Gordon Bremer to Captain Francis Neaufort, Hydrographic Office.* Sydney (on HMS Alligator): in Cameron, (1999), p. 58.

——, 9 February 1839. *Captain Sir Gordon Bremer to Secretary of the Admiralty.* Victoria: in Cameron (1999) p. 27.

——, 13 December 1838. *Bremer to Admiralty.* Historical Society of the Northern Territory ed. Victoria: in Cameron (1999) p. 19–20.

Brierly, O. W. B., 1848. *Journal of Oswald Brierly, H.M.S. Rattlesnake.* Manuscript, Mitchell Library, SLNSW.

Brock, J., 1993. *Plants of the Northern Territory.* Sydney: Reed.

Browne, C., 1871. *Letters and Extracts from the Addresses and Occasional Writings of J. Beete Jukes.* London: Chapman and Hall.

Buren, W. v., 1865. Quinine as a Prophilactic. see *Military Medical and Surgical Essays*,

United States Sanitary Commission, 1865, D, W.H. van Buren, M.D., Volume ch D, p. 13.

Cadell, F., 23 December 1878. *Cadell to King*. Adelaide: State Records of South Australia 83/1879.

Cameron, J., 1989. *The Origins of Australia's Capital Cities*. Melbourne: Cambridge University Press, Pamela Statham Ed.

——, 1999. *Letters from Port Essington, 1838–1845*. Darwin: Northern Territory Historical Society.

——, 2016. Stakes in a Ring Fence. *Northern Territory Historical Studies: A Journal of History, Heritage and Archeology*, 1(27), pp. 1–25.

Campbell, John, 1834. *Geographical Memoir of Melville Island and Port Essington, on the Cobourg Peninsula*, London: The Journal of the Royal Geographical Society of London, Vol. 4 (1834), pp. 129–81.

Campbell, Judy, 2002. *Invisible Invaders: Smallpox and Other Diseases in Aboriginal Australia 1780–1880*. Melbourne University Press.

Campbell, W. S., 1916. *The Earliest Settlements in the Northern Territory of Australia*. Vol. 3, pt. 3 (1912–13), p. 81–113 ed. Proceedings of the Australian Historical Society.

Carruthers, J. & Steibel, L., 2012. *Thomas Baines: Exploring Tropical Australia, 1855 to 1857*. Canberra: National Museum of Australia Press.

Chilsolm, A., 1966. *John Gilbert 1810–1845*. Hardcopy 1966, accessed online 26 April 2020 ed. Canberra: Australian Dictionary of Biography, National Centre of Biography, Australian National University, http://adb.anu.edu.au/biography/gilbert-john-2093/text2633.

Chronicle, 27 Jul 1844. *Statistics of the Colony*. p. 2 ed. Sydney: Morning Chronicle.

Colonist, 25 August 1838. Port Essington. *The Colonist*, p. 3.

Conigrave, C. P., 1941. *North Australia*. London: Jonathan Cape Ltd.

Conner, G., 1988. *Of the Hut I Builded: The Archeology of Australia's History*. Cambridge University Press.

Cross, J., 2011. *Great Central State: The Foundation of the Northern Territory*. Adelaide: Wakefield Press.

Currie, B., 2020. Personal [Interview] (6 April 2020).

d'Urville, J. S. C. D., 1839. *An Account in Two Volumes of Two Voyages to the South Seas by Captain Jules S-C Dumont D'Urville of the French Navy (Vol 2) to the Straits of Magellan, Chile, Oceania, South-East Asia, Australia, Antarctica, New Zealand and Torres Strait, 1837–1840*. 1 ed. in 'The Visit of the Astrolabe and the Zellee' by CC MacKight (Ed) 1969 'The Farthest Coast': MUP.

Bibliography

Day, M., 2010. *Victoria's secrets reveal death and noble failure.* Accessed 1 June 2020: The Australian, 30 October 2010.

Dermoudy, P., 1984. *Conservation of Historic Structures at Victoria, Port Essington, Northern Territory: a report for the Conservation Commision of the Northern Territory.* N.T. Library NTC 994.295 DERM.

———, 2020. *Personal Communication* [Interview] (2 June 2020).

Donovan, P., 1981. *A Land Full of Possibilities: A history of South Australia's Northern Territory.* University of Queensland Press.

Douglas, W. B., 7 November 1872. *Diary.* Palmerston: NT Archives.

Earl, G., 16 August 1830. *Letter: Earl to Capt. Washington, Royal Geographic Society, London.* Sydney: in Cameron (1999), p. 15.

———, 1837. *The Eastern Seas or Voyages and Adventures in the Indian Archipelago in 1832–33–34.* London: as quoted in Allen 1972.

———, 12 May 1844. *Earl to Captain Francis Beaufort, Hydrographic Office, London.* in Cameron (1999), p. 135 ed. Port Essington: Historical Society of the Northern Territory.

———, 13 July 1840. *Earl to Captain John Washington, Royal Geographic Society, London.* in Cameron (1999) p. 68 ed. Port Essington: Historical Society of the Northern Territory.

———, 17 March 1840. *Earl to Captain John Washington, Royal Geographical Society, London.* in Cameron (1999) p. 65 ed. Port Essington: Historical Society of the Northern Territory.

———, 1841. *An Account of a Visit to Kisser, One of the Serwatti Group in the Indian Archipelago.* The Journal of the Royal Geographical Society of London ed. London: Vol. 11 (1841), pp. 108–17.

———, 1846. *Earl, quoted in Powell, 2016 'World's End'.* Melbourne: Australian Scholarly Press.

———, 1846. *Enterprise in Tropical Australia.* (books.google.com.au) ed. London: Madden and Malcolm, .

———, 9 June 1841. *Earl to Captain John Washington, Royal Geographical Society, London.* in Cameron (1999), p. 86 ed. Port Essington: Historical Society of the Northern Territory.

Fensham, R., Bean, T., Dowe, J. & Dunlop, C., 2006. *This disastrous event staggered me: Reconstructing the botany of Ludwig Leichhardt on the expedition from Moreton Bay to Port Essington, 1844–45.* Cunninghamia. 9. 451–506. .

Fitzroy, C., 1 November 1846. *Sir Charles Fitzroy to Right Hon W.E. Gladstone.* Sydney: Historical Records of Australia, Governors' despatches to and from England /

[edited by Frederick Watson] Series 1, VOL 25, p. 783.

Flinders, M., 1803. *The Voyage of H.M.S. Investigator*. in CC MacKnight, 1969, 'The Farthest Coast', p. 61: MUP.

Foelsche, P., 1886. *The Australian Race: In Curr, Edward Micklethwaite (ed.). The Australian race: its origin, languages, customs, place of landing in Australia and the routes by which it spread itself over the continent.* [Online]
Available at: https://ia802205.us.archive.org/3/items/australianracei01currgoog/australianracei01currgoog.pdf
[Accessed 17: Foelsche, Paul (1886). 'Raffles Bay: The Unalla Tribe'. Nov 2019].

Gazette, 16 March 1850. *Death of Captain Owen Stanley*. Sydney: The Shipping Gazette and Sydney General Trade List, p. 76 .

Gazette, 17 September 1839. *The Sydney Gazette and New South Wales Advertiser*. Sydney: p. 4.

Gilbert, J., 28 June 1845. *John Gilbert diary of the Port Essington Expedition, 18 September 1844–28 June 1845*. in 'John GilbertA collector extraordinaire': https://trove.nla.gov.au/work/235958563.

Gipps, G., 1838. *Sir George Gipps To Marquess of Normandy*. Despatch No. 108, per ship Palestine. ed. Historical Records of Australia XXI.

——, 23 Sept 1838. *Gov Gipps to Lord Glenelg, per ship Marinus*. Volume VI,10, p. 591 ed. Sydney: Historical Records of Australia.

Glenelg, L., 22 Sept 1838. *Glenelg to Gipps*. Series I. Volume VI ed. p. 590: Historical Records of Australia.

——, 25 Jan 1838. *Glenelg to Gipps*, Series I. Volume VI: Historical Resources of Australia.

Goderich, 29 September 1831. *Viscount Goderich to Governor Bourke*. Historical Records of Australia, 1, xvi, p395.

Greenwood, J., 1863. *Curiosities of Savage Life Volume 1*. online at books.googleusercontent.com/books ed. London, p. 203: S.O. Beeton.

Grey,.H., 28 May 1847. *Earl Grey to Sir Charles Fitzroy, Despatch No. 157, per ship Eleanor Lancaster*. London: Historical records of Australia. Series I. Governors' despatches to and from England. Volume XXV, April, 1846–September, 1847 / [edited by Frederick Watson].

——, 18 August 1846. *Earl Grey to Sir Charles Fitzroy. (Despatch No. 21, per ship Wanner Castle.) Downing Street, 18 August, 1846*. London: Historical records of Australia. Series I., Governors' despatches to and from England / [edited by Frederick Watson] Vol XXVI, 1925.

Harris, J., 1985. *Contact Languages at the Northern Territory British Military Settlements 1824–29.* [Online]

Available at: http://press-files.anu.edu.au/downloads/press/p71761/pdf/article083. pdf [Accessed 5 May 2020].

——, 1990. Medlone also known as 'Jack Davis'. In: R. M. A. P. David Carment, ed. *Northern Territory Dictionary of Biography*. Darwin: NTU Press, pp. 203–4.

——, 1990. Memorimbo, also known as 'Flash Poll'. In: R. M. A. P. David Carment, ed. *Northern Territory Dictionary of Biography*. Darwin: NTU Press, pp. 204–5.

Hay, 21 Jan 1832. *Hay to Governor Bourke*. Mitchell Library SLNSW A1269.

Hepper, D., 1994. British Warship Losses in the Age of Sail, 1650–1859. London: Rotherfield: Jean Boudriot.

Herald, 17 September 1838. Sydney General Tradelist (Customs). *The Sydney Herald*, p. 2.

Herald, 30 June 1838. *Abstract of The Evidence Taken Before The Select Committee of The Legislative Council (Session 1848), on Steam Communication with England*. Sydney: Sydney Morning Herald.

Home, J. E., 19 April 1843. *Captain Sir J. Everard Home to Admiral William Parker, Commander in Chief, East Indies Station, Trincomalee*. in Cameron (1999) p. 124 ed. Port Essington: Historical Society of the Northern Territory.

Horden, M., 1989. *Mariners are Warned: John Lort Stokes and H.M.S. Beagle in Australia 1837–1843*. Melbourne: Melbourne University Press.

HRA, Series III, Vol VI: 643, 1824. *Historical Records of Australia*.

Huxley, T., 1848. *T.H. Huxley's Diary of the Voyage of the Rattlesnake*. Chatto and Windlass, 1936 ed. London: Julian Huxley.

Jack, R. L., 1922. *Northmost Australia*. London: Simson, Marshall et al.

Jones, W. H. B., 15 December 1845. *Medical Journal for H.M.S. President*. London: National Archives ADM 101/114/1/1.

JSTOR, 1898. *Obituary: Commander Crawford A. D. Pasco, R. N.* Accessed 23 Apr. 2020. ed. The Geographical Journal, vol. 11, no. 5, pp. 558–59.: www.jstor.org/stable/1774752. .

Jukes, J. B., 1848. *Narrative of the Surveying Voyage of H.M.S. Fly*. in Powell, Far Country, 1982.

Keppel, H., 1853. *A Visit to the Indian Archipelago, in H.M.S. Mæander: With Portions of the Private Journal of James Brooke*. London: R. Bently.

Kuper, A., 11 February 1840. *Captain August L. Kuper to Commodore Sir Gordon Bremer, Commander in Chief, East Indies Station, Tricomalee*. in Cameron (1999) p. 62 ed. Port Essington: Historical Society of the Northern Territory.

Lang, J., 1837. *Transportation and Colonisation*. London: s.n.

———, 1847. *Cooksland In North-Eastern Australia; The Future Cotton-Field of Great Britain: Its Characteristics and Capabilities for European Colonization. With A Disquisition on the Origin, Manners, And Customs of the Aborigines. By John Dunmop Lang, D.D., A.M.* https://espace.library.uq.edu.au/ ed. London: Longman, Brown, Green, and Longmans.

Laughton, J. & Lambert, A., 2009. *Bremer, Sir James John Gordon (1786–1850)*. Retrieved April 2020 ed. Oxford Dictionary of National Biography: Oxford University Press.

Leichhardt, L., 1847. *Journal of an overland expedition in Australia, from Moreton Bay to Port Essington .. during the years 1844–1845.* https://archive.org/details/b29336910 ed. London: T.W. Boone.

Lewis, J., 1922. *Fought and Won.* Adelaide: W.K. Thomas and Co.

Lubbock, A., 1967. *Owen Stanley R.N: Captain of the 'Rattlesnake'.* Melbourne: Heinemann.

MacGillivray, J., 15 October 1845. *MacGillivray to the Editor, Sydney Morning Herald.* in Cameron (1999) p. 155–59 ed. Sydney: Historical Society of the Northern Territory.

———, 1852. *Narrative of the voyage of HMS Rattlesnake.* 2 vols. London: Boone.

MacKnight, C., 1969. *The Farthest Coast: A selection of writings relating to the history of the northern coast of Australia.* 1st ed. Melbourne: Melbourne University Press.

———, 1976 . *The Voyage to Marege': Macassan trepangers in northern Australia.* 2017 ed. Melbourne: MUP.

Masson, E., 1915. *An Untamed Territory: the Northern Territory of Australia.* London: MacMillan and Co.

McArthur, J., 1 December 1846. *McArthur to Edward Deas Thomson, Colonial Secretary's Office, Sydney.* in Cameron (1999) p. 165 ed. Victoria: Historical Society of the Northern Territory.

———, 12 May 1840. *Captain John McArthur to Governor George Gipps, Sydney.* in Cameron (1999) p. 67 ed. Victoria: Historical Society of the Northern Territory.

———, 15 May 1841. *McArthur to More O'Farrall, Secretary of the Admiralty.* in Cameron 1999, p. 85 ed. Victoria: Historical Society of the Northern Territory.

———, 15 November 1848. *McArthur to Colonial Secretary.* Victoria: in Spillett (1972).

———, 16 October 1847. *McArthur to ------, Report on the buildings of Victoria.* Victoria: Historical records of Australia. Series I., Governors' despatches to and from England / [edited by Frederick Watson] p. 373.

———, 18 August 1848. *McArthur to Colonial Secretary.* Victoria: in Spillett (1972) p. 157.

———, 2 November 1840. *McArthur to Governor Sir George Gipps, Sydney.* in Cameron

(1999) p. 74 ed. Victoria: Historical Society of the Northern Territory.

——, 20 September 1842. *McArthur to Edward Deas Thomon, Colonial Secretary's Office, Sydney*. in Cameron (1999) p. 108 ed. Victoria: Historical Society of the Northern Territory.

——, 22 April 1843. *McArthur to Edward Deas Thomson, Colonial Secretary's Office, Sydney*. in Cameron (1999), p. 128 ed. Victoria: Historical Society of the Northern Territory.

——, 24 August 1843. *McArthur to Edward Deas Thomson, Colonial Secretary's Office, Sydney*. in Cameron (1999) p. 131 ed. Victoria: Historical Society of the Northern Territory.

——, 25 April 1845. *McArthur to Edward Deas Thomson, Colonial Secretary's Office, Sydney*. in Cameron (1999) p. 148 ed. Victoria: Historical Society of the Nothern Territory.

——, 25 February 1841. *McArthur to Governor Sir George Gipps, Sydney*. in Cameron (1999) p. 78 ed. Victoria: Historical Society of the Northern Territory.

——, 3 September 1841. *McArthur to Governor Sir George Gipps, Sydney*. in Cameron 1999, p. 96 ed. Victoria: Historical Society of the Northern Territory.

——, 7 November 1838. *McArthur to Captain Sir Gordon Bremer*. in Cameron (1999), p. 22 ed. Darwin: Historical Society of the Northern Territory.

McArthur, J. & McArthur, J., 1849. *Notebook of John McArthur and John McArthur Jnr., Kept at Victoria Settlement Port Essington, [Ca. 1843–1849]*. Darwin: Library & Archives NT, John McArthur. NTRS 3601, Reference digitised copy of notebook relating to the Port Essington settlement, 1838–1850.

McKenna, M., 2016. *From the Edge: Austalia's Lost Histories*. Melbourne: The Miegunyah Press.

Miller, J., 20 February 1874. Northern Territory Times and Gazette. *Trip of the Flying Cloud to Port Essington.*

Monitor, 7 Sept 1838. *Projected Departures*. p. 3 ed. Sydney: The Sydney Monitor.

Monthly Magazine, T., 1825. *The Monthly Magazine*. No 413.

Moodie, G., 2019. *At World's End*. [Online]
Available at: https://www.abc.net.au/news/2019-12-03/port-essington-worlds-end-failed-british-colonial-settlement [Accessed 5 Dec 2019].

Mulvaney, D. & Green, N., 1992. *Commandant of Solitude*. (including the Journal of Captain Barker): The Miegunah Press.

Murchison, R., 1845. President's Address. *Journal of the Royal Geographic Society*, Volume Vol. 15, pp. lviii–lxi.

Napier, F., 1876. *Notes of a Voyage from New South Wales to the North Coast of Australia.*

Sydney: online at http://bishop.slq.qld.gov.au/.

Nicholson, C., 26 October 1843. Report from the Select Committee, on the Proposed Overland Route to Port Essington. *The Australian*, p. 3.

NTTG, 10 March 1899. In the Northern Territory Buffalo Country. *Northern Territory Times and Gazette*, p. 3.

———, 16 December 1876. Port Essington—supplied. *Northern Territory Times and Gazette*, p. 2.

———, 20 February 1874. Trip of the Flying Cloud to Port Essington. *Northern Territory Times and Gazette Friday*.

———, 3 October 1874. Expedition to Port Essington. *Northern Territory Times and Gazette*, p. 3.

O'Brien, V., 1990. Edward William Price. In: R. M. A. P. David Carmet, ed. *Northern Territory Dictionary of Biography*, Vol 1. Darwin: NTU Press, p. 244.

———, 1849. *A Naval Biographical Dictionary: comprising the life and services of every living officer in Her Majesty's navy, from the rank of admiral of the fleet to that of lieutenant, inclusive.* https://archive.org/ ed. London: Cornell University Library, 1416 pages.

Olsen, P. & Russell, L., 2019. *Australia's First Naturalists: Indigenous Peoples' Contribution to Early Zoology.* NLA Publishing.

Orlovich, P., 1976. *Australian Dictionary of Biography*. http://adb.anu.edu.au/biography/roper-john-4503 ed. Canberra: ANU.

Pastmasters, 2016. *Pastmasters.* [Online] Available at: https://www.pastmasters.net/victoria-cemetery.html [Accessed 1 June 2020].

Pauling, T., 2020. *Personal communication* [Interview] (2 6 2020).

Pearson, M., 1992. *From Ship to the Bush: Ship Tanks In Australia.* Australasian Historical Archaeology ed. vol. 10, 1992, pp. 24–29.

Phelts, B., 2006. *Water and its Role in the Economic Development of the Northern Territory.* https://ris.cdu.edu.au/ ed. Letter from Sir James Stephen 1842 quoted: PhD thesis NTU.

Powell, A., 1982. *Far Country.* Darwin: MPU.

———, 2016. *'World's End' British Military Outposts in the 'Ring Fence' around Australia 1824–1849.* 1 ed. Melbourne: Australian Scholarly.

Pryor, G., 1990. *Confalonieri, Angelo Bernardo (1813–1848).* in Northern Territory Dictionary of Biography, Vol. 1: p 58–60, Edited by Carment, Maynard and Powell ed. Darwin: NTU Press.

Pugh, D., 2016. *Fort Dundas: The British in North Australia, 1824–29.* Darwin.

——, 2018a. *Escape Cliffs: The First Northern Territory Expedition 1864–66.* Darwin.

——, 2018. *Darwin 1869: The Second Northern Territory Expedition.* Darwin.

——, 2019. *Darwin: Origin of a City.* Darwin.

——, 2020. *Fort Wellington: The British in North Australia 1827–29.* Darwin.

Reynolds, F., 1797. *Cheap Living.* [Online] Available at: https://books.google.com.au/books [Accessed 1 June 2020].

Roberts, E., 1839. Letter. *Oriental Herald*, 4 July, pp. Vol 4, no. 20, pp. 1–11.

Roper, J., 1846. Letter to the society read by William Yarrell Esq. *Proceedings of the Zoological Society of London, (1824–1827)*(www.biodiversitylibrary.org/page/12862729#page/446/mode/1up), pp. pt.12–15.

Schauensee, R. M. D., 1957. *On Some Avian Types, Principally Gould's, in the Collection of the Academy.* Proceedings of the Academy of Natural Sciences of Philadelphia ed. Philadelphia: vol. 109, 1957, pp. 123–246.

Searcy, A., 1909. *In Australian Tropics.* London: George Robertson.

SFP, 25 January 1845. *News.* Singapore: Singapore Free Press.

Short, B., 2020. James Cook's first Pacific Voyage: alleged scurvy freedom unmasked. *Internal Medicine Journal*, Volume 50 (2020), pp. 378–380.

Sibbald, A. A., 1844. *Alexander Archibald Sibbald Diary.* NTRS541 ed. Darwin: Northern Territory Archives.

SMH, 31 October 1843. *Minutes of Evidence taken before the Select Committee on the Proposed Overland Route to Port Essington.* p. 4 ed. Sydney: Sydney Morning Herald.

Spillett, P., 1972. *Forsaken Settlement: An Illustrated History of the Settlement of Victoria, Port Essington, North Australia 1838–1849.* Sydney: Lansdowne Press.

Stanley, O., 1 November 1841. *Stanley to Captain John Washington, Royal Geographical Society, London.* in Cameron (1999) p. 99 ed. HMS Britomart, Singapore: Historical Society of the Northern Territory.

——, 10 June 1841. *Captain Stanley to Captain John Washington, Royal Geographical Society, London.* in Cameron (1999), p. 87 ed. HMS *Britomart*, Port Essington: Historical Society of the Northern Territory.

——, 12 May 1848. *Stanley to Colonial Secretary's Office, Sydney.* Sydney: The Australian p. 2.

——, 1841. *Hurricane at Port Essington.* London: The Nautical Magazine.

Stephen, 21 June 1841. *Under Secretary Stephen to Sir John Barrow.* Series 1 Vol 6 p. 414 ed. London: Historical Records of Australia.

——, 30 Nov 1841. *Under Secretary Stephen to Sir John Barrow.* Vol XXI ed. Historical

Records of Australia, Series 1.

Stewart, P., 16 November 1838. *Stewart to Sir Gordon Bremer.* Admiralty Records 7/766, 110–11, in Cameron 1999, p. 21.

——, May 1869. *Lt. P.B. Stewart's journal of an expedition into the interior of Cobourg Peninsula in May 1839.* Port Essington: in Cameron, 1999, p. 54.

Stokes, J. L., 1846. *Discoveries in Australia, With an Account of the Hitherto Unknown Coasts Surveyed During the Voyage of the HMS Beagle, between the Years 1837 and 1843.* Volume 1 ed. Cambridge University Press, 2011.

Street, T., 1990. *Northern Territory Dictionary of Biography: Vol 1, to 1945.* Edited by David Carment, Robyn Maynard, Alan powell ed. Darwin: NTU Press.

Sweatman, J., 1847. *The Journal of John Sweatman: a nineteenth century surveying voyage in north Australia & Torres Strait.* Edited by Jim Allen and Peter Corris ed. Brisbane: University of Queensland Press, 1977.

Taçon, P. S. C. & May, S. K., 2020. *Macassan History and Heritage: Rock art evidence for Macassan–Aboriginal contact in northwestern Arnhem Land.* [Online] Available at: https://press-files.anu.edu.au/downloads/press/p241301/html/ch08.xhtml [Accessed 15 May 2020].

Teggs, J., 1 January 1839. *Tegg's New South Wales Pocket Almanac and Remembrancer: Departures Of Vessels During The Year 1838'.* trove.nla.gov.au/version/260051650 ed. s.n.

TSR, 16 March 1844. *Torres' Straits—Important to Mariners.* Sydney: The Sydney Record p. 188.

Turnbull, P., 2017. *Skeletal Collecting Before Darwin. In: Science, Museums and Collecting the Indigenous Dead in Colonial Australia.* Palgrave Studies in Pacific History. Palgrave Macmillan, Cham.

Wallis, L., 2020. *Top End Plant Society* [Interview] (25 July 2020).

Watson, T., 1838. *Ship's Logbook: Essington.* on line accessed April 2020 ed. http://acms.sl.nsw.gov.au/_transcript/2010/D04420/a1490.htm.

Webling, A., 1864–66. *The Journals of Charles Webling: Narrating experiences and descriptions of early South Australia, particularly the Port Augusta Region, and the Escape Cliffs Settlement, Adelaide River, in the NT, from voyages aboard HM Schooner Beatrice 1862–1866.* Canberra: D'Arcy Webling editor 1995.

Webster, E., 1986. *Explorer at Rest: Ludwig Leichhardt at Port Essington and on the homeward voyage, 1845–46.* Melbourne University Press.

Whelan, P., 2020. *BITES (Biting Insect Technical Extension Services)* [Interview] (19 May 2020).

Wildey, W. B., 1876. *Australasia and the Oceanic Region: with some notice of New Guinea, from Adelaide via Torres Straits to Port Darwin, thence round Western Australia*. Melbourne: Ferguson and Moore.

Wilson, T. B., 1835. *Narrative of a Voyage Round the World*. This edition published by Franklin Classics ed. London: Originally published by Sherwood, Gilbert and Piper.

Index

3rd Regiment of Foot	9, 11	47th Regiment	232–3

A

abandonment xiv, xv, 13, 48–50, 110, 187, 193
Adam Head 5, 32–4, 40, **41**, **196**, 216, 218, **219**
Albion 79
alcohol xvi, 36, 81, 166, 214
Allen, Jim 47–8, 218, 234
alligator, (crocodile) 164, 213
Alligator xviii–xx, xxii, 18–22, 25–30, 37–8, 42, 45, 49, 54, 64, 73, 76–7, 238–40, 247, 251–5

Alligator Rivers 167
Alligator's log 18–9, **27**, 33, 53, 57, 64, 81, 101, 125, 175, 189–90, 238
Angelina 116, 150
anopheles mosquito x, xiv, 103
Anson 119
Armstrong, John xvii, 33, 96–7, 229
Arnhem (*Aernem*) 2, 247
Arnhem Land xviii, xxv, 2, 25, 83, **85**, 194, 200, 218, 221, 235
Australian xxv

B

Babar Island 37, 252
Backi-backi 137
Badtjala people 17, 252
Baines, Thomas 193
Balanda 137
banteng cattle 183, 235, **236**
Bapak Padu 43, 89–90, 247
Barker, Captain Collet 4, 31, 43, 48, 55, 83, 88, 247
bark painting **56**
Barlow, Captain Maurice 11–13, 247
Barnes, Capt. William 12, 18, 247
Barrow, Sir John 247
Battle of Trafalgar 7, 10, 247
Beagle xvii, xx–xxiii, 21, 58, 60, 62, 65
Beatrice 194–5, 209
Beaufort, Francis 16
Bermuda 7

betel nut 166
Bijenelumbo 146
Binanolombo people 151
Bintang 106, 108
Bissex, Mr 114, 123, 273
Black Point 162, 165, 167, 169, 215
blacksmith's forge **222**
Blackwood, Captain Francis 105, 107, 115, 154
'Bob White' 193–5, 160, 202
Bon Genie 7
Booby Island 27, 114
Borradaile, Edward 200, 286
Bourke, Governor Richard 12
Bowen Strait 43–4, 203
Brady, Bishop John 161
Bramble xxiii, xxiv, 103, 105–7, 123, 126, 153, 162–5, 182, 216, 244, 277

Bremer, Sir Gordon   xix, xx, xxv, **6**–14, 18–22, 27–8, 30–4, 40–41, 43–4, 48–50, 52–4, 64, 76, 78–9, 84, 89, 99, 111, 186, 208, 215, 247–9, 254, 256–7, 261, 264
  Edward, (son)   257
Brierly, Oswald Walters   175, **177**, 178, **179**, **186**
Bright Planet   30
Brisbane, Governor Thomas   8

Britomart   xix–xxii, 18–22, 28–9, 33, 35, 37–8, 42–3, 58, 62, 64–5, 68, 91, 96, 99, **128**, 175, 192, 240, 245, 247, 249–51
Brown, Harry   137
Bucki-bucki   277
buffalo   xx, xxi, xxv, 35–7, 55, 76, 110–11, 117, 134, 159, 195, 199–201, 205–6, 208, 214, 217, 235, **236**, 259, 264, 282
Bungaree   2
Bunn, Captain George   9

C

Cacique   174
Cadell, Captain Francis   194–5, 107
Cadell River   194
Cadet   xxiii, 113, 118–9, 122, 150, 160, 241
Calcutta   xxv, 14, 141
Campbell, Major John   12, 147
Canton   22, 29
Cape Croker   109
Cape York   1, 10, 27, 33, 115, 181–2, 192
Captain   7, 145
Castlereagh   162
Chameleon   xxii, xxiii, 79, 104, 246
Charles Eaton   17, 23–4, 28, 37, 255
Charlotte   23
Cheap Living   x, xxi, xxv, 63–4, 225
Chetwode, Captain Phillip   xxiii, 104, 106, 233, 246
Chilcott, Captain   114
Christopherson, Don   190
Cobourg Cattle Company   201, 203, 214, 283
Cobourg Peninsula   xiii, xxv, 3, 5, 8, 54, 88, 90, 106, 146–47, 150, 157–8, 167, 169, 183, 195, 200–1, 218, 221, 235, **236**
cockroach   xxiv, 163–5, 216

Coepang   xx, 96
Comet   290, **291**
Comus   7
Confalonieri, Father Angelo   xi, xxiv, 123, 150, **161**–63, 165–171, 234, 240
  map   **167**
  mission   162
Constable of Police   150
convict   x, xxiii, 3–4, 8, 10, 14, 17, 20, 24, 105, 107, 113, 122, 159
cookhouse   223
Cook, James   2
Cooper, Richard   105
Coral Bay   100, 104, 169, 178, 184–5, 277
Coringa Packet   xxiv, 114–5
Cornish chimneys   xiii, 34, 118, 221, **222**
corroboree   179, 189, **210–11**, 212,
Countess of Harcourt   9, 53
Crawford, Doctor John   xxiv, 130, 169, 174, 184–5, 189, 233, 243
Crocker Island   146
crocodile   26, 34, 156, 160, 217
Croker Island   x, xv, xxv, 28, 129, 158, 194, 255, 278, 277
Croker Island elder   157
Currie, Professor Bart   xiii, 108

D

d'Almeida, Antonio   xxii, 110–11, 117, 159
Dance, Henry   99, 245

Darling Downs   136
Darling, Governor Ralph   4, 12

d'Astrolabe	xx, 44, 220, 256, 262	Douglas, Bloomfield	197, 213
Dermoudy, Peter	ix, xxv, 218, 225, 229–31, 235, 245	Dunbar, Lieutenant George Sheddan	xxiv, 130, 184, 189–30, 243
De Weser	7	Duppar	24–5
diarrhoea	100, 113	d'Urville, Captain Jules Sébastien César Dumont	xx, 1, 7, 38, 44–5, 48, **66–67**, 220, 256, 262
didgeridoo, bamboo	**56**		
Dili	43		
d'Orley, Captain George	23, **24**, 25	*Duyfken*	xix, 1
Charlotte, wife	23		

E

Eagle	194–5	earthquake	xxiv, 80, 173
Earl Bathurst	8, 13, 18	Eastern Arnhem Land	158
Earl, George Samuel Windsor	xix–xxiii, 15–18, 29–30, 32, 34–8, 39, 40, 42, 44, 56, 73, 78–80, 88–90, 101, 103, 106–7, **120–1**, 122, 132, 145–6, 149, 159, 173, 240, 255	*Enchantress*	xxiv, 159–61, 240, 275
		Escape Cliffs	xi, 62–3, 193–4
		Essington	xix, xx, 21–2, **24**, 26, 28–9, 35–8, 42, 81
Earl Grey	142, 183, 265	Eyre, Edward John	131, 135, 183

F

Fagan, Reverend James	159, 161	Foelsche, Inspector Paul	158, 195, **196**, 197, 200, **210–11**, 214
'Fat Jack'	198		
Finniss, Colonel Boyle Travers	194	Forbes, Joseph	xix, xx, 37
First Northern Territory Expedition	63, 194	Forsaken Settlement	215
Fisher, Charlie	137	Fort Dundas	x, xix, 3–4, 11–13, 16, 122, 147–8, 186
Fitzmaurice, Lewis	62		
Fitzroy, Governor Charles Augustus	181	Fort Wellington	x, xix, xxv, 3–4, 12, 30, 44, 83, 107, 122, 132, 146–8, 202
'Flash Poll'	166, 194, 202–3, 205, 208–9, 213, 284		
		'Fought and Won'	**200, 201, 212**
Flora Kerr	105	Fraser, Eliza	17
Fly	xxiii, 103, 105–6, 114–16, 153–4, 182, 240, 244, 270	*Freak*	xxiv, 130, 185, 243

G

Garig Gunak Barlu National Park	xiii, 158, **216, 236**	Gipps, Governor Sir George	19–20, 22, 49, 72, 77–8, 91, 110, 117, 131, 136, 247
Gem	195, 197	*Gipsy*	116, **122–3**, 125, 127, 127–9, 168, 273, 275–8
Georgiana I	105		
Gilbert, John	xvii, xxi, 90–1, 93, 96, 136, 138, **139**, 140, 153	glass	36, 221, 223, 225, 227
		glass stoppers	**220**
Gilmore	xxi, 64, 71, 90–1	Glenelg, Lord	16–17, 19, 22, 247
		Gold, Doctor John	3

Index

Gothenburg 283
Goulburn Island 85, 168
Gouldian finch 93–4
Gould, John xvii, xxi, 91, 93, **94**, **95**, 140
  Mrs Elizabeth **94**
Government Gardens **69**
Government House **35**, 60, 68, 70, 77, 91, 118, 138, 173–4, 219, 221, 247, 263, 265–6
Great Barrier Reef 22, 159, 175
Gregory, Augustus 193
Gulf of Carpentaria 25, 132, 138, 175, 214
Gulnare 197, 207
Guy, Lieutenant Michael 194

H

Handy, Private William 33, 81, 218
headland **215**
health xxi, 4, 73, 99, 104, 106–8, 123, 141, 174, 185, 235, 258, 264
Hebe 109
Heroine xx, xxii, xxiv, 110–11, 117, 141, 159–60, 174, 180, 182, 205, 217, 275
Hobart xxiii, 9, 113, 118, 231, 233
Hogan, Reverend Nicholas 159, 161
Home, Captain Sir John Everard xxiii, 100–3, 263
Horton, Sir Robert Wilmot 16
Howard, Captain Frederick 194
Hunter, Lieutenant 79
Hutchings 188, 242
Huxley, Thomas Henry xxiv, 169, 175–6, 180–1, 192, 219
  Aldous 176
Hyderabad xxiv, 114–15

I

Iacama 32
Ince, Lieutenant 107
India and Australia Steam Packet Company 183
influenza xvi, xvii, 146, 150, 169
inscription 230–34
  Stiles' **231**
Investigator 2, 83
Ireland, John 23
Isabella, (*Essington*) 21, 23, **24**, 254
Iwaidja xvi, xix, xxiv, 3–5, 26, 31–3, 35, 39, 55, 57, 68, 80, 83, 89, 91, 118, 123, 145–58, 160–3, 165–9, 179, 187–9, 194–5, 196, 197–9, 202–3, 205, 207, **210–11**, **12**, 213–14, 221, 235
  and Macassans xiv, 68, 84–5, 89, 118, 145–6, 166, 197, 214
  and religion 165–6
  children 65, 123, 158, 163–4, 166, 168, 179, 187–8
  cicatrice scars 156–7
  corroboree 179, 189, **210–11**, 212
  creation stories 157
  dances 48, 189, **210–11**, 214
  death of a prisoner xxiv, 151
  first meeting 26, 35
  funery rites 179
  health 149–50, 158, 168
  known at Fort Wellington 3–4, 31–2, 44, 147–8
  language 146–7, 158, 161–2, 165, 167, 169
  musical instrument 149
  mutiny on the Gem 197
  payback killings xxiv, 151–6
  relationships with the British 31, 55, 91, 118, 145, 156–7, 160, 187, 189, 194, 207, 235
  shipwrecked on the *Herione* xxiv, 205
  spears 33, 48, **147**–8, 154–6
  trade 38–9, 85, 164, 212, 200, 233
  tribal groups 146, 167–8
  use of British cast-offs 39, 147, 155, 189, 221
  women 47, 68, 89, 147, 158, 164, 179, 187–9, 197, 213–4, 221

J

'Jack Davis' 157–8, 198–200, 202–3, **204**–5, 209, 213, 281–6
'Jack White' 160
Janszoon, Willem xix, 1
Jimbour jumpup homestead 136
' Jim Crow' 160, 191
John and Charlotte 170, 174
Juno 150

K

Keppel, Captain Henry **186**–9, 238, 245
    Keppel's journal **179**
Kew, Royal Gardens at 93, 96
Keys, Charles 62
Ki Islands 162–3
King George IV 10
King George the Third Island 2
King, Captain Phillip Parker xix, 2, 33, 92
Kissa xx, xxi, 36–7, 42–3, 76, 134
Knocker Bay 54, 91, 191, 209, 280, 282
Kuper, Captain Augustus Leopold xxi, 64, 68, 73, 76, 249
Kuringgai 2

L

Lady Jane 109
Lady Kennaway 22, 27
Lady Nelson 9–11, 37
Lambrick, Lieutenant George ix, xxiii, 55, 113, 120, **121**, 123–4, 130, 160, 163, 168, 173–4, 176, 184–5, 189–92, 209, 241, 267, 274–5
    Baby Emma ix, 122, 124, 191, **232**, 241
    George (Jnr) ix, 122, 124, **232**, 241
    Mrs Emma ix, 122–4, 230–1, **232**, 241
    Mrs Emma's grave **122, 228**–9, 230, **231**, **232**
    Reverend George 230
Lang, Dr John Dunmore 15, 131, 135
Langari 30, 145
Laws R.N., Captain John M. 13–14, 49
Le Breton, Louis **46**–**7**, 48, **69**, **86**–**7**, 256

Leichhardt, Dr Ludwig xviii, xxiv, 5, 100, **135**, 136, 137, **138**–**9**, 140–3, 159, 183–4, 193
leprosy 146
Levi, Charles 201, 203, 217
Lewis, Captain John xxv, 23–4, 103, **200, 201**, 202–3, 210, 214, 217, 221, 283
Limbakarajia people 146, 165
Limbapyu 146
Limbo Cardia 5
Ling Ah Loo 201
Liverpool River 8, 194–5
Lizard 22, 29, 125, **127**, 275, 277
Lord Auckland xxii
Lorence, Joseph 213
Lulworth xxi, 76, 96
Lynheer xxii

M

Macassan xiii, xiv, xvix, xxv, 2, 4, 33, 40, 68, 82–5, 89–90, 111, 118, 132, 145–6, 166, 197, 203, 214, 235, 270, 274
    camp **86**–**7**
    trading prahu (prau) 43, **88**
    trepang drying shed **85**
    (see also 'prau')
Macassar xxii, 79, 82, 85, 88, 90, 111, 133, 166, 197, 258, 271, 274
Macassarese 15, 89
MacGillivray, John xxiii, xxiv, **92**, 104, 106, 115, 146, 148, 151, 156, 166, 169, 175, 178, 181, 185, 189
Mackay, John 132

Index

Mackenzie, Captain Martin   159–60, 182
Maconochie, Captain Alexander   119
Macquarie, Governor Lachlan   2
Madagascar   53
Madras   14
magazine   **41**, 206, 218, **219**, 247, 268, 283
Maitland, Frederick Lewis   52, 77
Makassar   88–9, 166
malaria   x, xiii–xviii, 3, 103–4, 108, 110, 146, 150, 181
Male, Private Robert   80–81
Mallamay   39
Mamitba, Tim   157
Mangles   24
Manlius   xxii, 103
Maria   xxi, 64–5
Mariac   32
Marinus   247
Marsh, Captain   197–9, 207
Masland, Sargeant William   xxiv, 113, 151, 243
Masson, Elsie   208–9, 230
Mastotermes darwiniensis   173
McArthur, Captain John   iii, ix, xx, xxv, xxvi, xxvii, 5, 18, 29, 33–4, 53–64, **65**–87, **88**–105, 107–12, 114–17, 119–23, 125, **127**–9, 134, 137–8, 141, 145, **147**–51, 157, 160–2, 167–8, 173–4, 176, 178–81, 183–7, 189–91, 229–30, **232**, 234, 236, 238, 244, 249, 254, 263–9, 283, 288–90, **291**, 292–4
    James   18, 53–4, 78, 108, 110, **120–1**, 122, 238
John (Junior)   53, 100, 107–8, 110, 119–20, 122, **127**, 128–9, 148, 168, 190, 240, 273–9, 287–94
McArthur Map   **59, 271**
McArthur, Mrs   110, 190, 284
McArthur's house   **220**
McKinlay, John   183, 194
Meander   x, xxiv, **186**–90, 233, 247
melioid bacterium   108
melioidosis   xv, xvi, 108
Melville, Hardon Sidney   **120–1, 152**, 154, **155**
Melville Island   x, xix, 3, 8, 10, 12–4, 18, 48, 85, 199–200, 280, 282
memorial board in Victoria Cemetery   **229**
Memorimbo   123, 208–9
Mermaid   2
Mew, Corporal Richard   175, 239
Middle Head   57, 116, 125, **126**, 253, 257
Midge   114
Mildun, (see 'Jack Davis')   **204**, 205, 209, 211, 213, 230, 234, 283
Miller, James   197, 200, 207, 280, 282
Minto Head   33, 40, 70, 168, 226, 276
Mitchell, Sir Thomas   135, 183
Moa   xx, 37, 42–3, 76
Montreal   xxii, 115
Mount Bedwell   33
Mountnorris Bay   150, 194, 202
Mount Rose   33
Muran Clan   190
Murchison, Sir Roderick   182–3
Murray Island   22, **24**, 114

N

Nanyenya   210
Neinmal   xxiv, 151, **152**–4, **155**–7, 160
Nelson, Newfoundland dog   160–1, 217
Nemesis   153
Netherlands   17
New Holland   xix, 1, 8, 16, 52, 173, 254
Nicholson, Dr Charles   131
Nokodas   273
North Australian Expedition   193
Northern Light   200, 202, 283
Northern Territory Times and Gazette   198, 200–1, 203, 207, 217, 280, 282–3
North Star   xxiii, 100–2, 240

O

officers' mess	223, 227, 266–7
Ondenemer	xxi, 76
ophthalmia	146, 149
opium	79, 166
Opium Wars	76, 79, 235
orange footed scrub fowl	91, **92, 228**
Orontes	xix, xx, 20–2, 25, 27, 29, 30, 33, 36, 38, **39**, 45, 255–6, 258
Orontes Shoal	xxv, 141
Overland Route	131, 133–4, 183
Owen, Adjutant-General	186–7
Owen Stanley Ranges	192

P

Palmerston	171, 191–2, 194, 197, 201, 203, 282
Pasco, Crawford	57, 205
Pauling, Honourable Tom	ix, xxv, 226
Peacock	17
Pelacca	174
Pelorus	xxi, xxii, 64–5, 68, 70, **71**, 72, **73, 74** 75–7, 79, 99, 109, 233, 245–6
Permain, Thomas	200, 291
Phillip, Governor Arthur	2
Phillipus, Shadrack	101, 134
Piggott, Third Mate George	23
pineapple	221
Plasmodium falciparum	xv
Plasmodium vivax	xiv
Pobasso	83
Point Record	xx, xxiv, 5, 10, 26, 29, 33, 38, 42, 97, 163–4, 215–6, 253
Point Smith	28, 57, 104, 106, 141, 276–7
Point Vashon	280–1
Pope Gregory XVI	161
Port Adelaide	183
Port Albany	182
Port Essington	**xxvi–xxvii**, 5, **65**, 160, 197
pottery	82, 221
Powell, Alan	44, 93
prau	xv, xxi, 43, 82, 83, **84**–5, 88–90, 132, 166, 258
President	109
Price, Edward	213–14
Priest, Lieutenant Phineas	xxiii, 18, 34, **61**, 77, 101–2, 238
Prince George	xxiv, 115
Prisoners of the Crown	**102**, 107, 134, 244
Pyramis	105

R

Raffles Bay	x, xix, xxv, 3, 13–15, 30, 43–4, 48, 55, 83, 88, 96, 145–6, 194, 202, 218, 258, 260, 278
'Rambo'	137
Rattlesnake	xxiii, xxiv, 18, 28, 175, **177**, 181–2, 190, 192
Red Gauntlet	xxv, 141
Regatta	**128**
Regia	29–30
Reynolds, Frederick	x, xxi, 63
Reynolds, Honourable Thomas	283
Robertson, Captain James	114, 197, 199, 280–1
Robinson	xxv, 200, 202–3, 206–8, 282, 286
Roe, Lieutenant John Septimus	10
Roper, John	137, 140
Royal Geographical Society	12, 147, 176, 182
Royalist	xxiii, 104–6, 109, 114, 160, 233, 246
Royal Marines	xix, xxiv, 5, 11, 18–9, 27, 34, 50, 53–4, 72, 90, 95, 101, 103, 107, 112–13, 122, 130, 174, 186–9, 191, 205, 233, 235, 249, 269, 272

Index

S

Sandwich	7
Sapphire	159–60
Satellite	13
scurvy	xx, xxii, 3, 42, 49, 64–5, 100, 103, 223
Searcy, Alfred	xxv, 85, 209, 213
Selby, Edward	125, 127–9, 273–7
Select Committee on the Proposed Overland Route to Port Essington	131–33
Sesostri	xxi
Shamrock	114–5
Short, Captain Joseph	27, 38
Sibbald, Dr Archibald	xxiii, 105, 156–7, 179, 240
Simpson, Captain Thomas Beckford	193
Singapore	x, xxi, xxii, 15, 79, 89, 105, 110, 115–6, 125, 134, 153, 174, 182, 199, 270
Sir John Byng	174
smallpox	32, 146, 158–9, 194
'Smike'	199, 287
Smyth, Captain Henry	3, 32
Somerset, Queensland port of	195
Spear Point	33, 42, 185, 252
Spillett	118, 185, 215, 234, 245
sports day	62
Sri Singapura	116, 125
Stamford	15
Stanley, Captain Owen	x, xix, 18, 29, 39, 41, 60–5, 80, 84, 91, 126, 128, 145, 170, **175**, 182,192,226,249,263 'prying into all concerns' 170
steamship	153, 181–2, 194–5
Stedcombe	18, 23, 37
Stephen, Sir James	50
Stewart, Lieutenant Peter Benson	44, 55–8, 71, 256
Stiles, Tom	230, **231**, 233–4
Stirling Castle	17
Stokes, Captain John Lort	xvii, xx, 33–4, 58, 60, 64, **65**, 92, 97, 147–8, 173
stonemasons	9, 34, 244
storehouse	**61**
quartermaster's store	**228**
Strathfieldsay	105
Stuckey, (carpenter)	125–7, 274–7
sugar gliders	**95**
Supreme Court	151
Suwa	174
Swan River Colony	15, 30, 183
Sweatman, John	xxiv, 123, 149, 155, 159, 161, 163–4, 166
Sweet, Captain Samuel	197, 207
Sydney	xix–xxiv, 2, 5, 8–9, 11, 18–19, 21, 26, 28, **31**, 33, 38, 49–50, 62, 64–5, 68, 76, 91, 97, 101, 103, 105–6, 110, 114–5, 117, 119, 130, 132, 136, 141–2, 151, 153, 159, 162–3, 165, 170, 173–5, 180, 182–3, 187, 189–90, 192, 194–5, 205, 235, 247, 255, 265–7

T

Tamar	8–10, 186
Tam O'Shanter	174
termite	110, 119, 127, 173–4, 185, 219–20, 230
giant northern	173
Terrutong	146
Theatre Royal, Victoria	**63**, 65, 226
The Flying Cloud	197, 207, 213
Thomson, Surgeon John	176
Tilston, Assistant Surgeon Richard	xxiii, 113, 123, 150, 154, 169, 178, 184, 233, 241
Timor	xx, xxi, 11, 16, 36, 38, 42–3, 96–7, 133–4, 229
Timor Laut	xx, 23, 36, 134
Timor ponies	202, 205
Timpson, Lieutenant Henry	102, 240

Tiwi 3, 8, 85
tobacco 15, 20, 85, 149, 160, 166, 187, 190, 193, 202–3, 207–9, 214, 281, 284, 286
   pipe 209
   smoking 149, 166
Torres Strait xxii, xxiv, 9, 17, 22, **24**, 26–7, 29, 43–4, 105–6, 114–15, 153, 175, 182, 187, 197, 247, 254
Torres Strait natives 155
Torres Strait pigeon 157

Tor Rock 200
Tossell, Private James 130, 243
trepang xxi, xxv, 15–16, 18, 43, 83, 85, 88–9, 116, 132–3, 158, 194, 197, **199**–200, 202, 214, 257–8, 271, 281–2, 286
   trepang boilers **83**
   trepang fleet, Macassan 203, 209, 213
Trepang Bay 199–200, 202, 280–2
Trois Amos 195
Tyers, Charles 57, **58**

V

Van Diemen Gulf 146, 167
Vashon Head xx, xxii, xxv, 38, 141, 200, 285, **236**
venereal disease 146
Victoria Cemetery ix, xxv, 99, 108, 124, 198, 205–6, 225, 228, **229**–31, **232**, 236, 245

Victoria Hospital x, **102**, 118, **155**, 178, **224**, **225**
   kitchen **100**, **224**
Victoria Settlement 5, 207, 217
Victoria Square 72, **120–1**, 189, 193
Victoria Theatre Royal **64**, 65, 226
Vincennes 17

W

Wandy-wandy 197
Wanji-Wanji 30, 33
Wanji-Wanji Cove 33
Warramurrungunji 157
Washington, Captain 73
Watson, Captain Thomas xx, 21–4, 26, 28–9, 35–7, 81–2, 247
Wellesley 52, 76, 79
West Arnhem Regional Council 158
Western Arnhem Land 190

Whipple, Assistant Surgeon Frederick xxiii, 19, 34, 40, 104–5, 108, 239
Wickham, Captain John Clements xx, 21, 58, 62
Wild Duck 197
Wildey, William Brackley 214
Wilson, Dr Braidwood 132
Wood Duck 207, 280
Woolner 213
Wright, Lieutenant William xxiii, 113, 121, 165, 241

Y

Young Heroine 280

Yule, Lieutenant xxiv, 107, 153, 162–3, 182, 216

Z

Zélée xx, 44, 220, 256

Zoological Society of London 91, **92**

Further reading

FORT WELLINGTON
The British in North Australia, 1827–29

The Iwaidja woman, her belly opened by a bayonet, slipped below the dark water. Her 6-year-old daughter, Reveral, watched in terror. Her baby sister was already dead, hit by a slug in the first volley or drowned, but a young man lying on the sand with his intestines spilling out had to be finished off—out of mercy! Reveral, wounded in her side, was carried back to the fort in triumph, for she was worth a £5 reward from Commandant Smyth.

Capturing an Australian was how the British sought to make friends with the Iwaidja, on whose lands the new British garrison of Fort Wellington was being built. It was an appalling start, but eventually, with the remarkable Captain Collet Barker in charge, friendships were established. At last, it looked like a successful trading settlement would follow, the British would live in peace with the local tribe, and they would welcome, and protect the Macassan fishermen, who came annually to the peninsula for trepang.

But then, a twice ship-wrecked captain struggled ashore with the order to abandon the north coast altogether, and the soldiers, Royal Marines, convicts, their families, and even Reveral herself, wearily packed up the settlement and moved on, leaving the fort and its gardens to the Iwaidja. 'Another of our sweet, nice, wise, profitable, gingerbread, out of the way playthings is to go', rejoiced *The Australian*, in 1829.

This is the extraordinary forgotten story of the second attempt at settling Australia's north coast.

'an absorbing and detailed narrative' (Brian Reid).

www.derekpugh.com.au

ESCAPE CLIFFS
The First Northern Territory Expedition 1864–66

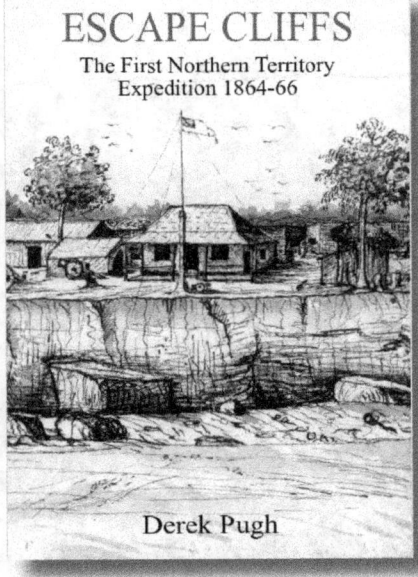

This is the true story of South Australia's first attempt at colonising their Northern Territory. It is a story of greed, courage, exploration, murder, wasted efforts, life and death struggles, insubordination, incredible seamanship, and extraordinary bushmanship, amid government bungling and Aboriginal resistance.

The South Australians wanted their state to be the *premier* state of Australia. The new settlement was expected to open up a trading route across the country, to Asia and beyond, and exploit the agricultural and mining opportunities of the interior. It was to be at no cost to the state, as the land was sold, unseen and unsurveyed, to investors in Adelaide and London, prior to the First Northern Territory Expedition even setting out.

The investors were already calculating their returns, but then, as the saying goes, the fight really started …

A fantastic read: insightful, cohesive, sequential, and well-paced. Loved it. Plenty of photos and maps to set the scene, with the addition of well researched complementary, first-hand accounts and primary records. Pugh has captured the essence of the time, place and characters: their personalities, hardships, successes and celebrations. I wanted to read it to find out what was going to happen next. Pugh's writing style is 'alive' and easy to read.   Jill Finch

www.derekpugh.com.au

The British in North Australia 1824–29
FORT DUNDAS

Fort Dundas was the first outpost of Europeans in Australia's north. It was a British fortification manned by soldiers, marines and convicts, and built by them on remote Melville Island, in 1824. The fort struggled on until February 1829, when it was abandoned and left to the termites.

The fort's purpose was twofold. First, it was a physical demonstration of Britain's claim to the New Holland continent, as far as longitude 129°E, and thus excluded the Dutch and the French from starting similar colonies on the north coast. It was the first of a series of fortified locations around the coast. Second, it would be the start of a British trading post that would become a second Singapore, and compete with Batavia.

The settlement was named in a ceremony on 21 October 1824, but it was not a success. From its short existence come tales of great privation, survival, greed, piracy, slavery, murder, kidnapping, scurvy, and battles with the Indigenous inhabitants of the islands, the Tiwi.

It was also the site of the first European wedding and the birth of the first European children in northern Australia.

None of the three military commandants who managed the outpost wanted to be there and all were gratefully relieved after their posting. They left

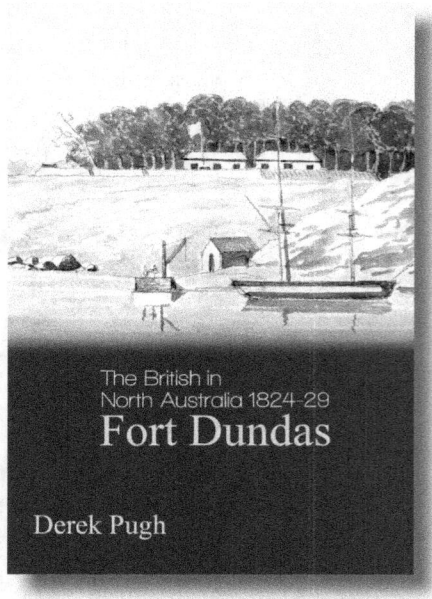

behind thirty-four dead—victims of disease, poor diet and Tiwi spears. Others died when the crews of the fort's supply ships were slaughtered and beheaded by Malay pirates on islands to the north. Two cabin boys from one of them, the *Stedcombe*, were enslaved by the pirates.

The story of what happened at Fort Dundas and why it was abandoned has been largely untold. Nevertheless, it is one of the most engaging stories of nineteenth-century Australia, presented here in Derek Pugh's usual captivating style.

www.derekpugh.com.au

DARWIN 1869
The Second Northern Territory Expedition

The Northern Territory had its beginnings under the governance of South Australia. Land was sold to investors, unseen and unsurveyed and in an unknown location. The sales raised the funds needed and The First Northern Territory Expedition was sent north to make it a reality, but it failed miserably, and the government faced huge losses with insufficient reserves to refund its investors.

To mitigate the loss, a new venture was envisaged—the Second Northern Territory Expedition, and there was only one man thought capable of ensuring a successful survey of the north: The Surveyor General, George Woodroffe Goyder.

Goyder was an extraordinary man, full of frenetic energy and with a phenomenal work ethic. The survey took him, and his expert teams of surveyors and bushmen, only eight months. It resulted in the laying out of the city of Palmerston (now called Darwin), three rural towns and hundreds of rural blocks, spreading over almost 270,000 hectares, all pegged out in the bush and Larrakia and Wulna lands—without permission or compensation—and conflict with the Aborigines was an ever-present danger. Two men were speared, one of them fatally.

Darwin grew from these somewhat humble but tumultuous beginnings. It was the only pre-Federation Australian capital established late enough to be photographed from its first settlement; and it is a survivor of challenges and privations unheard of in more temperate climes.

Darwin's story is written on its maps. Street names such as Knuckey, McLachlan, Daly, Wood, Bennett, Harvey and Smith Street recall the surveyors and their teams. Suburbs such as Millner, Larrakiyah, Bellamack and Stuart Park also remind us of the city's earliest days. It is the story of how the courage and diligence of a few led to the founding of the unique city of Darwin.

www.derekpugh.com.au

DARWIN: Origin of a City

A crocodile pulls a sleeping man into the river by one leg. Another breaks the neck of a swimming policeman. An out-of-luck miner drowns himself in the town's well.

Once called Palmerston, the City of Darwin was settled in the 1870s. It was a pioneer's paradise; sometimes as exciting as it was dull; full of potential but, too often, dangerous. Not everyone survived.

The first settlers arrived in January 1870, to find very little other than surveyed blocks of bushland sold to distant investors. It was a colony made from scratch, with little tangible reason for its existence until the Overland Telegraph Line came through from London and joined Australia to the rest of the world. Then gold was discovered, and hopeful miners rushed north from all over the country. Most went home disappointed; but only if they survived the privations of the bush and the distraction of the pubs. Then the government brought in Chinese 'Coolie' workers—and they kept coming, gold dust shining in their eyes, until, by the end of the decade, there were ten times as many Chinese as European settlers, and

Chinatown was the most vibrant part of the settlement.

Known as Palmerston until it was renamed in 1911, Pugh brings the early colony to life once again, through this delightful and colourful account of Darwin's fascinating, unique early history, and the extraordinary characters who pioneered the settlement of the north.

Shortlisted:
Chief Minister's Northern Territory History Book Award, 2020

www.derekpugh.com.au

Turn Left at the Devil Tree

A memoir and history set in the remotest parts of Arnhem Land. Derek Pugh, an ex-Kakadu ranger, teacher, naturalist, bushman, and historian, worked in several homelands schools and joined a lifestyle as old as time among the Indigenous peoples of central Arnhem Land.

His memoir is by turns reflective, tragic and hilarious and describes a life, in remote Aboriginal Australia, which gave him an insight into a traditional culture which has been witnessed by few outsiders.

Life there was 'frustrating at times, but always a challenge and Derek has recorded his experiences beautifully in this delightful book'. Ted Egan, AO

Spending more than twenty years among the people and wildlife of the Top End of the Northern Territory, Derek Pugh revelled in the lifestyle and freedom of the bush. Told with respect and candour

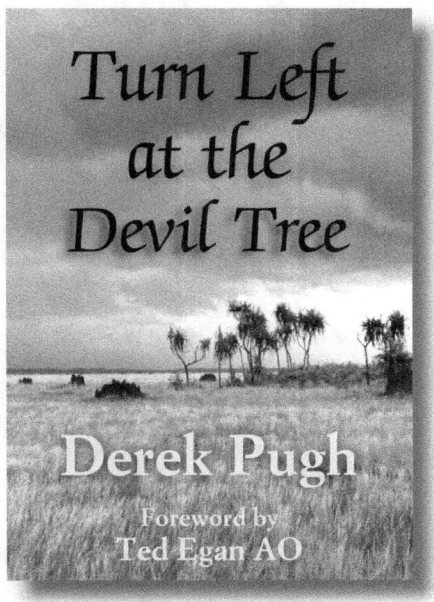

Turn Left at the Devil Tree is Pugh's 'slice of history'.

www.derekpugh.com.au

www.ingramcontent.com/pod-product-compliance
Lightning Source LLC
Chambersburg PA
CBHW060940230426
43665CB00015B/2010